To Marie –

Can you belie[ve] [...]
for over 50 year[s] [...]
enough for that? I have valued
our friendship and our heart-to-
heart talks.   Love –

Aunt Sherry's ™   Sherry

GOD CAN

Calm
the Chaos

GOD CAN
Calm the Chaos

BY

SHERRY LYNN BLAKE DRIVDAHL

VIERS JENSEN MILLER

"The tone and style of this manuscript are engaging and down to earth. The conversational syntax is encouraging and real, meeting the reader on the page with content that is often difficult but infused with hope. Both the tone and style create a comfortable and casual atmosphere for readers as they prepare to do some challenging but important work in their lives."
Jacqueline, Elite Editor

"Sherry does a great job. Tough subject matter but presented gracefully!"
Christian Ellis, Videographer

Press On
Publishing

Philippians 3:12–14

GOD CAN Calm the Chaos
© 2021 by Sherry L. Miller

Published by Press On Publishing
2207 Red Rock Xing
San Antonio, TX 78245

Scripture quotations, unless otherwise noted, are taken from the HOLY BIBLE, NEW INTERNATIONAL VERSION. Copyright© 1973, 1978, 1984 International Bible Society. Used by permission of Zondervan Bible Publishers.

All rights reserved.
No part of this book may be reproduced in any form without written permission from the publisher. Exceptions are the workbook pages specifically noted that copies are permitted and encouraged. Also excepted are brief passages for the purpose of review in a periodical.

ISBN: 978-1-7364656-0-8 (paperback)
ISBN: 978-1-7364656-1-5 (e-book)

First Printing, 2021
Printed in the United States of America

TABLE OF CONTENTS

Dedication   viii

Introduction   ix

Part One: Qualification   1

One: Hope   3

Two: Let Go   5

Three: The Good, the Bad, and the Ugly   7

Four: Press On   11

Five: Can I Get There from Here?   14

Six: Switching Gears   18

Seven: Peace and Contentment   20

Eight: How Is Your Life?   23

Nine: Time for Decision-Making   26

Ten: Time for Action   29

Conclusion   32

Part Two: Perspectives   33

Suicide Kills   37

Lingering Love   40

Normalcy in the Midst of Chaos   42

Father's Day   44

From the Heart   46

Bridging the Gap   50

Making Amends   53

Stepmother—Not So Evil After All   57

Joy—A Story of Faith	61
Holding On	69
Force Field	73
In God's Time	75
Establishing Relationships	82
What Is Family?	84
Angels Among Us	90
Against All Odds	92
Love Your Neighbor as Yourself	97
Innocence Lost	102
Foster Parenting Guide Dog Puppies	105
Good Boy, Cochise	108
Understanding	111
Part Three: Tools and Exercises	115
List of Contents	119
Part Four: A Biblical Path to Calm the Chaos	177
Introduction	183
Step One	193
Step Two	200
Step Three	207
Step Four	214
Step Five	221
Step Six	227
Step Seven	234
Step Eight	242
Step Eight A	250
Step Nine	259
Step Nine A	272
Step Ten	284
Step Ten A	290
Step Eleven	296
Step Twelve	304

Addendum One: Key Bible Verses   312
Addendum Two: House Cleansing Ceremony / Demon Release   315
Addendum Three: Memorized Prayer and Scripture   317

Index   325
About the Author   327

DEDICATION

This book is dedicated to God and the two men that He put in my life.
They were my saving grace.

To God, who calms my chaos every day.

To my husband, Jim, my Rock of Gibraltar
and my soul mate who just loves me.

To my dad, Bob Jensen, who healed my hurting heart.

And I want to thank all soldiers who have brought the symptoms of post-traumatic stress disorder and the hope beyond PTSD to awareness here on the home front. Whether the source of the trauma was the battlefield or circumstances here at home, the subsequent results and recovery are the same.

INTRODUCTION

This is the story of my journey to peace by learning to embrace who I am instead of defining myself by who I was. It is based on my compiled writings that came out of my recovery and discovery. It is a quick read but was a long study.

This book is written in four parts. With any self-help book, you, the reader, should be asking, "Who is this author? Can I trust her judgment?" In Part One I qualify myself as the author. I tell you my story, my downfalls, my victories, my recovery. You can judge for yourself if you want to take my advice. I can tell you this—I spent many years in recovery looking for magical answers, and there are none. What I have done here is to take out all the stuff that didn't work and offer you only the parts that did work.

Part Two is a group of short stories—perspectives in which I took the negatives in my life and discovered insights and lessons learned. These insights can be applied to many other parts of our lives. We can't change the past, but we can learn from it.

Part Three is a group of Tools and Exercises that I offer as a means to recovery. Some of these were suggested by others in the course of my recovery, some are well-known exercises, and many I made up as I went along in my recovery. They can be used alone or in conjunction with the Twelve Steps.

Part Four, "A Biblical Path to Calm the Chaos," is based on the Twelve Step Program of Alcoholics Anonymous, which is a proven recovery tool that has been applied to almost every type of addiction and disorder with great success. I have taken the effective Twelve Steps and applied biblical truth to each in a workbook format, creating a Twelve Step Bible Study from a Christian perspective. For each step I have indicated which Tools and Exercises from Part Three are effective in working that step. Even if there is no addiction or particular disorder involved in your life, these steps have a proven history, and I show through scripture how the steps are a valid biblical approach in restoring order to our lives—restoring relationships and restoring self-esteem.

The first clue that I have survived a dysfunctional life might just be the list of my last names as shown on the cover of this book. Blake is the name I was born with, the name of my biological father. He committed suicide when I was five. Drivdahl was the man who raised me, who never adopted me, but I used his name through all my school years, and then when he and my mother divorced, that relationship faded away. Viers was my first marriage—he had an affair and left me. Jensen was my third father, in whose house I never resided since I was an adult when he entered my life but who adopted me even though he didn't have to. And Miller is my second and current husband of forty-two years. He is my Rock of Gibraltar and my true love.

My pretty obvious addiction was compulsive overeating, but in time I learned that the effects of PTSD was the source of my addiction and my underlying fears. It is from those experiences that I write. Anyone who has ever dealt with an addiction or comes from a dysfunctional family or has had a loss of faith or has experienced emotional or physical abuse—oh heck, anyone who has lived life should be able to relate to this book on one level or another. Anyone who needs to repair relationships or restore love of self can benefit from this book. I am convinced that everyone can relate to my stories and then find their own insights from their life. I am also convinced that everyone can benefit from working the Twelve Steps. I have had friends who have said things like:

> *But I wasn't abused.*
>   *My parents were good to me.*
>   *I haven't experienced any trauma in my life.*
>   *I'm not an addict or alcoholic.*

Yet there were areas in their lives that needed repair, relationships that needed healing, self-esteem issues to be addressed, and a spiritual life to be revamped. Do not dismiss your life experiences as unimportant just because they may not have been as "bad" as someone else's. Working the steps is like giving your car a tune-up—it puts everything in working order and just needs to be done from time to time.

I spent at least thirty years looking for a magic cure—a pill or a program that would fix my overweight body. Mind you, I didn't really want to change my eating habits or fix any relationships; I just wanted God to make me thin. In a society that judges by outward appearances, I just wanted to look good, to be acceptable. I didn't realize that I needed to feel good too, and that I would actually have to work out so many areas of my life before I could even really approach the weight. I thought my weight *was* the problem. Not until I'd had a nervous breakdown and understood the connection to PTSD did I realize that the weight was a symptom, that the problems were underlying causes that I needed to fix. But was I really willing to look at something other than my weight? After all, I'd been making my weight the most complex problem of my life for over thirty years, and I was just sure that if I was thin, everything else would fall into place. That is some of what we will deal with in this book:

What got me to that point?
How did it manifest itself?
How did I identify the underlying causes, and how did I "fix" them?
Can we really achieve peace in the midst of this chaotic world?
What lessons have I learned?

It is my prayer and desire that my experiences in life will touch readers and inspire them to push past their own adversities and develop awareness and an ability to take action.

This book focuses mostly on how to live in this world—how to achieve peace in our everyday life. But as a Christian, I would be remiss in not mentioning the eternal peace beyond this world, and I will share in later chapters some of my journey in this realm as well. I do not want to suffer in death, but I do not fear death. Quite to the contrary, I anxiously await what is on the other side. John 3:16 tells us, "For God so loved the world that he gave his only Son that whoever believes on Him shall have eternal life." We are offered eternity in heaven as a gift, freely given, no strings attached, to anyone who chooses to accept it. That acceptance is the key to peace—what is there to worry about when our salvation is guaranteed? But it is in our human nature to want to be in control, so learning to rest in that assurance can sometimes be a struggle. If you have not accepted Jesus Christ as your personal Savior, I would encourage you to talk to a Christian friend or minister.

I want to thank first my husband. I'm sure he did not know what he was getting into when he married me, but he never wavered in this love and learned that he could not "fix" me but that he could love and support me. My husband chose me, but my daughter had no choice—I'm her mom. We have a great relationship and love for each other. I am so grateful that we were able to grow and learn together—much of my recovery was hers as well, and I love her for not placing blame and for loving me just the same. I thank all my family and friends for encouraging me, with special thanks to Cherie and Amber for their hours of editing.

Scripture quotations, unless otherwise noted, are taken from the HOLY BIBLE, NEW INTERNATIONAL VERSION. Copyright© 1973, 1978, 1984 International Bible Society. Used by permission of Zondervan Bible Publishers.

Occasional notes in brackets or italics within the passage have been added for clarification or emphasis.

PART ONE

QUALIFICATION

One

HOPE

Most people can change. Some people do change. If you are not happy with your life, you have the power to change it. I did. There is a country-western song called "Some People Change." That song gave me hope when I was at my lowest point, and it still encourages me every time I hear it. It recounts the bad circumstances in people's lives and the adversity they overcame. It encourages and provides hope that if they could change, so can you.

If you need to make changes in your life, I wish I could tell you that I have a magic answer or a magic pill. God knows how I prayed for those over the years. Miracles do happen, and some people, maybe, can experience an overnight conversion. However, for me it was a lot of consistent work—but it was worth it. What I am offering you is HOPE—some reason to hang on, to keep trying. God gives us hope so that we can cope.

How many times have you said things like:

When we get past this rough patch, life will settle down...
When we get that hospital bill paid off...
When I get past this cold...
When I get a new job...
When we move...

When...When...When. It turns into a never-ending cycle. I can remember being caught up in that—always thinking that my life would finally "settle," and then I'd have peace in my life. What I learned is that if we wait for it, we'll never have it.

We live in a chaotic world. We only *think* that we have control over our lives. Indeed, we have some control—we set the alarm, and we have a routine: kids to school, work, laundry, cleaning, kids' sports, practices, lessons. We make choices and set up our lives around those choices, and things go along pretty well for a while. But what happens when the unplanned events happen—a car accident, a health issue, a death in the family, the loss of job?

We are really defined by how we handle the unexpected happenings in life. There is always another glitch in our plan just around the corner. Rick Warren of Saddleback Church in Orange County, California, said, "Life is a series of problems. Every time you solve one, another one is waiting to take its place."[1] In other words, life will never really ever settle—we have to learn to live life in the midst of the chaos. Now, I personally don't believe that God gives us all our problems or illnesses. For the most part, they come about as a product of our free will and what that has created in this imperfect world. God could intervene and probably does more often than we realize. When He doesn't intervene in our adversity, He takes those painful experiences to mold our character and uphold our faith.

Why would God allow adversity in our lives? To test our faith, teach us obedience, strengthen us for greater usefulness, and enable us to comfort others. Romans 5:3–5 tells us that "we rejoice in our sufferings, because we know that suffering produces perseverance; perseverance, character; and character, hope. And hope does not disappoint us, because God has poured out His love into our hearts by the Holy Spirit, whom He has given us." As I said previously, God gave us hope so we can cope.

There were many times in my life when I really did not want to hear that. I felt as though I had already developed *plenty of character*—I wanted to bypass any more lessons. But today, I am thankful for all my experiences and God's direction in working through the chaos to help me to be a better person. Yep, I'm a character! A character with hope.

---

[1] Rick Warren, "Problems Force Us to Depend on God," *Daily Hope with Rick Warren,* www.PastorRick.com, May 21, 2014, Accessed 2015.

Two

Let Go

I attended a seminar one time where the speaker said something that has stuck with me. He said that the only thing we really have any control over is our attitude. We can choose to be angry when the unexpected happens or to say a prayer, hand it over, and let God be in control. That's when His peace comes into our life. When we try harder and harder to make a square peg go into a round hole, it just causes extra stress and frustration in our lives. But if we can ask God to show us what to do with that square peg and then let it go until He shows us the way, we have achieved peace. Frustration comes when we feel like there is nothing we can do about a situation or when we hate the options. Prayer is an action verb—we *are* doing something by praying.

My recovery has focused on three passages from the Bible. All three are from Paul's letter to the Philippians. I love Paul. Here is a man who at one time actually persecuted Christians and, with the intervention of Christ on the road to Damascus, became a model Christian—someone whom we can pattern our lives after (read Acts 9 for the full story). His letters to the Christian churches in Philippi, Ephesus, Corinth, and many others are filled with Christian principles and encouragement to live the Christian life. Yet he was imperfect—just like you and me. When he writes in Romans 7:15, "Why is it that I do what I don't want to do and cannot do that which I ought to do?" I see that he had the same struggles that we deal with every day. At times when I don't feel like I'm living up to God's expectation of me or my perceived expectation, I realize I'm not the only one who struggles and that it's OK to have doubts.

So the first passage, Philippians 4:6b–7 (RSV), states, "Let your requests be made known to God [*and then leave it there*]. And the peace of God, which passes all understanding, will keep your hearts and minds in Christ Jesus."

It's hard for me to pinpoint the exact moment when I finally achieved that peace that passes all understanding, but God has been faithful, and I experience His peace in my life every day. I've been at that place for at least the past fifteen years, it's a glorious place to be, and I know that it is mine forever.

Does that mean I never worry about anything? Of course not. The past few years I have dealt with health issues, financial problems, loss of loved ones, and a lawsuit. But I can honestly say that I don't fret. I deal with my feelings, take what action I can, and then let go by putting the rest to prayer. I truly step back *knowing* that God will take care of it and me. My world may still be in chaos, but my inner being is at peace as I work through the chaos.

The second scripture, Philippians 4:11b and 13, says, "I have learned to be content whatever the circumstances. I can do everything through Him who gives me strength."

Contentment. Over the past several years, my husband and I have had good jobs, we've been unemployed, we've had health issues, and we've had financial reversals. I can honestly say that I was content in each circumstance. Here we go again with the attitude choice. I could have complained all the way through it or, as the phrase goes, "Let go and let God." I chose the latter with an attitude of acceptance, and God rewarded me with His peace and a sense of contentment in every circumstance. But I couldn't have done that on my own strength—I was able to let go only through Christ, who gives me the strength.

The third scripture is Philippians 3:13b–14. Before I comment on that scripture, I need to tell you my story. And I need to tell you why I felt compelled to write this book and share my story with you. In 2 Corinthians 1:3–4 Paul writes, "Praise be to the God of comfort, the Father of compassion who comforts us in all our troubles *so that we* can comfort those in any trouble with the comfort we ourselves have received from God." I have written this book as a means of sharing my experience, strength, and hope as an obedient servant of Jesus Christ trusting that God will use my experience to strengthen and enhance your life.

Three

THE GOOD, THE BAD, AND THE UGLY

My life was a series of secrets and shame, and I kept them bottled up inside of me. I used to love the show *Touched by an Angel*. The recurring theme through all the episodes was the phrase "the truth will set you free," which is echoed in John 8:32. All those secrets and shame bottled up inside me were just festering and standing in the way of me have a fulfilling life. I had developed an eating disorder, binge eating, to keep the secrets and shame at bay. But no amount of eating made the shame go away. On the contrary, the fat that came with the eating only added to my shame. Eventually the truth did set me free, and I was able to achieve that peace and contentment I've been talking about. But it was a long road, and at times I didn't think I'd make it. Suicidal thoughts loomed on the surface—it seemed preferable to dealing with the secrets.

The only actual memory I have before the age of ten is of me standing on someone's front yard looking down the street at my house, where a police car was parked. That's it. No memories of anything else about that day, no other memories prior to the age of ten.

My father had committed suicide. I was five years old. No one told me the truth. No one told me anything. My dad was just there one day and gone the next. I was twenty when my mother finally told me how my father died, and then we never spoke of it or him again. It was a shameful secret best kept swept under the rug.

I have no memory of my mother dating or remarrying or of us moving to a new house or my mother having a baby. My memory just kind of picks up at age ten in a new house, with a baby brother and a man who was my dad but wasn't. And that was never explained either. I was also on a strict food regimen—a mother and doctor-controlled diet complete with diet pills. My binge eating and sneak eating had started after my father's suicide—my drug of choice, my way of exerting some control in my life, and my comforter. I don't remember that time, but school photos show a very normal-sized kindergartener, and then the next few grades show me a little heavier each year—until my mother and the doctor and the pills took control of my food, and then I looked normal again, like every other respectable ten-year-old girl. No one knew I didn't feel normal—all that mattered was that I looked normal, acceptable. Miranda Lambert has a song, "My Mother's Broken Heart," that describes the phenomenon of looking good on the outside no matter what you are feeling on the inside. If all looks good on the outside, everything must be good—right?

I did lose twenty pounds on that diet, and then, not long after, a neighbor began molesting me. My brain has a wonderful way of shutting out the things I don't want to remember, for I have very little memory of the details. In fact, I had nearly convinced myself it never happened. As a young adult, if anyone had asked if I'd been abused, I'd have said, "No, of course not." I think I would have known it was a lie, but I didn't want to deal with the truth. Then, at a gathering when I was about twenty-two or twenty-three, I found myself alone with this man, and he said to me, "I'm sorry for all the things I did to you." I had never acknowledged the truth to myself, let alone tell anyone else—I didn't know what to say, how to act. I think I said something like "Don't worry about it" and left the room. My binge and sneak eating increased after that, and I never spoke of it for another ten years.

At sixteen, a junior in high school, I was madly in love. We'd dated two years before we made love, and I got pregnant right away. This was an era when no one talked about sex or birth control or options. The only thing that was said about sex was "don't." Nobody told my molester. It wasn't a long stretch from being molested to having consensual sex.

My mother was unmerciful to me and oscillated between silent treatments and continual barrages of, "How could you do this to me?" One more shameful act to be hidden away and not talked about. Suicide sounded surprisingly good.

But I did marry, had my baby, and raised a delightful daughter named Amy. I chose that name because it means "greatly loved," which was nothing like I felt but what I wanted for her more than anything. From that day forward, my mother lied about my age so no one could do the math and figure out our secret. I had remained thin the rest of my childhood under the watchful eye of my mother, but when I married and left home, my mother was no longer in control of my food, and my binge and sneak eating increased. My marriage failed, and the eating worsened again.

For the first time since the age of ten, my weight yo-yoed out of control. As a fat person I hated myself, and eventually I'd pull myself together enough to lose fifty pounds or so. I'd look good, feel great, and the men liked what they saw too. My past left me on shaky ground with respect to sexual boundaries. I'd feel vulnerable and uneasy with the attention, and I'd get fat all over again. I developed a lifetime pattern of "fat and safe" or "thin and vulnerable." I didn't realize why I was stuck in this pattern until many years later—I just knew I was out of control and didn't seem to be able to help myself.

In one of my thin times, I was date-raped. The term "date rape" didn't exist in those days, and I just figured I was stupid for letting myself get into a position for it to happen. I figured I got what I deserved.

In one of my fat times, I tried hypnosis to get control of my eating, only to have the doctor fondle my breasts while I was under hypnosis. I remember knowing it was happening but not being able to respond. Always the victim, I said nothing. I just didn't go back. And my eating progressed; only now I didn't feel safe thin or fat—I just always felt vulnerable and always wanted to eat to stuff down the feelings.

At age forty with another fifty-pound loss under my belt, my life careened out of control. The weight was coming back on—*again*. I couldn't stop the freight train. In desperation I started forced vomiting and abusing laxatives and diuretics until one night I lay on the cold bathroom floor sure I was dying as my body convulsed as a result of the abuse. I probably should have gone to the hospital, but I was too ashamed to tell my husband (by this time I'd been remarried for ten years). I survived the night and dropped the destructive behaviors (except the eating, over which I had no control), and the pounds increased as my self-esteem plummeted.

I found myself rocking in our overstuffed rocking chair for days, unable to respond, unable to do anything. The only thing that kept going through my mind was suicide. And the only thing that kept me from doing that was knowing how

9

my father's suicide had affected his loved ones. I couldn't do that to my husband and family.

My relationship with my mother had not been the best, and she did and said some things that I truly had to forgive her for. But she also gave me a wonderful gift. Her father died when she was just a teenager; her husband committed suicide and left her with two toddlers when she was twenty-six; she got breast cancer at the age of thirty-three. Her marriage failed shortly thereafter, and her cancer went into and out of remission three times until it finally claimed her life at age fifty-one. But I never saw her faith waver. The wonderful gift she gave me was the gift of a loving, compassionate, forgiving Heavenly Father and a friend, comforter and companion in my Savior, Jesus Christ. She gave me the gift of faith. Consequently, I'd always had a strong personal relationship with Christ and felt the love of a compassionate God—that was the only thing that kept me going all those years. But all those years I'd also been praying for help with my eating to no avail. I know now that my prayers had really been *make me thin, but don't make me have to change my eating.* My sneak and binge eating were my comfort and the only place in my life where I allowed myself to be rebellious. But at that point, I really felt like God had abandoned me and was choosing not to help me. I felt not only abandoned but rebuked.

In that rocking chair, I could not pray any longer. I was experiencing a spiritual death, separated from my relationship with God for the first time in my life, and that was the scariest thing of all.

Four

PRESS ON

It was mid-November. My husband nursed me through the holidays and on the second of January took me to the hospital for a voluntary thirty-day commitment. I'd had a nervous breakdown and needed to revamp my life. Alone in my hospital room the first night, I felt totally abandoned by everyone, everything. A stack of books was on the side table—a thirty-day program based on the Twelve Steps of Alcoholics Anonymous.

I opened the Twelve Step book. "Step One—We admitted we were powerless over our lives—that our lives had become unmanageable." Yep, I could agree to that. "Step Two—Came to believe that a Power greater than ourselves could restore us to sanity." My breathing became labored. "Step Three—Made a decision to turn our will and our lives over to the care of God as we understood Him." Tears poured down my face as I practically screamed, *"Nooooo—God and I have gone our separate ways—I can't do this."* But I did.

Now I look back at that thirty-day program of thirty years ago as a life and soul saver. Those thirty days plus the next five years, on and off, helped me come to terms with all my secrets and shame. As the angels, Tess and Monica, from the TV show *Touched by an Angel* had said, the truth did set me free.

I learned that ultimately it didn't really matter how I had gotten to this point, who had done what to me, what my past indiscretions had been, or who had hurt me. I had to finally stop playing the blame game and accept responsibility for who I was and what my actions were now. I had to choose to accept responsibility for myself each day. I had over thirty years of bad habits, and although there might have been good reason for them at some time, it was time to let them go. Old habits are certainly hard to break, but I finally chose to make decisions with my eyes wide open and with conscious thought. I would no longer blindly react to long-ago feelings and hurts.

I came to the understanding that I had been unable to be honest with myself, let alone anyone else, about what I was doing, why I was doing it, and how I had gotten this way. I became willing to look at my problem behaviors honestly. It took a lot of fact-finding, and I had to learn to let go of the anger, the guilt, and the shame. I became able to put the issues in perspective, to learn from them, to forgive others, and, even more importantly, to forgive myself.

But it did not all come about overnight with a single decision. I was finally aware and willing, but it took time and hard work to bring about the change. The years of "pulling myself together" were not always easy. I sometimes just wanted to stop trying, but I stayed on track no matter how slow the progress was—and there was always progress, even if it felt minute at times.

And that brings me back to my third scripture, Philippians 3:13b–14. Paul writes, "Forgetting what is behind and straining toward what is ahead, I press on toward the goal to win the prize for which God has called me heavenward in Christ Jesus."

I never stopped trying. I kept straining forward. I have a friend who has been clean and sober for many years with Alcoholics Anonymous. One of the things they say in each meeting is something like this, paraphrased: "Rarely have we found anyone who cannot succeed in this program unless they are constitutionally incapable." On one of my days when I felt like I just couldn't keep moving forward, I told her that I thought I was "constitutionally incapable." She just roared with laughter, and I was put in my place. And so I was reminded of this passage and kept moving forward.

I did many years of therapy, and I developed a list of Tools and Exercises that can be done to get past issues of anger, hurt, anxiety, and low self-esteem (see Part Three). When one stopped helping, I tried another. When I ran out of exercises given to me by therapists, I started making up my own. Every step of the way was preceded by prayer, and I felt God's hand every step of the way. When I was at an impasse, I'd think back to that overstuffed rocking chair and instead of seeing myself in it alone, I imagined God sitting in that chair with me on his lap—rocking me, comforting me, making me feel loved. I'd never had that in an earthly father, and it warmed my soul to drift away in that rocking chair with Him. As my Christian friend Ellie had advised, I "stopped struggling and started snuggling."

Five

CAN I GET THERE FROM HERE?

O ne exercise I did involved a doll. In my thirty-day hospital commitment, in a group session, the therapist simply asked us to close our eyes and think back to our earliest childhood memory. The sight of myself standing on the grass of a neighbor's yard drifted into my mind's eye. There was a police car down the street. Then I was standing in front of a closet door. I pushed the door aside, and huddled inside was a little girl. She was about five years old with blond ponytails, wearing a light-blue jumpsuit. The hanging clothes softly brushed the top of her head. She was curled up in the corner, her knees pulled up against her chest, her head resting on her knees, and she was crying. I guess I started to cry, too, because ever so softly I felt a hand on my shoulder and a soft voice telling me to keep my eyes closed and to just tell her what I saw. "Me," I said, "hiding in the closet."

It was a pivotal point in my recovery, and after I left the hospital, I decided I wanted to make a doll that would represent that time. Well, I didn't want to really make it myself, but I wanted to find someone to make it for me. I found several crafters who made dolls to order, but for one reason or another, it never worked out to get one for me. God was putting up one roadblock after another. You see, He wanted *me* to make the doll. I finally agreed to tackle the project, and in the end, I had reinvented myself—God had a purpose in having me do it myself.

That was the beginning of self-acceptance for me. I had never loved myself or thought I was good enough. But I learned that God loves me just the way I am. Can I improve? Of course, and God wants that for me, but for today, He loves me just the way I am—today. I came to this self-acceptance with the help of several Tools and Exercises from Part Three: Personalize Your Bible, GOD CAN, Ghost Chair, Writing, Fill in the Blanks, and God Talk. God Talk involved a notebook that I kept at my bedside. I started a nightly routine in which I imagined myself on God's lap in that rocking chair again while I verbally reviewed my day with Him—what I had done, had not done, ways I had succeeded and failed. And then I picked up my pen, and God wrote me messages in my notebook. He'd write:

Sherry, you were so thoughtful when you comforted that woman at the car wash.
Sherry, I'm so proud of how you stood up for yourself at work today.
Sherry, I really like the new outfit you bought—you look great.
Sherry, I forgive you for...

Learning to see my words and actions through His eyes and to rejoice with Him over even the smallest victories began a process of self-acceptance.

And then there was the act of forgiveness—that was an area of my life that I did readily for others on a daily basis, but I was so hard on myself—I just couldn't forgive myself for *my* indiscretions. Then, in a group therapy session, a woman said that she'd been reading her Bible, and it just suddenly came to her that if God could forgive her, "who the heck do I think I am to not forgive myself?" She said if she didn't forgive herself after God had, it was like she was putting herself above Him. That really sank in for some reason, and I started a whole campaign of forgiving myself that allowed me to love myself. I used the bedside notebook to reinforce this in my nightly God Talk.

Forgiving those who hurt me took a bit more—I thought I had forgiven them but had really just dismissed myself as not being important enough to bother with. I used several exercises to fully express my anger. Until I could get in touch with the anger, there was nothing to forgive. It was agonizing to express my feelings, but I was important enough to go through the process. I was finally able to truly forgive them, which felt like a breath of fresh air.

Tools and Exercises that were especially helpful were the Ghost Chair and GOD CAN. The other exercise that was helpful was spending hours Personalizing My Bible. For instance, John 5:6 reads, "When Jesus saw him lying there and learned that he had been in this condition a long time, He asked him, 'Do you want to get well?'" I put lines through the pronouns and actions and wrote in my name and appropriate actions so that it now reads, "When Jesus saw Sherry lying there and learned that she had been addicted for thirty years, He asked her, 'Sherry, do you want to get well?'" And Psalm 142:6 reads, "Rescue me from those who pursue me for they are too strong for me." My version reads, "Rescue me from compulsive overeating for the urges are too strong for me." I had to learn to love myself as God loved me.

Another thing that helped my recovery was gathering information with the Fill in the Blanks tool. Finding out as much as we are able about a situation may help to put things into proper perspective. My aunt was a fountain of information about my biological father, which helped fill in the gaps in my memory. I had always felt abandoned by my father, somehow feeling that I was not loved enough for him to stay around. In going through my mother's things, I found a poem that he had written on a scrap of paper when I was a baby. It is entitled simply "Sherry" and can be read in Part Two.

That poem let me know that I was loved. He struggled with bipolar disorder in the days before they even had the term *bipolar* and before there was any understanding or medicine for what he was dealing with. It was easier to forgive him with that knowledge.

After several years of therapy and working a Twelve Step program, I had come to an acceptance of my past, I loved and accepted myself the way I was, I had forgiven others, and I was forgiven myself. I was in a surprisingly good place, but I still had three distinct problems—disturbing dreams, paranoia, and panic attacks.

All my life I'd had disturbing dreams—three, to be exact, always the same three dreams. Two were a variation of the same dream. I was alone on a typical neighborhood street, fearfully running from someone I never saw. In one variation the houses were all dark, with no one home to help me. In the other variation, the house lights were on but then would go off as I approached for help. The other dreams were rape dreams. I would awaken with a sudden panic, out of breath and terrified.

In addition to the dreams, I had unfounded fears and felt unsafe. When I was out in public, I oftentimes felt like I was being followed. I was panicky getting the keys into the car door or house door before "they" could get me. Once in the car or house, I was fearful that someone was inside. In the car I would check the back seat and then, as I drove, watch to see if someone was following me. Once in the house, I had to check every window and door lock and then check every nook and cranny before I could relax and feel safe. It was exhausting.

The overwhelming panic attacks would surface without warning. I would suddenly feel short of breath with a heaviness on my chest; I'd feel lightheaded with waves of heat and nausea. I was unable to concentrate or focus until the symptoms subsided.

Six

SWITCHING GEARS

In spite of the fact that I still had those problems, my life had improved so dramatically, and I was just tired of working on myself—I felt like I needed a break. One day, at my nephew's soccer game, I saw a woman with a dog wearing a special vest. After talking to her, I discovered that the dog was a guide dog in training and that the training institute was just about an hour from my home. I'd wanted a dog for some time, but we weren't home enough to really care for one, but this dog could legally go with us everywhere. This was not a dog I'd have to leave at home. Of course, I knew I'd fall in love with it and then have to give it up, but I felt the risks were worth the rewards. It was time for me to be doing something for someone else.

So my husband and I launched into a ten-year adventure of raising six guide dogs for Guide Dogs of America in Southern California. We originally thought we'd do just one, but when you have to give up one dog, getting another puppy just feels right to fill the void.

About twelve months after we got our first dog, Cochise, a yellow Labrador retriever (you keep them about eighteen months), I noticed that I wasn't checking the house for intruders and I wasn't panicking at the door. I mentioned it to my husband, and he said he'd noticed it too. We went on to our second dog, and after about six months with Zuni, a black Lab, I noticed that I hadn't had a disturbing dream in quite some time. We moved on to Denali, a yellow Lab, Cheyenne, a chocolate Lab, and Kosi, a black Lab. I still had panic attacks, but the paranoia and dreams had not returned for about eight years at this point. Then along came Kiva, a black Lab. He was my dog from the very beginning. He stayed by my side and snuggled at my feet. When he was about six months old, he started pestering me on occasion—sitting in front of me, staring at me, pawing at my leg. I just thought he wanted attention, but then my husband started noticing that every time he did that behavior, I would have a panic attack shortly thereafter. We started taking note of it, and he was right. Eventually, I learned that if I paid attention to Kiva and stopped what I was doing, took a break, did some deep breathing and a little writing, I could avoid the panic attack. When I didn't pay attention to him, about thirty minutes later, I'd have a full-blown panic attack. I haven't had a panic attack in about fifteen years now. I was seeing a psychiatrist at the time, and when I told him about Kiva he said, "You need to keep this one for yourself." I told him that I'd love to keep Kiva, but a contract is signed when you take on a guide dog puppy, ensuring that you will give him back. So when it came time to take Kiva back to the Guide Dogs of America, I did just that. About a week later, I got a call from the school. They were sorry, but Kiva would not be able to be a guide dog—he had a small cataract, and they couldn't take a chance on it getting worse. "Ah gee, that's too bad," I said, "I'll keep him." I always say that God intended Kiva to be mine all along. He was by my side for over twelve years as my PTSD companion.

So I started an adventure that I thought was to help others and ended up getting the very help I needed as well. Never think that your options are closed—you never know what is around the corner.

Sherry and Kiva

Seven

PEACE AND CONTENTMENT

So my recovery was just about complete. I had dealt with all my secrets and demons. I finally loved myself and was at peace with myself and with God. My relationships were all in good shape. My paranoia, panic attacks and dreams were things of the past. I no longer did any binge eating, but I have to admit that I still struggled somewhat with my comfort foods.

In 1 Corinthians 10:23, Paul writes that "all things are permissible for me, but not all things are beneficial." I learned to apply that principle to my food and to all avenues of my life. "Ok," I say to myself, "I can have cake, but is it beneficial?" It's a different perspective than saying, "I'm on a diet, and I can't have that." I lost seventy pounds fifteen years ago and have maintained that loss for all fifteen years. My food is not perfect, and I'd still like to lose another fifteen pounds, but my food does not control my life anymore.

I found that growing spiritually was and is the key to continuing peace and contentment. Growing indicates a continuing process. Plants continue to grow, and when they quit growing, they become stagnant and die. I am a project-driven person. I like to take on projects and see them through from beginning to end. I enjoy the process and feel a real sense of accomplishment with the outcome.

But I found those two concepts to be at odds with each other. I recognized the need to grow spiritually, and so I became more involved at church and at work by joining Bible studies. I went along for quite some time being content with that, feeling like I was growing spiritually and becoming more at peace in my life. But somewhere along the way, I began to feel agitated and restless. I felt frustrated and couldn't put my finger on the reason. So I started writing and discovered that I wanted to know the ending. I was approaching this part of my life like a project, and projects have an ending. This growing spiritually was a continuing, ongoing forever project. That concept overwhelmed me for quite some time and almost made me want to just walk away from it all together. But I just knew that God did not want our relationship to be so complicated.

When I need to work out a problem, Writing is my go-to exercise. In doing so, I started thinking about my salvation. For as far back as I can remember, my salvation was never in question. I had a really hard time functioning in this world and made life overly complicated, but I was secure in the next world. I viewed salvation as an uncomplicated gift that God had given to me long ago. I had no intention of giving it back, and I knew that God would never take it back either. He loves me, He sent His Son, I believe Christ is my Savior, I am saved. Ephesians 2:8 tells us that "it is by grace you have been saved, through faith—and this not from yourselves, it is a gift of God—not by works."

Somewhere along the line, I had confused my spiritual relationship with my salvation. My earthly brother, Bill, will always be my brother. Whether I choose to have a close relationship with him or not is another matter—but he will always be my brother (we do have a close relationship—love you, little brother). My salvation is secure. Whether I choose to have a close relationship with God is also another matter. Now, once you have been saved, it is only natural to want a close relationship with Him, and so I choose to maintain a close relationship, but my salvation is not dependent on that. There was a certain peace that came with that realization.

I realized that my previous attempts to forge a spiritual relationship were more of a "religious" attempt than a personal attempt. It was at that point that I began simply walking daily with my Lord. Now, that does not mean that my life became easy with no problems. It meant that I had a new BFF (best friend forever)—someone to confide my innermost feelings to, to cry with, and to talk to when lonely. I could ask for advice, share happy events, and share my victories. The Holy Spirit lives within me, so I am always with the Lord. I do read my Bible regularly, but it has taken on a whole new meaning. I no longer do so because I feel I should. I read the scriptures as a conversation with God. It is a means by which to strengthen our relationship and for Him to talk to me. In thinking of our relationship, I thought about my earthly relationships. Would it be much of a relationship if we never talked, never got together to do things, never shared our feelings with each other? God created us to have a relationship with Him. I confide in Him, and in His time, I hear from Him in a Bible passage, a magazine article, a billboard, a whisper in my ear, an innermost feeling, or a sermon at church.

No matter how the daily struggles play out, I am secure in Jesus. Knowing that my salvation is secure allows my day-to-day experiences to take on a proper perspective that allows me to experience hope instead of despair and move into victory instead of defeat. I just keep handing it over to God and live in His peace and contentment.

Contentment—I can honestly say that I am content in all circumstances; I don't necessarily *like* all circumstances, but I can be content. It's an attitude choice. I could have complained all the way through my recovery or chosen an attitude of acceptance. I chose the latter, and God rewarded me with His peace and a sense of contentment in every circumstance. But I could not have done that on my own strength—I was able to do that only through Christ, who gives me the strength.

Eight

HOW IS YOUR LIFE?

A re you living in peace and contentment? You could be. You may have demons like I did, shameful secrets, addictions, and failed relationships. Or you may just not feel like you are on the right track. Or you may think you've got it all together but cannot explain why you are not happy. Or you may be struggling in your relationship with God.

Are you struggling with an addiction or obsession? Are you happy with yourself and your relationships? For this, you need to be critically honest with yourself, or you may need to ask those around you and be prepared for an honest assessment.

I will use the terms *addiction* and *obsession* and *habit* interchangeably, as they are all degrees of the same issue. And they are only an issue if they interfere with other aspects of your life and/or those around you. If you find that they do interfere with your well-being or the rights of those around you—guess what, you need to address the problem. Consider the following:

Food was my problem. So am I addicted to food? I certainly hope so; it sustains life. So in that respect, addiction is not a bad word. But the way I ate was inappropriate and took on an addictive quality. Almost anything can be an obsession or addiction. Chewing gum can be an addiction. But is that a bad obsession? If the dentist is not noticing any problems with your teeth, if TMJ or jaw ache isn't an issue, if you can afford the habit, and if you are not driving your family crazy with smacking, then you are probably OK. But if you are experiencing jaw ache, headache, and tooth decay and/or if you are driving your family crazy—then you may need to address the problem.

In Ephesians 6:12, Paul tells us that "everything is permissible but not everything is beneficial." He was responding to questions of forbidden or permissible foods, but the logic can be applied to most situations. Certainly, chewing gum is permissible for most people, but maybe for you, it is not beneficial.

Drugs are permissible and beneficial under certain circumstances—pain control after surgery or for a disease. Most people can "do drugs" in that capacity. But for some, "doing drugs" is not beneficial. Alcohol has its benefits as well—a single calming glass of wine with dinner, for instance. But for many, it is not beneficial and therefore not permissible.

Food is a complex issue. Of course, food is permissible and beneficial, and you cannot just stop eating. For many, though, it's a powerful psychological addiction, and gaining control is quite complex.

My point is that almost anything can be an addiction—if not for us, then perhaps for others around us. Romans 14:17–21 tells us,

> The kingdom of God is not a matter of eating and drinking, but of righteousness, peace, and joy in the Holy Spirit, because anyone who serves Christ in this way is pleasing to God and approved by men. Let us therefore make every effort to do what leads to peace and to mutual edification. Do not destroy the work of God for the sake of food. All food is clean, but it is wrong for a man to eat anything that causes someone else to stumble. It is better not to eat meat or drink wine or to do anything else that will cause your brother to fall.

So if what you are doing is beneficial to you and is not creating problems for you or others in your life, then what you are doing is probably OK. But, for instance, if alcohol is OK for you but will be a challenge for your friend's hard-fought sobriety, then you should refrain from drinking when with that friend. No matter what the behavior, if it presents a problem or temptation for those around us, then we should refrain from that behavior for their sake.

You must be critically honest with yourself here. In my life, I had to admit the extent of my problem and how it affected others. I tried to convince myself that it only affected me—*my* life, *my* health, *my* appearance. But I had to honestly look at the money I spent on binge foods, the risk to my health and possible premature death, or other health problems by being overweight—diabetes, high blood pressure, high cholesterol—the emotional highs and lows that my loved ones had to live with, the cost of diet programs and the downsizing and eventual upsizing of clothes. Everything we do affects others, and we are responsible for our actions. If what we are doing, in spite of the benefit, is detrimental in any way to ourselves or those around us, then it is a problem to be addressed.

In spite of the benefit? What benefit could there be to overeating, being fat, drinking into oblivion, or doing drugs? For me, it started out as a comfort to feeling abandoned, and as the years went on, it just turned into habit. It was also a safety net for me. Although I didn't like looking and feeling fat, it did make me feel safe from sexual predators. When I finally saw how my actions had affected others, at first it only added to my guilt and shame. But as Christ and the *Touched by an Angel* angels promised, the truth did set me free—just not immediately. Working a Twelve Step program helped me to put it all in perspective.

Nine

TIME FOR DECISION-MAKING

For some people, a commitment to Christ with a daily recommitment may be enough—an instant healing, a miracle—it is so totally possible. But it doesn't always happen that way; many times, God has another agenda for us. We may not understand why, but we can trust and move forward in His will. For many, working a Twelve Step program is a wonderful way to put our lives back on track. It focuses on, first, putting ourselves right with God; second, repairing relationships; and third, accountability for our actions—past, present, and future.

Whatever your situation, there is probably a Twelve Step group out there—alcohol, drugs, gambling, sexual addiction, pornography, approval addiction, depression, fear, anxiety, control, anger, rage, lying, perfectionism, codependency, divorce, loss, or grief. The only problem I have with some of the programs is that they have to remain so general about the identity of God, and they don't include Christ, so as not to offend non-Christians. I was able to work through the program with my Christianity intact; in fact, it restored my relationship with Christ. But if that is a worry to you, there are two other ways to work the steps other than the traditional Twelve Step meetings.

"A Biblical Path to Calm the Chaos" is my Twelve Step Bible Study from a Christian perspective that can be done from home and is included here in Part Four. But I only recommend working the steps that way if you have an accountability partner. An accountability partner is someone with whom you would share your work and ask advice and someone who will keep you honest. We will discuss how to choose that accountability partner in Part Four. For now, suffice to say you should carefully consider who you include in your inner circle. Confidentiality is essential, as is the character and faith of that individual.

There is also a Christian Twelve Step program called Celebrate Recovery,[2] which is open to all disorders, addictions, and behaviors. It is a nationwide recovery program that primarily meets at churches, but it is not required that you attend that church, and it is open to the public. You can find a meeting place by looking them up on the internet.

If you are unsure about working a Twelve Step program, let me offer some scripture in support of that decision. In these programs, the steps are all worked with a sponsor (what I call an accountability partner) and stress the importance of accountability for our actions. This is to keep us honest with ourselves and to get honest encouragement. Pride often stands in the way of recovery, as we often resist answering for our actions. But Ephesians 5:21 tells us to "submit to one another out of reverence for Christ." And James 5:16 tells us to "confess your sins to each other and pray for each other." Recovery is not meant to be done alone—we need our Christian brothers and sisters to hold us accountable. Although Christian accountability involves confronting sin, its primary purpose is not to dwell on the sin but to encourage and strengthen one another and, through forgiveness, to put that sin behind us.

A major part of these programs is making amends to those we have hurt or harmed. Colossians 3:13 tells us to "bear with each other and forgive whatever grievances you may have against one another. Forgive as the Lord forgave you." There are many more scriptural references in support of a Twelve Step program, and I would encourage everyone to participate. The Bible Study in Part Four includes a series of steps and actions that can help with the forgiveness process.

For the past several years, God has had it heavy on my heart to write this book. The 2 Corinthians passage that I shared earlier that says that we should share "*so that we* can comfort those in any trouble with the comfort we ourselves have received from God" convinced me of that, so in gratitude to God, I have completed this book. I cannot and will not believe that I have worked through all my issues

---

[2] Celebrate Recovery, www.celebraterecovery.com

just to take care of myself. Others who have experienced anything even remotely similar need hope and encouragement. That is why, through Christ, I have made my life an open book and share my experience, strength, and hope. I will never allow anyone to make me feel rejected, dirty, unloved, abandoned, or angry again. God loves me, and through Him, I love myself.

Ten

TIME FOR ACTION

My overall message to you is summed up below in three take-action paragraphs. The first two are directed at your life. I prayerfully hope that you will act on them and put your life in a position to allow God to calm your chaos each and every day. The last one is directed at the lives of others and calls for us to think beyond our own front door and look at what is going on around us.

#1—If you have issues that stand in the way of a rich and full life and/or if you need to make some changes in your life or relationships, then I am calling you to action to make the necessary changes. Whether you choose to effect those changes through a Twelve Step program or counseling or Bible Study, I encourage you to make a decision and start on that journey. I encourage you to just never give up. Keep moving forward, keep trying, and you will reap the benefits of peace and contentment through Christ.

#2—This is really just a continuation of #1 above, but I believe it has enough significance to be addressed separately. If you have childhood issues that you have never faced, do not let them continue to fester. Deal with them once and for all, and I promise you that the truth will set you free. For some issues, you might want to include professional counseling along with your recovery program.

And #3—We need to think beyond ourselves. Abuse, whether it be sexual, physical, verbal, or emotional, is a major epidemic in our nation. Statistics are difficult to obtain because so much of it goes without being reported, and the definition of abuse varies from report to report. But several large studies suggest similar findings that one in ten children are abused every year in the US. A report of child abuse is made every ten seconds (and what about the ones not reported?). Almost five children die every day as a result of child abuse, and more than three out of four of them are under the age of four. It is estimated that there are sixty million survivors of childhood sexual abuse in America today. Most of them exhibit long-term post-traumatic effects, including fear, anxiety, depression, anger, hostility, inappropriate sexual behavior, poor self-esteem, substance abuse, and difficulty with close relationships. Over 60 percent of people in drug rehab centers report being abused or neglected as a child.[3]

The first time I went to group therapy for my weight, I learned that 90 percent of the women there had been sexually molested as children. I was flabbergasted, disgusted, and appalled. And those were just the women who turned to food to deal with the unspeakable. What about the ones who turned to alcohol or drugs or never sought help at all and continued destructive behaviors or committed suicide? The numbers are staggering. It is an epidemic that just cannot be tolerated! It is truly a national disaster. We need to help those who have been victims like I was, but even more, we need to stop the *crimes*!

How can we just sit back and pretend that it's not happening? I am asking you to be vigilant. We all have children in our lives—our own children, nieces and nephews, our children's friends, and grandchildren. If you are an educator, you have dozens of children in your life. Take a few moments and think of all the children you know—name ten of them in your head. See each one's face. Which one out of the ten is being sexually abused right now? See the faces again. Imagine what they are going through right now, and then look twenty years down the road and realize that each one of them will probably deal with some sort of addiction or destructive behavior because of these acts against them as children.

If you know a child who has been a victim of emotional, physical, or sexual abuse, encourage the family to get counseling. Every victim needs to be assured that what was done *to* them does not define them or make them a bad person. They need to be assured that they will be safe and given tools to safeguard them from

---

3 "Statistics and Facts About Child Abuse in the U.S.," www.americanspcc.org, *American Society for the Positive Care of Children*, accessed 2015; "Child Abuse and Neglect Fatalities 2012," www.childwelfare.gov, *Child Welfare Information Gateway*, accessed 2015.

future travesty and to have healing programs available to them so that they will be able to heal from the past abuse in a positive manner. A traumatic event can be put into proper perspective if dealt with in a timely manner. But if the situation is swept under the rug, that child *will*—not may, but *will*—develop unhealthy habits or attitudes to deal with it. PTSD is not just for soldiers; the effects of PTSD can manifest themselves in anyone who has experienced trauma.

See those children's faces again. If you ever think that something is not right in a child's life, do not be afraid to speak up. Monitor the judges in your district. If a particular judge is being lenient on sentencing child molesters, lobby to get him out of office. It's not a pleasant subject, but it is even less pleasant to the child being abused. If you would be interested in donating time or money, look for organizations in your community that focus on the rights of children, the recovery of child victims, and abuse prevention. Ten percent of the sale of this book is donated to organizations such as Alliance for Children's Rights and World Vision for Sexually Exploited Children.[4]

Also, remember to put the problem to prayer. Make it part of your daily prayers, and we can make a difference. Don't be complacent. Remember, prayer is an action verb.

Pray for God to lead you through this program for *your own* healing and for Him to reveal when the time is right and what your actions should be regarding the national disaster of child abuse.

May God bless you in your recovery and self-discovery.

---

[4] Alliance for Children's Rights, 3333 Wilshire Blvd, #550, Los Angeles, CA 90010, www.allianceforchildrensrights.org, 213-368-6010; World Vision, Sexually Exploited Children, POB 9716, Federal Way, WA 98063, www.worldvision.org, 888-511-6548

CONCLUSION

Perhaps there is no real ending to my story, as our lives are always evolving. But if you would like to embark on a recovery process of your own, I can tell you that the journey is well worth the effort. I can honestly say that I wish much of my past did not exist and that I had not had to endure some of my experiences, but I can also tell you that I would not be the person I am today without them. Not that I am without flaws, but I know that I am a kinder, gentler, more patient and loving human being as a result of my experiences. I will never know what my path might have been without them. We cannot change our past, and we can let it define us, or we can learn from the experiences and be the best version of ourselves that God would have for us today.

On Good Friday, we remember the sacrifice of our Lord and Savior Jesus Christ. On that day, a great sadness comes over me as I read the words and really understand the pain and anguish that Christ endured for me. And if that were the end of the story, it would be so very tragic. But that tragedy turns to absolute joy on Easter Sunday when we acknowledge the risen Christ and the gift of eternal life that is offered to us. In the same way, we endure hardship and pain and injustice in our lives here on earth, but God can take those experiences and turn them to good in us. David's song of praise in 2 Samuel 22:29 says of God, "You are my lamp, O Lord, the Lord turns my darkness into light." He has done that for me, and He can do that for you.

Part Four of this book, "A Biblical Path to Calm the Chaos," is one way to approach your life's tune-up or recovery. An addiction is not necessary to work the steps. They are effective tools for doing a tune-up of your life, putting your life in balance, and restoring relationships with or without an addiction. What I have done is present the Twelve Steps from a biblical perspective so that you can apply the principles to your need. These steps are effective to any recovery or tune-up and are worth the journey.

PART TWO

PERSPECTIVES

PERSPECTIVES

Compiled Writings of Sherry Miller

Following are short stories and poems that I wrote in the course of my recovery while working through the Twelve Step program. Writing is such an effective tool in recovery to uncover feelings, discover forgotten incidents, make sense out of the chaos, and forgive others and ourselves. With each story, I learned something about myself and discovered lessons that I could use to live a productive and positive life for the rest of my years. I hope they will touch your heart, and perhaps my perspectives will spark insights of your own. For the most part, each story is inspirational with an emphasis on a positive outcome, a lesson learned. There are, however, a couple that some may find disturbing—I hope so. Each leaves us with insights that carry over into all avenues of our lives and impact those around us. As you read my perspectives, it is my hope that they will inspire you to include Writing as a tool with your recovery and discovery. We cannot change the past, but we can learn from it.

The obvious tool used in these perspectives is Writing. But other tools were employed in coming to an understanding of the circumstances. I have noted at the end of each perspective what other Tools and Exercises from Part Three were employed.

Hopelessness

Suicide Kills

SUICIDE KILLS

Someone is in pain tonight.
He thinks it affects only him.
But little does he know, my friend,
the lives that his actions will dim.

Friends spent the evening with him that night.
They didn't suspect a thing.
He counted trump and played the hands
like he was Pinochle King.

I watched next day from down the street
as the police car drove to my door.
What could it mean—I'd never seen
One at my door before.

Mommy, Mommy, why all the tears?
Why is everyone crying?
Where is Daddy? Mommy, please tell.
What's all this talk of dying?

Innocence lost, no more a child,
For tonight I am in pain,
because suicide kills not just the one.
What did he hope to gain?

This was written before I had any understanding of my father's suicide. Healing started when I found the poem entitled "Sherry," which was written by my biological father, Richard Dale Blake.

Tools employed:

Fill in the Blanks	Ghost Chair	GOD CAN
Let Yourself Grieve	Prayer and Meditation	
Talk to Someone	Up in Smoke	

Full Circle

Lingering Love—Sherry

Normalcy in the Midst of Chaos

Father's Day

From the Heart

Bridging the Gap

Making Amends

Stepmother—Not So Evil After All

Joy—A Story of Faith

Lingering Love

But five I was when I lost my dad,
No memory of him still lingers.
What was he like? His touch, his smile.
Did he love me? The thought lingers.
Scrapbooks and photos offer some clues,
but the question of his heart still lingers.
A scrap of paper found under the stack
warms my soul in a way that lingers.

Sherry

A cry, a wail in the dark of the night.
Papa wakes and jumps in fright.
First the bottle, then the cream.
A rush against time—a wail, a shout.
First you feed, and then you burp.
Change her clothes, then comes the work.
Six paces to the left, three to the right.
Change a diaper, turn off the light.
Back to sleep, and in the morn'
I'm awfully glad my Sherry was born.

—RDB

I wrote "Lingering Love" after finding the "Sherry" poem among my mother's things shortly after her death in 1981. "Sherry" was written by my biological father, Richard Dale Blake.

Tools employed:

Fill in the Blanks   Ghost Chair   Talk to Someone
Visualization

Normalcy in the Midst of Chaos

I was five years old and did not understand what was happening. Everything seemed wrong; people were upset, nobody was talking, my mother was crying. My father had committed suicide.

In the midst of chaos, however, there was a sense of normalcy—Grandma (my maternal grandmother) was there. Meals were served, beds were made, laundry was done, the house was cleaned, and the cards were shuffled for a game of Go Fish. I was tucked into bed each night with a prayer and a kiss. This, I was to learn, was Grandma's job—to create a sense of normalcy even in the midst of chaos.

This scene was repeated when my brother was born; when measles and mumps ran through the family; when my mother was diagnosed and underwent surgery and treatment for breast cancer; and when, as an adult, I was divorced with a two-year-old daughter to care for. Grandma returned with each occasion and created a sense of normalcy. The only thing that changed was the game for which the cards were shuffled. We graduated from Go Fish to Canasta to King's Corners. She was, for me, a symbol of stability and security, and I loved her dearly.

Grandma was a good, stout, German farm girl with a rich Lutheran heritage who had no time for pity parties. She just rolled up her sleeves and did what she could. That attitude, I'm sure, started in her childhood when, at the age of twelve, she lost her own mother to TB. She and her sisters had to take over the running of the household, which included cooking for the farm hands, raising the smaller children, and all the daily cleaning and washing chores. There was no time to feel sorry for herself.

When asked what she admired most about her father, she said she was so thankful "that he kept us all together after my mother died." In those days, children were often farmed out to relatives when the wife died. Consequently, family meant a great deal to her, and she and her sisters had a special emotional bond, perhaps from working as a team to run the household. She was in attendance for the birth of every one of her grandchildren, a fact that she held dear.

I felt blessed when, in her late nineties, I was able to give back just a bit of what I'd received. Going to the nursing home every week was sometimes heartbreaking. She was not particularly happy there, she could no longer care for herself, and she'd sometimes question, "Why doesn't the good Lord just take me?" But true to her nature, she never complained and was grateful for every little thing that was done for her. The smile that radiated from her face when she saw me walk through the doorway was worth every trip.

I was given the opportunity to create a sense of normalcy in the midst of her chaos. I wrote letters for her, manicured her nails, fixed her hair, and shuffled the deck of cards. She died at one hundred years and eight months, and I miss her very much. But her legacy continues.

My best friend Linda died of breast cancer at the age of forty-eight. I could not cure her. I could not take away the pain. I could not answer the question of "why?" But I could manicure her nails, style her wig, decorate for the holidays, and bring a smile to her face. I was able to create a sense of normalcy for Linda in our weekly visits.

I watched my best friend deteriorate, and it broke my heart. But through my grandmother's example, I was able to focus on what I could do instead of focusing on what I could not do. When I think of my grandmother, her presence said, *Everything will be OK.* I can physically feel myself taking a deep breath of fresh air at the thought of her. The world in which we live will always have elements of chaos, but we can experience peace in the midst of that chaos through the choices we make and by the grace of God.

Tools employed:

The Breaststroke	Deep Breathing	GOD CAN
Self-Affirmations		

FATHER'S DAY

My biological father's suicide when I was five left me feeling as though I'd done something wrong, that if I had been better somehow, maybe he'd have stayed around. My mother remarried shortly thereafter, and this man was my dad until I was nineteen. I called him Dad and used his name all through school. But when he and my mother divorced, the relationship gradually disappeared. Once again, I wondered what was wrong with me that I couldn't keep a father.

Mother remarried again, and Bob was a wonderful, kind man. I was twenty now and no longer living at home, but I felt a great love and attachment for him. A few years later, my mother was diagnosed with cancer and was not given long to live. Several months before she died, Bob came over to my house alone one day. We talked about a lot of things, and then he told me that he wanted me to know that he would always be there for me, even after Mother was gone. Then he asked if he could adopt me.

I could hardly believe my ears. Tears streamed down my face. He wanted me—me! This man had no obligation to me, but he was reaching out from his heart, and I accepted. During the adoption proceedings, the judge commented on all the undesirable duties of his profession and then, with a tear in his eye, thanked us for brightening his day as he pronounced us father and daughter. I was twenty-seven and married with a daughter of my own, but I was his little girl.

Five short years later, Bob, too, was diagnosed with cancer and was gone within the year. At first, I was hurt and angry at God for taking this father away from me too. But eventually the love and acceptance that I felt from Dad came through again, and I became, once more, grateful for the years we had.

On Father's Day, I always reflect on what I've learned about fatherhood. I've learned that it is not dependent on biology or even on raising a child. Fatherhood is a matter of the heart. Bob's gift from the heart will warm my soul for eternity.

Tools employed:

The Breaststroke	Fill in the Blanks	Ghost Chair
GOD CAN	Hurt List	Let Yourself Grieve

FROM THE HEART

S iblings by blood. Siblings in Christ. Siblings by marriage. Sisters by adoption. We are all of that—Jann, Sherry, Cindy, and Bill. We are all siblings in Christ. Sherry, Cindy, and Bill are siblings by blood. We three girls are sisters by marriage and adoption. But most importantly, the four of us are siblings by choice.

These are the facts (and if you are old enough, you know that phrase comes from the black-and-white TV show *Dragnet*).

Jann was born in 1950 and grew up in a middle-class home in Orange County, California, with her dad, Bob, and her mother, Wanda. Her mother died of breast cancer in 1968.

I, Sherry, was born in 1951, and Cindy was born in 1955. Our father died when I was five and Cindy was one. Our mother, Mavis, remarried, and we grew up with a stepfather and a new baby brother, Bill, who was born in 1961. We also grew up in a middle-class home in Orange County, California. Mavis also developed breast cancer and had a mastectomy of one breast in 1963, but she survived. Our mother and stepfather divorced in 1971.

In 1973, the stars aligned just right to bring us all together. Jann and Mavis met at work at the now defunct Broadway department store. As fate would have it, they struck up a friendship, and Jann eventually introduced my mother to her father. Before long, we were planning a wedding.

My mother seldom opened up to me on personal matters, but she was now, like me, a single divorced woman, so we had a common bond that we had not had before. She talked to me about dating Bob like we were girlfriends. We giggled and shared tender moments—a time together that I cherish. One night as we talked, she broke down in tears. She and Bob had not yet been intimate, but she could tell things were moving in that direction, and she just sobbed as she asked me, "How do I tell him about my mastectomy?" Then I cried too.

Mavis had always been attractive. She dressed well, and her hair and makeup were always done. I remember the first time she tried to buy a bathing suit after the mastectomy. They did not do reconstructive surgery in those days like they do today. We shopped for hours, and she did her best to keep the tears at bay as one bathing suit after another was tossed in the *no* pile. We finally found one that did a side sweep over one shoulder and left the other shoulder strapless, but it was for the wrong side. But that gave her hope, and she went home and made one that very day. We had a pool in our backyard, and we entertained often, so it was important to my mother to dress appropriately and look good.

I told my mother she'd just have to tell Bob about the mastectomy and that if he really loved her, it wouldn't make any difference. I could understand her fear, though. Then she told me that his first wife had died of breast cancer. That shed a whole new light on things. No matter how much he loved my mother, would he be able to get past the emotional scarring from his first wife's death? We cried and prayed about it.

The next week, she came to me with a smile and said, "You'll never guess what he said. He said he loves me, not my boob (or lack thereof)." So they were married in 1973, and Jann, Cindy, Bill, and I became siblings. At this point, Bill was the only one still living at home, so we never really bonded as siblings with Jann. We liked each other and had a good time together at holidays and such, but that was about it. The four of us had never lived together, so we had no history. We lived several hours apart from each other, and there had not been any time for us to really get to know each other.

A little over a year later, Mavis was diagnosed with cancer again. They had taken her in for a routine hysterectomy, and she was so full of cancer that they just closed her back up. They gave her six months to live, but she was a fighter. Chemotherapy was pretty new at that time and not an option, but she sought out unconventional doctors and tried many experimental trials. She far outlasted the doctor's prediction but finally succumbed six years later. She was healthy and happy for most of that time frame, but the last few months were really hard on all of us.

I honestly do not know how Bob held up through it all. He had lost his first wife to cancer, and then, hardly past the newlywed stage, it was thrown in his face again. As a true testament to his character, he held it together and was there for her to the very end. But it was another gesture of love before my mother died that touched my heart forever, when he gave himself to us kids through adoption. We were now four siblings instead of three, and Jann was no longer an only child.

The next six years scooted along quickly. Dad (Bob) moved from the house into an apartment. Jann had moved to Colorado, and Cindy was overseas with her husband's job, but they came for visits when they could. But mostly it was just Dad, Bill, and me and our families. Dad came over to visit often, and we enjoyed our time together as father and daughter. He played golf regularly and even started dating a lady from church we all approved of wholeheartedly. We all got together and played penny-ante poker and watched the TV show *Murder, She Wrote* every Sunday evening. It was a good time.

Then he too was diagnosed with cancer—colon cancer. After watching two wives fight valiantly to the end, he had no energy left for himself and was gone within the year. For a while, it really hurt that I had finally found a father and that he was now gone too. But it was in that time frame that a sisterhood with Jann really began to blossom.

Jann made more frequent visits to California while our dad was ill, and she phoned often for updates. When she visited, Dad was not always up to playing host, and she and I would sit and chat. We shared stories of our childhood and, having grown up just a few miles apart, found so much common ground. We shared our faith and our commitment to Jesus Christ. We were now forming a basis for a lasting relationship—truly as sisters. Our phone calls moved from just health updates to genuinely caring about what was going on in each other's lives. We prayed with and for each other and were genuinely concerned about how the other was dealing with the impending passing of our father and the hurt that still lingered from the loss of our mothers.

When I revealed, for the first time to any family member, that I had been molested as a child, Jann was beside herself to learn that there was someone she could talk to about her childhood molestation. There is no doubt we were brought together for more than just sisterhood. We really needed each other.

As Dad was nearing the end, our sister Cindy flew in from South Africa. We four siblings spent many nights into the wee hours really getting to know each other. We were like kids again, hanging out in the family room developing the relationships that we didn't get by living together as kids. Dad was quite ill by this point, but he told me how he loved listening to our chatter as he lay in bed. He was glad to know he wasn't leaving us alone, knowing that we had each other.

Bob warmed my heart with his gift of adoption, and the few brief years we had as father and daughter were healing for me. I don't know if Dad actually realized just how far-reaching his gift really was. I believe that God planted a seed, and with no knowledge of the consequences, Dad just acted from his heart. Just as he had given himself to us as our mother was dying, he had brought the four of us together to be there for each other. Dad gave us the gift of sister and brotherhood that is an ongoing, constantly evolving relationship. It is truly the gift that just keeps on giving.

Tools employed:

GOD CAN   Let Yourself Grieve   Prayer and Meditation

BRIDGING THE GAP

I sat alone in the hospital room. Committed for thirty days. How had I let my life get to this point?

My weight was only a symptom of underlying problems. I'd spent years dieting, exercising, praying, soul searching, and berating myself for all the failures. I'd recently lost fifty pounds and felt on top of the world until the pounds started migrating back—again. I couldn't stop it; it was like a runaway train that I was trying to stop with a Superman stance. Laxative and diuretic abuse was my desperate attempt to gain control until the night I thought I was dying on the bathroom floor. In the predawn hours, I had locked myself in the bathroom until the shock waves passed, too ashamed to tell my husband what I had been doing to myself.

After I survived that night, I rocked for hours and days in our overstuffed rocking chair, thinking only of suicide. Voices from the past floated through my consciousness.

We never suspected a thing.
Your mother was devastated.
We played cards with him just the night before.

Knowing how my father's suicide affected my family, I knew I couldn't do that to my husband and children. So there I sat in the hospital, alone, scared, and desperate. God had always been a part of my life, but now I felt abandoned even by Him.

The thirty days included education, spiritual renewal, and intense therapy. In one session, I "found" my child self hiding in the closet (see Part One, Chapter Five). What I had discovered was my little five-year-old self who'd been lost in the aftermath of my father's suicide. With writing, talking, prayer, and continued therapy, I came to terms with my past: my father's suicide, my feelings of guilt and confusion, and habits that I had developed as coping tools (such as comfort eating).

I decided that I wanted to make a doll that would represent the bridge from my lost childhood to reconciliation. The only problem was that I hated to sew. I was a crafter, but I tried to take on only projects that did not require the use of a sewing machine. So for the first year after my discharge, I looked for someone I could pay to make the doll for me. I visited craft fairs, doll shops, antique malls, and craft and fabric stores. I talked to several crafters and got phone numbers for others. I was willing to pay whatever they wanted but could not find even one interested party. I prayed and talked to God. Surely, He could see the healing power in having the doll. Indeed, eventually He made me aware that He could see the healing power in *me* making the doll. So I began.

Joann's Fabrics netted a wealth of patterns, fabrics, and yarns from which to choose. Fabric paints, brushes, stuffing, and thread completed the shopping list. I worked on the doll every evening after work and weekends. I was still no master seamstress, but it turned into a labor of love. I took my time and enjoyed the process. The sewing machine even cooperated with no binding bobbins or puckered seams.

The day came that the body, extremities, head, and hair were done. All that remained was to paint the face and then the clothing, of course, but I was putting off even thinking about the clothes until later. I was really worried about ruining all my work so far by botching up the face. I considered asking someone else to help but by now realized that God had me doing this on my own for a reason. I said a prayer and worked on her eyes and then her eyebrows. Another prayer, and her nose. Yet another prayer, and her mouth completed the face. And then it happened—a drop of dark pink paint on her hand. I blotted it off the best I could, but there was no getting rid of it. I just sat and cried. I had ruined all my hard work.

Why was God putting me through this impossible exercise in futility?
Should I toss her out and start all over?
Was all my work for nothing?

I've always known that God put my husband into my life as my Rock of Gibraltar, and he came through once again. Jim passed through the family room where I sat crying, doll in lap. Once he understood my dilemma, he simply took brush in hand and painted a beige Band-Aid over her boo-boo. "All better," he said with a kiss to my hand. It made me realize that God has never given up on imperfect me, so for my doll to have a flaw just made her perfectly imperfect.

Next, I had to consider her clothing. *Do I really have to sew those too?* I prayed. God let me off the hook and led me to a Gymboree children's clothing store, where my little girl was a perfect newborn size with a size-two infant shoe. The sales-clerk, who had as much fun as I did, found matching ponytail bands to complete her outfit.

Today I am grateful for that nervous breakdown. I am grateful that God blocked my quest to find someone else to make my doll for me. And I am grateful for every stitch in my Sherry doll that helped me bridge the gap from age five to forty-five.

Tools employed:

Fill in the Blanks   GOD CAN   Make a Project

MAKING AMENDS

My Side of the Street

I n working a Twelve Step program, one of the essential parts of the program is about making amends. In order to move on in life with a clear conscience, it is imperative to right any wrongs we have done. I am a pretty humble person and generally have no problem admitting when I am wrong. Saying I am sorry is not difficult for me, and then I can put the matter to rest—unless the other person will not forgive. It is difficult for me to let go if the other person will not accept my apology.

In a situation with my paternal grandmother, I learned that a person can be genuinely repentant but have no control over the recipient of our repentance. I had heard often, "We can only take care of our side of the street." What is meant by that is that no matter how genuine our repentance may be, they may never be able to forgive us, and we will just have to live with that. If we have sincerely taken care of our side of the street, we will have to move on with our life knowing that we did the best we could with the circumstances. How they deal with things on their side of the street is their business, and we cannot tell them how to live.

I was on the phone with my paternal grandmother.

"Look at the mess you've made. You're not even twenty years old, and you're already a mother and a divorcee."

"If your mother had been a better mother..."

"You know it's your mother's fault that your father is dead..."

"If he'd been here..."

"Your mother kept you girls from us..."

"Obviously she doesn't care if you get your father's share..."

I was in shock. I couldn't believe the words coming out of my grandmother's mouth. I was so taken by surprise that I couldn't even respond. I have no recollection of how the phone call ended, only that I sat numb for what seemed like hours. *Why was she attacking my mother? What did she mean about my mother's fault? What was the significance of "my father's share?" Why didn't I defend my mother?*

I had heard that when you are confused or hurt, it could be helpful to sit down and write a letter to that person. So I did. I wrote a letter to my grandmother defending my mother and saying some hurtful things. I was young and naïve and misunderstood that the intent of the letter was supposed to be to help you vent and identify your feelings but that it should not be mailed—at least not that first draft. Well, I vented quite well and got in touch with my feelings, but it was very wrong of me to mail such a hurtful letter. Even before it probably reached her, I was miserable and considered how I could possibly retrieve it.

It bothered me so much that I finally had to talk to my mother about it. My father had died when I was five, and now at age twenty, I still knew nothing surrounding that time frame. It had never been discussed, and I had always somehow known it was something that we just did not talk about. When I told her about the phone call and the things my grandmother had said and what I had done, she told me to go get my sixteen-year-old sister.

When we came back, my mother was crying. She apologized for not telling us sooner about our father's death—his suicide. Carbon monoxide poisoning. She cried some more. Fifteen years after the fact, my sister and I sat there dumbfounded. In answer to my questions, she finally went on to explain that our grandmother had always blamed my mother for his suicide (many years later, I learned that he had been bipolar) and that over the years, my grandmother had threatened to withhold our "father's share" of the inheritance if my mother restricted our visits with her at all.

My mother told me that I had made a mistake in trying to defend her, but I should only pursue the matter if I was truly sorry and wanted a relationship. She warned me to never seek the relationship just for the money my grandmother had always used as leverage. I was terribly sorry, so I wrote the letter of apology, and I never heard another word from her again. I tried to call several times over the next several months, but each time my grandmother just hung up on me.

I knew I had done wrong. The grandparents I remembered went to church and made a big show of their church affiliation, so I did not understand why they couldn't or wouldn't forgive me or at least talk to me about it. And it bothered me that they had not only walked away from me but had also cut off all communication with my sister. She had not done anything wrong, so it made no sense that they were punishing her too. Had my grandmother just been looking for an excuse to walk away? The idea haunted me and made me sad. I sought forgiveness from God and tried to be content with that.

Eleven years later, as my mother was dying of cancer, she asked me if there was still no reconciliation with my grandmother. She told me that no one should die with anger in their heart and suggested I try one more time. And so I wrote one more apology letter. This time I got a response. I let my sister know, and she too wrote a letter and included photos of her two sons, one of whom bears a strong resemblance to our biological father.

For about a year, polite letters were sent back and forth, and then I asked if we could visit her in Arizona as we passed through from California to Texas to visit my husband's parents. She responded in the positive and asked us to stay the night with her. I had mixed feelings about spending the night, but I did not want to upset the apple cart, so we accepted the invitation. I found myself praying as the miles passed, asking God to give me the words to say and the actions to take that they would be acceptable in His sight. I asked Him to help us start with a fresh, new relationship.

She greeted us with guarded cordiality. The atmosphere seemed to warm some as my husband, my fifteen-year-old daughter, and I shared family photos and gave updates on our activities. Then she said that it was a shame that my grandfather had died before this reunion took place. I made a simple, short apology and refrained from saying anything about her refusal to accept my previous apologies and tried to move the conversation along. The edge in her voice was making it plain that she had not forgiven me, and the next thing I knew she was making small snide remarks about my mother again. I responded only that my mother had died of cancer several years ago, hoping to quietly put an end to the whole thing. But it continued. I excused myself and went to the bathroom. I needed time to regroup and think this through. I did not want to act in haste as I had years before. I prayed for guidance and felt a sense of calm come over me. *Have you forgiven her?* I sensed. *Yes,* I had. *Then extend the forgiveness.*

I returned to the living room, and she continued with little polite digs and barbs. It was as if she were baiting me. But I did not take the bait. Now I knew that to do so would seal my fate, just as a fish seals his fate when he takes the bait.

Being uncomfortable, I considered going to a motel for the night, but I feared that doing so would only add to the tension. Our luggage had already been brought in, and she had rooms set up for us. So we spent the night. Once alone, I asked my husband and daughter if I was being too sensitive, and they both responded in my defense at the appalling way this woman was talking to me.

Over breakfast the next morning, I asked for the date of her birthday. "You don't need to know," she responded. "I don't want any meaningless cards." I didn't know how to respond. Again, it seemed as though the bait was dangling, tantalizingly so. *Why?* I asked for the addresses and phone numbers for my aunt and uncle—her children, my father's sister and brother, and my godfather. She refused.

We left with a promise to stay in touch, and she gave me a kiss on the cheek. We wrote cordial letters for another year or so, and then my letters started being returned. I suspected she might have died or gone into a nursing home or to her children in California, but I had no way of finding out.

Several years later, we found ourselves traveling through Prescott, Arizona again and on an impulse drove to the only address I had for her. The people said they knew my grandmother and confirmed that she had died a few years earlier.

That concluded a chapter in my life, but the conclusion came with no satisfaction or sense of resolution. The life lesson I learned is that I can only take care of *my side of the street* and need to be content with that. I cannot control the actions of others. My mother's words kept ringing in my ears: "No one should have to die with anger in their heart." She was right—no one should have to, but many do. I will not.

Tools employed:

Ghost Chair	GOD CAN	God Talk
Hurt List	Mirror Talk	Self-Affirmations

Stepmother—Not So Evil After All

Being a stepmother can be challenging, frustrating, hurtful, confusing, and, yes, rewarding. In my generation, our parents most often stayed married. A typical household consisted of a mom, dad, and two to four children who worked, loved, and fought but ultimately worked together for the common good of all in the household. Growing up, I didn't know anyone who had to shuttle between households or forgo events in order to go visit their dad. I didn't know what alternate weekends meant.

I married and had a daughter, and when he left me for another woman, I found myself in the midst of a divorce. I was a single mother to Amy for eight years before I met my second husband, Jim, who had two children from his first marriage, Lisa, nine, and Kevin, six. I knew how to be a mother and assumed that stepmothering would be about the same. I had no idea that it required such different skills and emotions.

For the first two years, Lisa and Kevin lived with their mother. We attended events in their hometown forty miles away and had them at our home alternating weekends. Being a stepmother under those conditions wasn't too alarming. I knew my place—I was just a weekend mother who could love, nourish, enjoy, and then return them to their "real" mother. But when she voluntarily relinquished custody to us and they came to live with us full-time, I found my parenting skills challenged.

I was, for all intents and purposes, their mother. I fed, read to, and tucked them into bed. I did their laundry, helped with homework, and bandaged their scrapes. I attended parent-teacher conferences and school events and coached Little

League teams. I loved and disciplined and tried my best to balance the two. We attended church as a family, vacationed as a family, and sometimes fought as a family. I wiped away tears, read bedtime stories, and loved them very much. How was that any different than how I treated my own daughter? In the day-to-day operation, there was no difference. Consequently, I would start to feel like their "mother."

But then the phone call or letter from their "real" mother, now two thousand miles away, would come, and the relationship got all stirred up for a few days. Lisa, who had just introduced me to friends as "Mom," now screamed, "You're not my mother!" Kevin, who had curled up next to me for a story just the night before, didn't even want me to tuck him into bed. A few days would go by, and then I'd be "Mom" and storyteller again.

I knew how difficult it was for me to bounce back and forth and worried about how the children were dealing with it. Jim and I tried to be sensitive to their feelings. We counseled with our minister and spent a lot of time in prayer. Eventually, we seemed to strike a healthy balance of contentment and acceptance. The phone call and letter interruptions were less severe and stirred things up only for the day, and then we'd be back to "normal." The quick recovery rate seemed to indicate that the children had adjusted, and I continued the dual role of mother/stepmother trying not to cross over the emotional boundary.

Just about the time I felt we'd truly settled in, their mother sued for return custody. We retained an attorney, feeling that what the children needed most was a settled home life, which we had finally been able to provide for them. We felt that if custody changed, it would only put the children's lives in upheaval again.

I was reminded of my parenting status as the court proceedings began. Regardless of any care I had given to the children the past few years, I was, after all, only their stepmother and had no voice in the proceedings. I was not allowed to accompany my husband into the judge's chambers—I was a "disinterested" party.

In the end, against our wishes, the children were returned to the custody of their mother and transported to their new home with a new stepfather two thousand miles due east. More than anything, what Jim wanted for his children was a stable and secure home life. Recalling the difficulty they had settling in with us, he decided not to hinder their ability to settle into their new home.

Our hearts ached, but we made no contact for several years, allowing them to have a stable life with their mother. It was a sacrifice that we questioned many times. Several friends reminded us of the solid foundation we had with Lisa and Kevin and tried to console us with the concept that in the full circle of life, we'd be reunited with them again. It was difficult to trust, and many hours were spent in prayer as a result of that decision.

Lisa left her mother's home at eighteen and joined the air force. She contacted Jim from boot camp, managed a base assignment back out to California, and spent the next Thanksgiving with us. We had been planning my daughter Amy's wedding. Excited to have her sister back, Amy asked Lisa to be a bridesmaid, and she accepted. This opened the door for Kevin to reenter our lives as well, and at Amy's wedding, the full circle came about. We cherish that reunited family photo.

It took time for relationships to reestablish, but for Jim, their father, it came about rather quickly, naturally. Reestablishing my relationship was harder, mainly because I wasn't sure what it was. Just what is a stepmother to grown children? There did not appear to be any animosity, so slowly a stepparent/friendship developed.

When Lisa announced her engagement, she asked me if I would plan the wedding. I was overwhelmed with feelings of love and acceptance and wanted more than anything to say yes. But this being an honor that is usually reserved for the mother, I told her I could not. She insisted, so I told her to talk to her mother about it, and we could talk again in a couple of weeks.

Two weeks later, Lisa came into the house, sat down, took my hands, and said, "Now will you plan my wedding?"

"Your mother?" I asked.

"It's OK," she said, "my mother will not even be attending the wedding." My heart just broke for her, and I ached to pull her into my arms and hold her close. But Lisa never has and did not then show any anger or emotion in matters concerning her mother—at least not in front of us. A carryover, I believe, from the hurt of divorce felt by a sensitive little girl made tough to deal with the pain. So I simply said how sorry I was to hear that and asked if she was OK.

"I'm fine," she said. "Now will you plan my wedding or not?" We laughed and hugged and launched into wedding plans. I still had some confusing emotions. After all, I'd spent a great deal of time drawing that line between being a mother and stepmother, and now, here I was crossing over the line.

Plans moved along like all wedding planning, and I enjoyed every minute of it. Picking out her gown was the most pleasurable of all—I wouldn't trade those memories of shared love and dreams for anything. However, as wonderful as those memories were, another memory was to top them all.

At the wedding rehearsal, the minister said, "Who gives this woman in marriage?" and then he stopped to give some instructions. He said that I should step out into the aisle with Lisa and my husband, Jim, and that Jim should respond, "Her mother and I." I thought that perhaps the minister had made a mistake, so I looked over at Lisa for advice. She just smiled, nodded, and motioned for me to join them. I knew then that our prayers had not gone unanswered. I knew then that, in spite of my mistakes and misgivings, this beautiful young woman was able to accept my gift of love.

To this day, thirty years later, I cannot recall that moment without tears coming to my eyes. It was as if every struggle I had ever felt about where I fit into the relationship puzzle was resolved. The puzzle was complete, and the finished product was beautiful.

I am a stepmother, a loving, caring stepmother. Lisa has her own separate relationship with her mother defined by whatever boundaries they choose. I am privileged to also have a relationship with Lisa defined by whatever boundaries we choose. What more could a stepmother ask for? Well, maybe just one more thing—between my three children, I have five adorable children who know me as "Grandma."

Tools employed:

Bible Reading	Boundary Setting	The Breaststroke
Ghost Chair	GOD CAN	Hurt List
Prayer and Meditation	WWJD	

Joy—A Story of Faith

The phone rang, and when I answered, he asked for Amy, my teenage daughter. It was the call we had been anxiously awaiting all day. One look at my daughter's expressive face as she held the phone to her ear told me the news was good. She had been accepted to an ecumenical musical touring company for which she had auditioned the day before. The company was a separate entity from any local churches but rehearsed at a local church and received financial support from three separate Christian denominational churches in our desert community of Lancaster, California. My husband and I hoped this would be a faith-building experience for Amy, but never did we dream it would come about as it did and so profoundly affect us all individually and as a family.

Parents and student members anxiously attended the first meeting of the season. We thought we would find out just what the season would consist of, what each parent could do to help, get the tour schedule, and in general just get to know one another. Instead, we were faced with the news that the church at which the company had always rehearsed and whose bus the company used on tour was withdrawing its support—unless, that is, the company would become a part of their church. The members of the company would be expected to attend their church services and attend their youth group activities, and the company itself would come under the direct control of their church.

We were all devastated. What had attracted most of us to this company in the first place was its ecumenical nature and the spiritual growth that each member of the company ultimately found as they reached out in performance to share their Christian faith, regardless of what denomination of Christianity they chose. We consulted with the other two churches that had pledged financial support in the past. Basically, they did not approve of the actions this church was taking, but they did not want to get in the middle of things either. Therefore, at a company meeting, we chose to forgo the support of this church, seek out another rehearsal space, and pray for a solution to transportation needs. With this resolve, the director and officers informed the church of our decision.

Then this church tossed out some other news to us. They told us that we were free to leave, but they would retain the name of the company and all its equipment (staging, lights, sound system, etc.). *How could they do this?* Many hours were spent in meetings and prayer, but the church would not budge. We either had to give in to their demands or walk away with nothing. We considered yet another option—taking them to court. They were literally stealing from the company, and what they were doing was not in accordance with the bylaws that governed the company. But when we considered it further, we asked ourselves, *What would we gain?* It could easily take years to get through the courts. What would happen to these twenty-five teenagers who had so joyfully auditioned for a company in which they would share their Christian faith? And what kind of example would we, their parents, set for them in taking that kind of recourse?

Reluctantly, the director resigned his position. And after many hours of prayer, my daughter resigned as well. We discovered that about three-fourths of the company had resigned. *God*, I prayed, *what will these children do now? How will this affect their faith?*

Start a new company, He told me. The very thought of it was so overwhelming that I could hardly even entertain the thought. I worked full-time, had three active children, and was active at church and Little League. I didn't have the time or knowledge to launch such an endeavor. But God kept tugging at my heart. Finally, I sent out a letter to all the students who had left the original company and their parents. I invited anyone interested in forming a new company to attend a meeting. Of course, I really didn't expect anything to come of it, but maybe God would let up on me if I made this attempt. I called the director to see if he would consider taking on a new company that had no budget. To my surprise, he said yes. And as an added surprise, fifteen students and their parents showed up at the meeting. By the end of the meeting, we had a new company with a director, fifteen teenage student performers, a parent executive committee, and no money. *Oh, Lord*, I prayed, *what have you gotten me into?*

At the next meeting, a name was chosen for the company. It was suggested that since so much grief had been encountered getting to this point, what the company really needed was joy. And so the name became JOY Company (Jesus Over Youth). In the next few weeks, the company began rehearsal of the musical, *Godspell,* and a tour schedule was set up that remarkably only put us one month behind what the original tour schedule would have been. Behind the scenes, we were busy too. Within a few months, we got JOY Company incorporated, obtained our nonprofit status, obtained a rent-free rehearsal area, constructed scenery and tin-can lighting elements, and begged and borrowed sound equipment. We held fundraisers and developed a new constitution and a set of bylaws. With every step of the process and in each meeting, we kept asking ourselves if this could really be coming together. Each time we came up against a brick wall, we simply said that if it was God's will, it would work out. And it always did.

Money, or rather a lack of money, continued to be a thorn in our side. Our treasurer asked if we were willing to put our faith to the test. He quoted Luke 6:38 (NIV): "Give, and it will be given to you. A good measure, pressed down, shaken together, and running over, will be poured into your lap. For with the measure you use, it will be measured to you." He asked us to commit to tithing 10 percent of all our income. *Was he kidding?* We didn't have enough money to do even 10 percent of what we needed, let alone give 10 percent of that away. In the end, he convinced us, and we were blessed with the decision. We donated money each month from our meager income. To a family whose house had burned, to the family of a critically ill child, other youth organizations, etc. We especially liked the idea of reaching out in our own community. It became a joy each month to decide where our 10 percent would go. All the members became active by keeping their eyes and ears open to the needs of others. I sensed a real community growing within these teenagers who had almost not gotten the opportunity to ever get to know each other. And I learned a lot about faith and tithing. God continued to meet the needs of JOY Company.

The last elements to come together were transportation. We used the station wagon of one of the members' families, and a different church who had watched our efforts let us use their passenger van with no strings attached. Now we needed a vehicle to carry equipment—staging, lights, sound equipment, costumes, props, and luggage. My husband and I had a 1955 GMC truck. I offered the truck and my driving services. It was not our first choice—the bed was open, and the truck was old. We decided we would pray for another means of transportation but if nothing else came forth, we would use the truck.

Our touring season would consist of an Easter week tour of Northern California, where we would present *Godspell* at eight locations. Then, April through June, we would perform three out of four weekends each month in southern California. Finally, the big day came—our first tour. We loaded the station wagon, passenger van, and, yes, my truck. God had been leading us every step of the way so far, so I figured, who were we to question? The truck was old but had been well cared for and completely checked out by a mechanic and tuned up before we left. On that fateful Saturday, we left Lancaster, California, caravan style with the truck bringing up the rear. It was 1983, in the days before cell phones, so before leaving, we agreed on a rest area about four hours up the road to be our first stop.

My daughter Amy and Kathy, another student member, kept me company in the truck. We sang as we moved along the freeway and thanked God for good weather. Our first performance would be that very night in Newman, California. We had allowed plenty of time to arrive, eat, set up, relax, and have devotions before the performance. Suddenly, the truck began to spit and sputter, and then it shuddered and just cut out altogether. As I pulled off on the freeway shoulder, I flashed my lights and honked my horn at the passenger van in front of us. But they did not notice. I reminded the girls that the rest stop was only about twenty minutes ahead, and surely they would return for us when we didn't show up there. There was, of course, still the problem of the stalled truck. Try as I might, it would not start.

Thankfully, a man stopped to help us—he was a mechanic. "God at work again," I told the girls. He thought he knew what the problem was but needed a part. He said if I'd give him twenty dollars, he would go get the part and come back. *Should I trust him, Lord?* I thought. I felt absolutely foolish trusting this man to come back, but I gave him the twenty dollars, and off he went. I reasoned that surely by now our caravan must have realized we didn't make it to the rest stop. Later we would find out that one of the student members of the company erroneously reported seeing us bypass the rest stop and go on without them. Not until they arrived in Newman and found that we were not there did they realize we were in trouble.

An hour passed, and I felt even more foolish as no mechanic returned to us. In the meantime, another car had stopped to help, and we asked them to find a pay phone and call AAA for us. This second car had just left when the mechanic returned. I had to ask God to forgive my little faith. Not only did he bring the part, but he brought cold drinks for us. He had gone to four parts stores before he found the right part. Thirty minutes later, however, he had to admit defeat. The part was installed, but the truck still would not start.

Now I was beginning to panic. The others had not come back for us, we were due to perform in just five hours, AAA still had not arrived, the mechanic was stumped and had finally left to call AAA again, and the weather, which just hours before had seemed glorious, was now extremely hot! I began to run a timetable in my head. Even if we could get to a garage, even if they could work on it immediately, even if they could locate the source of the problem immediately, we would never make it in time. We were still three hours from our destination. The only chance we had of making it would be to get back to the closest town and rent a vehicle. My head began to swim—I couldn't personally afford this expense, and the company surely didn't have extra funds for this. *Have we, the company, misinterpreted God's intent for us?* I began to wonder.

I ran the timetable. It was now 2:30 p.m. If AAA arrived by 3:00; if AAA could get us to a rental lot by 3:30; if a vehicle to fit our needs was available and we could transfer the load to the rental vehicle and be on the road again by 4:00; if we encountered smooth sailing on the road; if, if, if,—then we could still make that night's performance. *Do you approve and bless our efforts, Lord?* I asked. *If you do, please give me a sign!* I shared the timetable with the girls, and with another glance at my watch—2:58 p.m.—the AAA truck pulled up. He pulled us into the rental lot at 3:27 p.m. They did not have a truck for us, but they did have a cargo van. That was what we had really wanted all along. While the girls transferred the load, I called my husband to let him know the situation and to come pick up the truck.

Amy called ahead to the church where we were to perform that night. She only got the answering machine but left a hurried message that we were OK and *would* be there by performance time. I used my personal credit card to cover the $500 it was costing to rent the van and prayed that no one would get angry at me or think me crazy. By now, I was so energized that I had almost forgotten about the timetable. But as we pulled out of the lot, Kathy asked the time—it was 4:00 p.m. exactly.

We made it to the church on time—almost. When we arrived, tears, hugs, and helping hands were there to greet us, and not just from our own company members. The entire church had been praying for us all afternoon. The office had been closed, and no one had thought to see if there were any messages on the machine. So until we pulled up, they had no idea what our fate had been. The police had even been notified.

The entire congregation had the equipment unloaded in minutes, and they helped set the stage for us while our student actors changed into costumes. We spent some time in a prayer of thanksgiving, and then, believe it or not, the curtain went up only thirty minutes late. I believe it was the best performance the company ever gave.

In all the excitement, no one had even questioned my decision to rent the van. We split up and spent the night in the homes of church members and then met together again at the worship service the next morning. It was then that the director of JOY Company asked me about the expense. I told him that for now it was covered, but I did not tell him the amount. He assured me that the company would cover the expense somehow. That morning from the pulpit, the pastor (after talking to me and putting all the pieces together) related the series of events to the congregation. He never mentioned the amount of the added expense of the rental van. After the service, a woman approached me, asked to remain anonymous, handed me an envelope, and quietly dismissed herself. I stood in awe for a moment and then opened the envelope which contained $500. I just stood there and cried.

These life-changing events took place over thirty-five years ago, but the lessons learned have stayed with us over the years. I never learned the name of our financial benefactor or the kind mechanic who tried so hard to help us. He wouldn't take any money for his services, asking only that I help others in need—I have and continue to do so. It was a faith-building lesson learned by all the JOY Company members. In those times when my faith grows weak, I think often of those events and know that God is always at work in my life. He surely blessed me with *joy*.

"The Lord said to me, 'My grace is sufficient for you, for my power is made perfect in weakness.' Therefore, I will boast all the more gladly about my weaknesses, so that Christ's power may rest on me. That is why, for Christ's sake, I delight in weaknesses, in insults, in hardships, in persecutions, in difficulties. For when I am weak, then I am strong." 2 Corinthians 12:9–10

Tools employed:

Bible Reading	Conflict Resolution	Ghost Chair
GOD CAN	Prayer and Meditation	WWJD

I'd love to hear from you if you remember or were a part of this story in any way. Email me at auntsherry@auntsherrysgodcan.com
Or post on my website www.auntsherrysgodcan.com

A Note about Tithing

Luke 6:38: "Give, and it will be given to you. A good measure, pressed down, shaken together, and running over, will be poured into your lap. For with the measure you use, it will be measured to you."

Wanting God to take care of you financially should not be the motive for tithing. The reason to tithe is because God wants us to. When we are obedient to God in all areas of our life, He does bless us in ways we cannot imagine.

Because of our experience with JOY Company, my husband and I decided to tithe personally, and we have done so to this day. But when my husband was injured ten years later, our resolve was shaken a bit. His income had halted while the attorneys decided who was at fault and other legal issues, and I couldn't work because he needed me as his nurse the first year. We had some savings, but they would not last long. We finally decided that we had to trust in God to provide for us. We used our savings at first, and then the county (my husband's employer) sent his stored sick leave account. It wasn't much, but we needed every penny, so taking 10 percent off the top and giving it away was really hard. But we did. Every now and then, a little pot of money would be freed up as the attorney worked on our behalf. We kept tithing, continued to put our trust in God, and our needs continued to be met. God was faithful in seeing us through—emotionally, physically, spiritually, and financially.

Standing Firm in the Faith

Holding On

Force Field

In God's Time

HOLDING ON

I was thirteen, my sister nine, and our brother just three years old when our mother was diagnosed with breast cancer. In 1964, before the advent of chemotherapy, they performed a radical mastectomy, prescribed cobalt treatments, and told her if she could survive ten years, she could consider herself cured. We all felt the cloud lift as that tenth anniversary finally came to pass. Perhaps that feeling of being "cured" was one reason the next diagnosis of cancer less than a year later was so devastating. My mother was a strong Christian woman and a survivor determined to raise her children. In later years, she told me of her barter with God to let her see her children grow up. He was faithful to His promise. My sister and I had both married, and then my brother was married in July 1981, and my mother died that November.

You would think that with all that warning, we would have left nothing unsaid, nothing unresolved, nothing undone—that mother would have left this world leaving us with no regrets. But that was not the case for me. Despite our love for each other, our ending years were tumultuous as I struggled to discover my own identity, to make my own decisions, to sever the umbilical cord. My mother hung on so tight and was so controlling that I hated her at times. At the time, all I could see was a very controlling woman who was making my life exceedingly difficult. What I didn't see, until later, was a woman afraid to let go—afraid because the time she had bartered for was coming to a close. Her children were grown; her time was up. Perhaps without even thinking about it, she felt that if she kept me dependent on her, God would still have a reason to leave her here with us.

I was sad at her passing but even more sad that we did not part with a more loving, respectful relationship. It bothered me terribly that we were not able to resolve our differences before she died. I struggled with guilt for many years after her death.

She had a long, hard struggle, but her faith never wavered. Regardless of our mistakes, my mother left us one invaluable gift—that is, her faith. She never doubted God for a moment, and it was her strong faith that gave her endurance, hope, and joy. She had no worldly inheritance to leave us, but the gift of her example by faith was worth so much more than silver or gold. In coming to terms with our relationship after her death, I wrote the following poem. In doing so, I realized the depth of her faith and the agony of letting her children grow up and leave home.

LETTING GO

We watch our little ones grow up
and shed a tear or two.
We want to keep them always young,
enjoying all they do.

But they spread their wings
as we let them go a little at a time,
assured each day that no matter what,
our love will prove divine.

Her prayers became more fervent;
something's tugging at her soul.
Did she love her children more than most?
She's afraid to let them go.

She had three little ones at home,
but the disease knew not her goals.
So she made a deal with God on high
to stay with them till grown.

One daughter now is married,
but it's hard to let her go,
for her children are her lifeline.
One child's grown, two more to go.

The Mother of the Bride once more,
her children keep her sane.
God's promise has been good thus far;
one son at home remains.

It's been a very long, long time,
and she's healthy as can be.
Perhaps the warning from so long ago
has decided to let her be.

She had three little ones at home,
but the disease knew not her goals.
So she made a deal with God on high
to stay with them till grown.

But back it came with such a force,
it drove her to her knees.
Fear not, she heard from God on high,
I'll give you what you please.

The Mother of the Groom this time,
for that little boy so dear.
All three children on their own,
The time is drawing near.

God is great, God is good.
His promise He kept dear.
Her children now in loving arms
as His arms hold her near.

She had three little ones at home,
but the disease knew not her goals.
So she made a deal with God on high
to stay with them till grown.

Tools employed:

Conflict Resolution   Fill in the Blanks   GOD CAN
Let Yourself Grieve   Prayer and Meditation   Talk to Someone

FORCE FIELD

ddiction. It had a force field of its own, invading every aspect of my life. There was not a day that went by that I did not wake up and go to bed thinking about my next fix. Just as soon as I would get one fix, I would already be thinking of the next—when I was alone, when I was out running errands, when I was tired or bored, when I felt overwhelmed, when I was in a social setting, at work, during church. My mind became preoccupied with how and where I could get the next fix. Money was not a problem. Not that I was rich, but almost anyone could afford a few candy bars or some Mrs. Field's cookies or Winchell's Donuts. Food, you say? Yes, every bit as addicting as drugs or alcohol. Anything that you cannot control and that threatens to control you is a problem.

When *Star Wars* hit the big screen, I stood in line with everyone else. Now I was watching it on TV and wondered if the Force could be with me. Not literally, of course, but it got me thinking.

I imagined a glass jar that encapsulated me with a layer of strength warding off the food that beckoned to me each day, each hour. Every morning, I envisioned that jar around me and then went about my day. The cake called my name; the ice cream enticed me; the chocolate pleaded with me; the pizza begged me; the fast-food restaurants seduced me at every corner and along every block that I traveled. But the jar surrounded me. I could see them through the jar. They looked really good. But their allure could no longer penetrate my boundary jar. Their seduction became more frantic, their enticement more cunning, their pleading more frenzied, their temptations more subtle. But the boundary of strength held firm. The truth of the deception became more and more apparent. They pretended to be my protector from the past that I did not want to deal with, but they were really predators.

My breathing became labored as I realized the extent of the hold that they'd had on me, as I realized the seductive lies that I had accepted. I thought they'd keep me safe from sexual predators, from myself, from manipulators. They sought me out most vehemently when I was alone, recognizing my weakness, preying on me as a wolf preys on a wounded deer. Their seductive dance threatened to overwhelm me until I remembered my boundary jar, until I felt that layer of strength and stood my ground. No longer was I willing to let them take advantage of me.

Those scenarios played themselves out daily, hourly. The layer of strength continued to build with each victory. Every time I could turn away from them, my resolve strengthened and my breathing relaxed. I was breathing deeper, pulling the strength inward, no longer willing to dance to their lies. The layer of strength afforded me by the all-encompassing boundary jar began to migrate to within my being. No longer was the strength simply a covering like a sweater against the cold. It now generated within my being. The glass jar was shattered as the Holy Spirit replaced it with an inner force field that was totally impenetrable. The cookie crumbled; the candy melted; the pizza went stale; the cake fell; the beacons of the fast-food restaurants were extinguished. They no longer had any hold on me. With the help of the Holy Spirit, I had taken control. Using the strength of the Holy Spirit, I could now beckon food upon my command and partake when and as I pleased, but it no longer had any control over me.

My breathing was regulated, normalized. A sense of calm enveloped me. I felt a freedom knowing that I would live, that they could not destroy me. My health was ensured, my self-worth was preserved, and my sanity and faith restored.

This was all possible only through my Lord and Savior Jesus Christ. I thank Him for those times when He carried me through the storms, the insanity. I thank Him for assuring me that He will always be by my side ensuring my force field of strength through the Holy Spirit. I thank Him for the spiritual gift of self-control.

Psalm 5:12: "For surely, O Lord, you bless the righteous; you surround them with your favor as a shield (or boundary jar)."

2 Timothy 1:7: "For God did not give us a spirit of timidity, but a spirit of power, of love and of self-discipline."

Tools employed:

Bible Reading	GOD CAN	God Talk
Personalize Your Bible	Prayer and Meditation	

IN GOD'S TIME

We joke about the devil. We dress like him at Halloween. We use him in cartoons depicting our "bad" side. But it is all in fun. What if it was real?

I grew up in the Lutheran tradition. My ministers spoke of a loving and caring God, the Father; a Savior in Jesus Christ who promises a heavenly home; and a Holy Spirit who dwells within us to guide and comfort us. I was promised love, hope, forgiveness, and grace as a Christian. I am thankful that I was not subjected to the fire and brimstone version of God, although, having studied the Old Testament, I know that side exists as well. The devastation of Sodom and Gomorrah justifiably attest to that side of God.

The devil, Satan, and evil spirits were acknowledged in my church upbringing, but there was no real focus on that subject matter. There was an acknowledgment of "evil" in general in our world today, but actual demons and demonic forces were not taught as being actively alive and well in our world today.

In Mark 5, a man asked Jesus to remove the demons that were in him. Jesus sent them into a herd of pigs. In Matthew 17, a father brought his demon-possessed son for Jesus to heal. Jesus rebuked the demons, and they left. Looking in my Bible concordance, I found at least forty scripture references to demons and demon possession. I find it hard to believe that they were alive and well then and not now. I don't see how we can deny their existence. If we accept the Bible and its teachings, we cannot just decide to ignore that part. Yet we do so by ignoring the issue. Exorcism is practiced in an extremely limited capacity, but for the most part, people's view of that is of the movie *The Exorcist* or *Rosemary's Baby*. It is not a socially acceptable topic.

With all of that being my background, it is amazing that I actually knew what to do when I was confronted by Satan.

Three significant events precede my story. First, my father had committed suicide thirty years prior to this, and I had never come to terms with that. Next, my mother had died of cancer about four years prior. When someone dies, there are often loose ends, things that we wish we'd said or hadn't said, things we wish we'd done differently. Unfortunately, my mother and I had more than our share of unresolved loose ends. And lastly, for the previous two years, I had begun to experience the fullness of the Holy Spirit. I was brand new in allowing the Holy Spirit to guide my life and in recognizing spiritual gifts.

It was at this juncture in my life that I began to see spirit-like visitors at night. I would be home alone and something would awaken me, but I was not startled. At the far corner of the room, many white, misty, somewhat illuminated transparent faces would drift toward me and dissipate as they crossed the room. The first time, I was quite surprised but not shocked. I did not feel anything threatening, it was over almost as soon as it started, and there was nothing more to the experience than that.

This repeated itself over the next year with no regular frequency and with months in between, but always when I was home alone. My husband worked the graveyard shift, and my daughter was a social butterfly with many sleepovers, so the opportunities were abundant. I wondered if this could be from the Holy Spirit. I toyed with the idea that perhaps this could be a means of communicating with my mother and father—a way to settle those loose ends and relieve me of the guilt I carried. I shared these experiences with my husband—he did not doubt me, but I think he was glad he wasn't there when they happened. I did not share with my sixteen-year-old daughter; I did not want to scare her.

Each time the faces appeared, my hopes grew. But each time, always in the still of late night, the misty white, indistinct faces only showed themselves. There was no contact, no voices. That made me even more curious. I nervously spoke out a couple of times, but there was no response. It left me yearning for more.

I considered seeking a mediator, someone to help me communicate with these apparitions. Although a part of me knew it was something I should have no part of, I couldn't deny their presence, and there was nothing evil or threatening about them. I figured, *What could be the harm?* I could only see the possible good of healing relationships with my mother and father.

Curious, one night I spoke out to the apparitions. I said, "If you are of God, show me your purpose." I think I was hoping for something rather grand to happen, but they just floated and dissipated as usual.

But the very next night, I awoke to a knife penetrating my back. There was no pain, but I could literally feel the blade piercing the denseness of my flesh and the tissue parting as the knife plunged deeper and deeper. All around me (not off in the corner of the room) were the misty faces I'd been hoping to talk to, but this time they were crimson red. I instinctively knew what was happening and rather calmly spoke aloud, "In the name of Jesus Christ—be gone." And as if someone had flipped a light switch, they were gone, and I could feel the tissue in my back knitting back together.

I felt a calmness and peacefulness as I lay there in absolute wonder at the experience. There could be no fear in the midst of that power from God. I praised God and thanked Him for His faithfulness. And then I wondered, *What does one do after a demonic experience?* I actually thought about rolling over and going back to sleep, I felt that much peace. But I kind of felt a need to touch base with human reality. But who do you call at 3:00 a.m.?

I called the sheriff's department where my husband worked as a deputy sheriff. He'd be in the field, I reasoned, but at least I could leave a message for him to call and hear the human voice of the deputy on watch. To my surprise, the deputy said, "Oh, here he is now" and handed the phone to my husband. I briefly told him what I'd experienced, and he said he could not get by the house until he was done with a booking and asked if I'd be OK until then. I told him that in spite of everything that had happened, I was at peace and felt fine.

I wasn't exactly sure of what to do next, but I was sure of where to start—I got my Bible and a booklet from a Bible Study I'd been attending and cuddled up on the couch. The Bible Study booklet was open to a page that was referencing Ephesians 6. So that is where I turned, and this is what I found in Ephesians 6:10–18:

> Be strong in the Lord and in His mighty power. Put on the full armor of
> God so that you can take your stand against the devil's schemes. For our
> struggle is not against flesh and blood, but against the rulers, against the
> authorities, against the powers of this dark world and against the spiritual
> forces of evil in the heavenly realms. Therefore, put on the full armor of
> God so that when the day of evil comes, you may be able to stand your

ground, and after you have done everything, to stand. Stand firm then, with the belt of truth buckled around your waist, with the breastplate of righteousness in place, and with your feet fitted with the readiness that comes with the gospel of peace. In addition to all this, take up the shield of faith, with which you can extinguish all the flaming arrows of the evil one. Take the helmet of salvation and the sword of the Spirit which is the word of God. And pray in the Spirit on all occasions with all kinds of prayers and requests. With this in mind, be alert and always keep on praying for all the saints.

Wow—I was blown away. Shivers ran through my body as I whispered, *Thank you, Lord*. I had read that passage many times, and it is funny how you think you understand something until it truly touches your life. God had given me those tools all my Christian years growing up, and I had used them that night. I can't tell you how much my faith was strengthened when I realized I had stood strong in the faith and had taken up the sword of the Spirit to overcome the evil one.

The Holy Spirit led me to other scripture until I understood that Satan is always looking for areas of weakness where he can present himself in the light and then devour us as a roaring lion. I was led to 2 Corinthians 11:14: "For Satan himself masquerades as an angel of light" and to 1 Peter 5:8: "Your enemy the devil prowls around like a roaring lion looking for someone to devour."

Satan had seen a weakness he wanted to exploit and a strength he wanted to prevent, and he was cunning in his approach. My weakness was the guilt and doubt I had surrounding the death of my parents. Satan saw that as a way into my life. And my strength? I think that Satan could sense my ever-strengthening relationship with the Holy Spirit, and he tried to intervene. He wanted to prevent that relationship from growing stronger and use my weakness as a stronghold for him. I was weak in the flesh and had a lot of guilt and shame to work out in my life, but Satan greatly underestimated my faith and my Christian foundation. In time, I realized that the root of my faith lay in my mother, and I was eventually able to move past her weaknesses and focus on her strengths. I learned that if I am faithful to the Lord, He will never fail me.

I had pretty much finished what I felt I had been led to read when there was a knock on the door. God's timing had been perfect. I shared the entire experience with my husband, and we reread some of the scripture together, and his faith was strengthened as well. We spoke about how God's timing had been perfect that night and came to the realization that, although we might not always see the purpose or understand the long-range plans, we were now more willing to wait for God's time in all aspects of our lives. My husband was still on duty and had to get back into the field, and when he left, I simply went to bed completely secure in the Lord and drifted off to sleep reciting, *Now I lay me down to sleep…*

Believe it or not, the devil did not stop right away. Four or five times over the next few months, the faces appeared again, in white, across the room. I immediately repeated, "In the name of Jesus Christ, *be gone*," and they were. And then they were no more. Two things that I learned from my experience are that first, they (evil spirits, the devil) really *do* exist. And second was that I need only to call upon my Lord, and He will be there for me. Christ was faithfully there in my moment of need, and the Holy Spirit was there to guide me to understanding.

Sharing my experience has been…interesting. Some people do not want to hear it, they do not want to believe it, and they want to dismiss it as a dream. But I guarantee you—it was very real. Consequently, I became selective with whom I shared my experience. And I still did not tell my daughter. She was sixteen, and although I was very much at peace with the whole experience, I was not sure how she would deal with it. Years later when she was an adult, I did share the experience with her.

She believed every single word. Not just because she believed me, but because she told me she had seen those same faces in her room! Not with as much frequency or over as long a time span and never in red, but, yes, she had experienced them too. I asked her why she never told me, and she said that nothing ever came of it, and then they just suddenly quit coming, and she kind of forgot about them. Gee, I wonder when they quit appearing?

A few years later, she was living in Italy with her navy husband and new baby when she called me in California in the middle of the night. She had awakened to those apparitions hovering over her bed. She called out, "In the name of Jesus Christ, *be gone*." And they were. Her mothering instinct was on high alert, and she wanted something to make sure they were never going to appear in her life again. I met with my Bible Study group and shared my story, and one member had a two-page document for me with scriptures, prayers, and a room-to-room cleansing ceremony (see Addendum Two).

My daughter and her husband in Italy and my husband and I in California cleansed our homes and have never encountered them again. But if they ever decide to rear their ugly heads again, we are ready! "Therefore, put on the full armor of God so that when the day of evil comes, you may be able to stand your ground." Ephesians 6:13.

Tools employed:

| Bible Reading | Deep Breathing | GOD CAN |
| Personalize Your Bible | Prayer and Meditation | Up in Smoke |

Relationships

Establishing Relationships

What Is Family?

Establishing Relationships

Relationships don't just happen. We need to foster and refuel them. We have to give them attention, or they die away. If the relationship is important, you have to make an effort.

My husband, Jim, and his father, Bill, had a unique relationship of admiration and love. Bill was a stern father, but evidently the love came through, because Jim considered his dad to be his role model. They had a kind of game of their own that they played called "between us we know everything." If Jim was asked a question that he could not answer, he'd simply say, "That must be something Dad knows," and vice versa. With Jim in California and Bill in Texas, they could pretty much get away with the bluff most of the time.

I had joined the family through marriage only a few months past and was still trying to find a way to fit in and establish relationships with long-distance relatives I hardly knew. My only meeting with Jim's parents had been the few days around the wedding. They seemed nice, nothing to dislike, but I hardly had enough time to get to know them and establish any relationship. It was important to me to find some common ground in which to foster a relationship, but with the distance, I wasn't sure how I was going to do that. And then the opportunity presented itself, and I seized the moment.

One day, as Jim and I traveled across the southern California desert, we came upon a sign that said, "Visit the Historic Town of Temecula." I asked Jim if he knew the history of Temecula. "Don't know," he responded, to which I quipped, "Oh that must be something your dad knows, huh?"

"Guess so," he said. We laughed, and I'm quite sure that Jim thought that was the end of it as our conversation moved on to other things. But, unbeknownst to him, I was calling their bluff. I wrote a letter to Bill telling him about our day and asking if he knew the history of Temecula.

You can imagine our surprise when we received a two-page letter detailing the entire history of the tiny desert town of Temecula. I'd bet that he came up with historical details that were unknown even to Temecula's historical society. Jim's mother, Mary, later told me that Bill spent several days at the library researching the history of Temecula—anything to keep the legend alive. If Jim had admitted not knowing, then he was honor bound to come up with an answer.

What that taught me was that relationships don't just happen. We have to put an effort into our relationships if we want them to remain vibrant, caring, and loving. Mary told me several times over the years how that simple gesture had brought them closer to me and launched a real relationship. I'm so glad I took the initiative and the time to find a way to fit in. Bill and Mary have been gone for many years now, but I will forever be touched by the warmth of their hearts, their genuine excitement about family get-togethers, and their gratitude for even the smallest of gestures. I'm glad I found the Miller family.

Tools employed:

| Fill in the Blanks | Have a Plan | Live for Today |
| Relationship Affirmation | | |

WHAT IS FAMILY?

F amily is flying across the country with two little ones to be consoled by loved
ones.

When my father committed suicide, understandably, my mother, only twenty-
six, was left with raw feelings and an uncertainty as to how to proceed alone in life
with two small children. It is often in these types of circumstances that we reach
out to family. We were in California, and my mother had brothers in Minnesota
and North Dakota, so off we went. It was a time of healing that my mother desperately needed and a time to escape the uncertainties of the things that I could
not understand. We played with our cousins, swam at the lake, and pretended we
were on vacation.

Family is piling three adults and four children into a car for a cross-country trek
because a loved one is in need.

When it was time for us to leave Minnesota and North Dakota, my Uncle
Harvey did not take us to the airport for our return trip home. No, he piled three
adults (he and his wife, Aunt Gerry, and my mother) and four children ages one
through seven (my mother's two and his two) into the car for a cross-country trip
to California. My Aunt Gerry told me many times that she remembered that trip as
being one of the best trips of their many vacations. I like to think that was because
it was a trip made in love.

Family is piling three adults and four children into a pickup truck with all their
belongings to get one ailing family member to a drier climate.

My husband's family lived in West Virginia. The family consisted of Grandpa
Miller; Bill and Mary (Dad and Mom); and four children, JoAnn, Tony, Sue, and

Jim (my husband), aged thirteen to three. Bill had served in the army in World War II and then returned to work the farm and work in the coal mines. He contracted black lung disease, and at that time, 1949, the only hope was getting to a dry climate. The family never even considered whether the move was practical or whether they could afford it. One family member was going to die if they did not make the move. So, as the *Beverly Hillbillies* TV show song goes, "They loaded up the truck and they moved." But instead of Beverly Hills, their destination was Arizona or New Mexico.

They loaded three adults in the cab of the pickup without seat belts and the kids in the open bed of the truck along with the mattresses and whatever else they could fit. The rest was left behind with various relatives. Jim recalls a cigarette butt that flew into the bed of the truck and started a fire in the mattress.

When they reached El Paso, Texas, just short of New Mexico but just as dry, the truck broke down, and there was no money for repairs. So that was where they stopped. Their first home was a dirt-floor one-room cabin at the edge of the cotton fields where they all got jobs picking cotton. Even three-year-old Jim was picking cotton, and he says today that if he was starving, he'd just go ahead and starve to death before he'd ever pick cotton again!

They nursed Bill back to health and worked hard to get back on their feet. And they did just that. El Paso became their new home; Bill regained his health and eventually became an insurance agent. Mary told me many times that looking back, she was so glad that welfare did not exist at that time. She said that they were so destitute that they surely would have ended up on the welfare rolls and then probably would have been stuck there. "We had no choice but to pull ourselves up by the bootstraps and do whatever it took to get back on our feet," she told me. I admired Jim's family for their pluck and get-it-done attitude. The dry climate did the trick for Bill. He lived a long, healthy life and died at the age of eighty-two.

Family is aunts and uncles who lovingly remember all the little things about their niece's childhood.

I lost a lot of memories of my childhood due to my father's suicide and the ensuing trauma. I do remember that we got together a lot with my aunts and uncles and cousins. We gathered to celebrate all the holidays and birthdays with my mother's California siblings and their families. As a kid, I just remember they were there—always there for us. As an adult, I loved to sit and just chat with them because they remembered everything about my childhood. My mother had died of cancer before I finally sought counseling to come to terms with my memory loss and my father's suicide. But they were there to help fill the gaps and put my childhood back together again. I love them for loving me.

Family is a grandmother who puts everything else aside to go stay with family members in need.

My maternal grandmother's husband died when she was only in her mid-fifties, but in those days (1946), the oldest son generally took care of his widowed mother. Consequently, Grandma moved from North Dakota to California to live near and eventually with her son, my Uncle Roy. Uncle Roy's service to his family did not go unnoticed, as Grandma picked up from there and provided service back to all her children. When she was not at Uncle Roy's, you'd find Grandma moving about the country, giving service to her children. She attended the births of all of her grandchildren, offering service in the home to the new mother and everyone else in the household. See the story "Normalcy in the Midst of Chaos."

Family is delaying Thanksgiving dinner while sixteen people gather in the small den around a TV to watch one family member's performance on *Bowling for Dollars*.

Grandma Smith was a bowler and continued bowling clear into her eighties. When she lived with me and my daughter, she was left home alone all day while I was at work and Amy was at school. Grandma did all the cooking, cleaning, and laundry. And then she went bowling and to activities at the senior center. With no one to provide transportation, she hauled her bowling ball with her to the corner and took the bus each week. At that time, *Bowling for Dollars* with Chick Hearn was a popular show on TV, and Grandma sent her name in to be a contestant once a week for several months. I didn't know it, but she was sending my name too. I bowled occasionally, but I was not a real bowler and didn't even have my own ball or shoes. So guess who got the call to be on the show? Yep—me. Grandma was so excited that you would have thought they'd called her. And they should have. I was just an average twenty-four-year-old. She was an active eighty-something— she would have been a more interesting contestant by far, and she probably would have done better than I did.

I drove the thirty miles into Hollywood, California, with Grandma and my daughter, Amy. I was taken to an area for the contestants where they provided shoes and bowling balls. But we did not get any practice time. Grandma and Amy were seated in the audience. The format of the show had Chick Hearn interview the contestants and then ask if they had anyone with them that day. When it was my turn, the camera panned out to the audience, and Grandma and Amy stood as I introduced them. Grandma didn't make it on the show as a bowler, but she did make it to the small screen. She was so excited I thought she was going to forget to breathe. And then it was my turn to bowl. I could throw the ball two times. If I got a strike with the first ball, I would win fifty dollars and not need to throw the second ball. If I got a spare (all ten pins in two balls), I'd win twenty-five dollars. If I didn't make the spare, I would win one dollar per pin. Even by 1973 standards, the winnings were not worth the trip, but hey, you got to be on TV, and it made my grandmother so proud. She was proud of me even though I only got nine pins for nine dollars. It didn't even pay the gas and dinner out, but it was worth it.

That was in the days before VCRs. If you didn't see it on TV at the prescribed day and time, you didn't see it at all. Before we left the TV studio, they told us when the show would be aired—on Thanksgiving Day. We had Thanksgiving at my Uncle Roy's house that year, and everything about that day revolved around *Bowling for Dollars.* Everyone needed to arrive at least an hour before the show so we could get our gabbing out of the way and get settled in for the show. Aunt Bernice had to time the dinner around the show's schedule. Now, of all the houses to have Thanksgiving that year, Uncle Roy had the smallest TV room. They did not watch TV much, and it was just the two of them at home, so the twenty-inch TV was in the den. We squeezed all sixteen of us into the den and hooted and hollered as we watched Sherry, Grandma, and Amy on TV. Then we had our Thanksgiving dinner, and the conversation relived every moment of what we had just watched. Grandma was in her glory. And everyone agreed that even though I only got nine pins, I had great form.

Family is not necessarily blood relations. Sometimes it takes the form of "adopting" nieces and nephews.

My daughter's friend suffered a series of tragedies shortly after giving birth to her only child—a son. Within a six-month period, she lost her dog, her grandmother, her mother, and her father—all to death—all unexpected. So her son is now my "nephew." I have always been an active aunt. I try to remember my nieces and nephews for all occasions. I want them to know that they are special and that they are greatly loved. Ultimately, I want them to know that about themselves. I want them to know the love of God. Christina was devastated with all the losses she had suffered, and I felt it only right for me to include one more nephew in my life, one more child who deserves to know how special he is.

We may not all be blessed with loving, caring families. Many times, "family" relationships come out of our friendships. Do you have a story that exemplifies what family is to you? Email it to me at auntsherry@auntsherrysgodcan.com or post it on my website, www.auntsherrysgodcan.com.

Tools employed:

Fill in the Blanks	GOD CAN	Live for Today
Relationship Affirmations	WWJD	

Be Ready for God's Calling

Angels Among Us

Against All Odds

ANGELS AMONG US

It seemed as though my mother had been dying most of my life, as she battled cancer or the effects of treatments for sixteen of my thirty years. She lingered her last couple of months at the local hospital in our small town. Family gathered, and at first, her room was bright with sunshine and bouquets of flowers. As time passed, however, the room seemed to dim along with her chances of survival. The room became dark and heavy with a pervading sense of death.

In the months that followed her passing, I found myself going out of my way to avoid the intersection where the hospital was. I didn't want to relive those last months with my mother. But living just four blocks away in a small town, I found it impossible to avoid the intersection all together. Each passing of that intersection seemed to bring back the hurt and kept the wound festering so that it couldn't heal.

I put extra effort into my work and children to still my mind. But on one day in particular, I felt overwhelmed, and it seemed that I needed to just pull away from the world. I called in "sick" to work, got the children off to school, and curled up in our oversized rocker.

The phone rang. I really didn't want to be bothered, but I had three children in school, so I reluctantly answered. It was Barbara, the mother of one of my daughter's friends. "I'm at AV Hospital," she said. "They've released me, but I can't get ahold of my husband. I wonder, since you live so close, if you'd be able to pick me up?" *Why did she call me?* I seemed to scream inside. We really didn't know each other that well, and I absolutely did not want to go back to that hospital!

"Sure," I heard myself say. "Room 227? OK, I'll see you in a bit."

As I approached the intersection, my stomach felt queasy. The familiarity of the parking lot, the front doors, the lobby, and the elevator took my breath away.

The elevator doors closed, and I stood there frozen, suffocating, and unable to push that familiar button for the second floor.

The hallway sign indicated that room 227 was to the left, one more turn of familiarity. I wasn't sure I could walk down that hallway again. I moved forward slowly, cautiously—221, 223, 225—and then my breathing stopped. I couldn't move. I wanted to turn and run. Barbara was waiting for me in my mother's room. *How is it that I didn't remember my mother's room number?* I whispered to myself. I surely would not have come had I realized that some demented twist of fate had put Barbara in that room. *And just where is her uncaring husband anyway?* I fumed. I just couldn't enter that chamber of death.

A passing nurse remembered me and offered to help, but I had a sense that somehow, for some reason, I had to do this. I thanked her and told her I'd be fine. One step forward, then another, and I entered a bright and cheery room bathed in sunshine and daisies. My mother was not there, for she was and is in God's arms. I always knew that, but somehow I had gotten stuck in the night she died. The queasiness passed, my breathing returned to normal, and I no longer go out of my way to avoid that intersection.

I had planned on reading my Bible and some self-help books that day, but God had another plan. He knows that, for me, actions always speak louder than words. We know not where angels tread and do not always recognize them when confronted. They may come in the form of Monica and Tess,[5] or yes even Barbara.

Tools employed:

Bible Reading	The Breaststroke	Deep Breathing
GOD CAN	Let Yourself Grieve	Live for Today
Prayer and Meditation	WWJD	

---

[5]   from the TV show *Touched by an Angel*

AGAINST ALL ODDS

Fractured skull. Crushed eye socket, nose, jaw, and cheekbone. Broken neck. Shattered pelvis and hip. Her leg nearly ripped off at the knee. And yet, when I entered the room where my sister was with the nurse, what I saw and heard gave me hope. The nurse was rubbing Vaseline all over my sister's hand, saying apologetically, "We have to get this ring off, but your hand is swollen, and I don't want to hurt you."

Cindy responded, "Oh, go ahead, I hurt so much everywhere else maybe it will take my mind off the other pain for a few minutes."

I knew right then and there that, despite warnings from the doctors, my sister would certainly survive. She had her wits about her and a sense of humor. The doctors were not so optimistic and had their doubts regarding prognosis, but I knew that she would not have brain damage or be paralyzed and that she certainly would walk again. She has met and exceeded all those expectations.

But it isn't just her physical recovery that makes Cindy a remarkable person. Her inspiration to others comes from the grace with which she accepted her situation, her unwavering faith through the years of recovery, the positive attitude she exhibited every day, the strength with which she endured, and the way that she continued to reach out to others when she certainly could have taken time just for herself.

I'm just sure that if I'd had to endure her same journey, I'd be crying on everyone's shoulder, asking, "Why me?" and I'd certainly be having quite the pity party. But from Cindy, you heard things like "I'm better today than yesterday; I'm so glad it was me instead of anyone else in the car; and God is so good" as she shared the tiniest of victories.

In some ways, I guess I shouldn't have been surprised. She was an upbeat, inspirational gal even before the accident. She and her husband coached a high school hockey team. They were great coaches with a winning record, but that is not what set them apart from the other coaches. They really gave of themselves to those young men. They taught them integrity, sincerity, honesty, teamwork, and friendship. Some of the kids came from dysfunctional homes, and even kids from functional homes sometimes need an outside source of inspiration. Cindy opened her heart and home to them all. Her house in Orange County, California, was home to all of them—a safe haven, a good meal, and lots of discussions in which those kids were inspired to think for themselves, to question and find answers, and to be good citizens and friends.

Cindy, her husband, Gary, their son Jeff, and his EMT friend Ryan had been to an out-of-state hockey tournament in which they took their seven-passenger SUV with their camping trailer in tow. The winds had been moderate but hardly noticeable as they drove through a desolate stretch of canyons in Utah—until a semitruck passed them on the right. It momentarily blocked the wind, created suction, and then, as the truck completed its pass, unleashed a gale force blast from the passenger side. They lost control of the SUV and, with the trailer attached, rolled down the steep center embankment. Cindy's middle seat had only a lap belt, and she was tossed around like a rag doll and then sucked right out of the lap belt and thrown partially through a closed window. Miraculously, Cindy was the only one injured. Ryan literally held her fractured skull together in his hands as paramedics arrived and transported them to a small rural hospital. Since they were unequipped to deal with her injuries, she was flown to a Las Vegas trauma center.

When we got the news in California, there was no questioning the trip to be at her side. Eight of us converged in the parking lot of the hospital and set up camp with my brother's motorhome. We rotated around the clock so that someone was by her side twenty-four seven. That is but one definition of family—being there when someone is in need.

Ten major operations, forty days of drug-induced coma, many months of physical therapy, and one year later, Humpty-Dumpty was back together again. She was of sound mind, had all her physical capabilities, and, although she had a severe limp, she walked. The conventional doctors were astounded at her recovery and had done all they could for her. She was by all rights a walking, breathing miracle. She was all put back together and was functional but not pain free. Her hip was fused, causing walking challenges. She had drop foot[6] in her right foot, and the lower part of her right leg was numb but with stabbing nerve pain in her foot. I asked her to describe the foot pain, and she said, "It feels like someone is holding a hot poker to my foot." I just wanted to cry, but she reminded me how much better she was than just even the previous week. She was comforting me!

The conventional doctors might have been done with her, but Cindy was determined to keep exploring her options and prayed for guidance. One day she was led, through a series of unlikely events, to a woman who was doing a new procedure called Frequency Specific. Simply stated, it works with sound waves and breaks up the scar tissue that is putting pressure on nerves and vessels. My husband, Jim, accompanied her to Portland, Oregon, for a week of treatments, and by the end of the week, she was rotating her hip and tossed away her cane. But the best thing of all was that the searing pain in her foot was gone—totally gone. The doctors there were so impressed, not just with her physical recovery but with her inspiring attitude, that they pictured her on the front of their new brochure with her quote "I'm pain-free—finally!"

She still deals some with the drop foot issues and some other complications, but with foot massages and continuing at-home frequency treatments, she is still improving. She is quick to share her improvements with you but never complains about any remaining problems.

All of us have challenges and conflict in our lives, and I am no exception. When I start to feel overwhelmed with the day-to-day challenges, I just think of my sister and say to myself, "If Cindy can do it, so can I." Having seen her incredible recovery, it is amazing how that perspective helps.

One year into her recovery, a friend encouraged her to attend a healing service at Saddleback Church in Orange County, California. There, her friend prayed for her complete recovery. At the time, Cindy says that she thought a complete recovery was a pretty lofty request and dared not hope for all that. But today, fifteen years since the accident, she continues to improve, so she holds on to that prayer knowing that it has, is, and will continue to come about—completely. Cindy is no

---

[6] Drop foot is a general term for difficulty lifting the front part of the foot, which can lead to tripping.

superhero—just an average woman who was able to lean on her Christian faith and learned to live her life on two biblical principles:

"I can be content whatever the circumstances. I can do everything through Him who gives me strength" (Philippians 4:11b and 13) and "In everything, do to others what you would have them do to you" (Matthew 7:12).

Rick Warren of Saddleback Church stated on his Daily Hope website, "The starting point for all happiness is shifting the focus away from yourself. If all you think about is yourself, you're going to be a pretty miserable person. If you truly want to be happy in life, you have to care about the needs of those around you."[7]

Cindy has truly accomplished that as she places God at the center of her life with a daily morning prayer, "I am available, Lord, use me." I think her accident and recovery just became a new catalyst for her to reach out to others in new and exciting ways. Cindy not only helps others, but she also treats them with dignity, as did Christ in His dealings with the everyday people. Cindy serves as an example that through Jesus Christ, we all have the ability to persevere and to not only survive but thrive.

Tools employed:

| Bible Reading | GOD CAN | Live for Today |
| Personalize Your Bible | Prayer and Meditation | WWJD |

---

[7] Rick Warren, "Forget Yourself, and look to the Needs of Others," *Daily Hope with Rick Warren*, www.PastorRick.com, June 11, 2014, accessed 2015.

Call to Action

Love Your Neighbor as Yourself

Innocence Lost

LOVE YOUR NEIGHBOR
AS YOURSELF

Suicide has been in my thoughts since I was sixteen years old, even before I discovered that my biological father committed suicide. I was in high school and six months pregnant. I was very much in love with my boyfriend. He was supportive, loving, kind, and wanted us to be married. He was, at that point, the only person who knew of my condition. If it could have remained that way, perhaps suicide never would have entered my mind. I was a mature teenager, and the responsibilities of marriage and motherhood did not scare me. Telling my mother did.

Connie Stevens, Sandra Dee, and Natalie Wood portrayed girls like me in several movies. One gave her child to her mother to be raised as a sister so the world wouldn't know her sin; one sought an illegal abortion in dingy back rooms; the other attempted suicide. All of them were testimonies of how the world viewed my situation in 1968. How could I tell my mother in a world where outward appearances, what other people thought, and scrutiny of the masses outweighed any personal feelings or needs?

I stood with a razor blade in hand but couldn't make myself slash my wrist. I stood with gun in hand and could not pull the trigger. I considered abortion but didn't have any idea where to even begin to search for one of those dingy back rooms. And, oh yes, my mother did suggest that I be sent away until I had the baby, and then she would raise the baby as my sister—just like the movies.

Once my sin was confessed at six months pregnant, my mother oscillated between the silent treatment and continual barrages of rebuke. I was not allowed to attend high school classes or participate in anything on campus—school rules as well as my mother's. Friends were not allowed to visit or give me a baby shower.

The ladies at church held a baby shower without me and sent the presents over to my house in secret. I wasn't allowed to attend services at my church. The only church services I was allowed to attend were at the local drive-in church complete with window-mounted speakers just like the drive-in movies. Basically, I wasn't allowed to be seen in public.

I did insist on making one decision. I kept my baby and got married. But we were only allowed to get married at night and with only our parents in attendance.

I was not surprised by my mother's reaction—it was exactly what I had expected. With the absolute certainty that all of that would be facing me, I could not even fathom an answer to the frequent question, "Why did you wait so long to tell me?"

For twenty years thereafter, it seemed as though I couldn't do anything good enough and I wasn't good enough. Yet as I looked back over those years, I discovered that I was a good mother, wife, and worker. I was responsible, productive, and supportive. I always had good jobs, volunteered at church and Little League, and instilled good values in my wonderful, independent daughter.

But in the midst of those years, none of those actions felt good enough. Suicidal thoughts would creep in fleetingly, only to be dismissed because of the daughter I cared for. After she left home, however, suicidal thoughts became stronger, harder to ignore. Now it was for my husband that I clung to life. I just couldn't inflict the hurt on him that my father had on our family with his suicide.

In the hospital with a nervous breakdown, I was finally able to begin the process of letting go. I was able to let go of the hurt and pain from others, but I couldn't be as kind and forgiving of myself because shame and guilt lingered on. I was able to practice only half of what Jesus called the second-greatest commandment in Matthew 22:39: "Love your neighbor as yourself." I could and did love others, but not as I loved myself. That would have been a pretty miserable attempt at love. I gave to others in abundance what I could not give to myself. I forgave others but could not forgive myself.

I asked Pastor Bill Ankerberg of Whittier Area Community Church if he had any thoughts on why, even when we believe God has forgiven us, we have so much trouble forgiving ourselves. He said, "One of the hardest things to do is to live in grace, which is unmerited favor. God can forgive us for the sin, but generally that doesn't change the consequences. As we deal with the consequences, we are reminded of the sin." He went on to say, however, "that we have been created to rise above the struggle."[8] I guess that was what had kept me moving forward all those years.

I had been raised a Christian, and I knew that no matter what, God loved me and accepted me just the way I was. Nevertheless, I didn't seem to be able to do the same for myself. In a group therapy session, a woman shared that she had awakened that day to the realization that "if God can forgive me for my past and love me just the way I am, then who am I to dispute His good judgment?" She continued by saying, "If I don't forgive myself when God does, it is as if I am putting myself above Him." Those words stuck with me, and slowly I began the process of getting to know that wonderful person within myself and began, as Pastor Bill said, "to rise above the struggle."

I allowed myself to return to that teenager who desperately needed love, understanding, acceptance, and forgiveness. I rummaged through yearbooks, photo albums, and mementos. There had been only one person who had approached me with loving kindness—my drama teacher. He had given me a card with the only kind words I heard at the time. Their meaning, however, had been tucked away with all the other mementos.

> Either God meant what he said, or He didn't. If you accept any part of Christianity, then you must accept His promise. So now is the time for grateful rejoicing! When fear, worry, or regret try to barge into your mind uninvited, remember His promise and send those evil thoughts on their way with a prayer of thanksgiving.

As I reread those words, I cried and was finally able to understand the meaning of the words and accept his gift. Thank you Mr. Schlatter.

My father, I've learned, was severely bipolar in the days before the term even existed. There was no medication to help him, no understanding of his symptoms. That knowledge helped me to better understand the reasons for his suicide and allowed me to take it less personally. Mental illness continues to be difficult to

---

[8]   Pastor Bill Ankerberg quoted, from personal interview, with written permission.

diagnose. Because of my father's diagnosis, doctors wanted to go down that path with me but finally agreed on a diagnosis of PTSD and obsessive-compulsive disorder (OCD). Medications have helped to relieve my OCD symptoms, and I accept that I need them just as a diabetic needs insulin.

But a pill is not a cure-all, and life is still difficult for me at times. Fleeting suicidal thoughts continued to surface. Today, however, with a prayer of thanksgiving, I am able to send those evil thoughts on their way and continue to choose life, only now I choose life for myself. I've learned to be kind and loving and generous to myself. I still give my time and talents to others but have learned to reserve a healthy portion for myself. These days, as I practice the second-greatest commandment, I am able to practice both halves. I am able to finally love others *as I do myself.*

Tools employed:

Fill in the Blanks	Ghost Chair	GOD CAN
God Talk	Hurt List	Let Yourself Grieve
Talk to Someone	Up in Smoke	

A Call to Action

Suicide is not a comfortable topic, and most every family who has been affected by it tends to bury the memories away rather than deal with them. In 2013, according to the CDC, someone in this country died by suicide every 128 minutes. And for every suicidal death, it is estimated that there are ten to twenty attempted suicides. But that is just an estimate because no one really ever talks about it much. It is the third-leading death among our youth ages fifteen to twenty-four and the tenth cause of death among all Americans.[9] Maybe we just need to be willing to talk about it.

---

[9] "Understanding Suicide," www.cdc.gov/violenceprevention, *Center for Disease Control,* accessed 2015; "Facts and Figures," www.afsp.org, *American Foundation for Suicide Prevention,* accessed 2015.

Teens today face the same challenges that I did and many more. I don't want any of them to succumb to suicide. There is nothing beautiful or romantic about it. If you are troubled, find someone to talk to. Adults, talk with your children or the other children in your life even if they don't seem interested. If you see troubling signs in your child or anyone in your circle of family and friends, go ahead and meddle. Talk to them, help them to find the right person to talk to, tell a friend or family member who might be better suited to talk to them, but do something.

Even better than approaching them at the point of suicide would be to talk to them regularly about what is going on in their lives. Suicidal thoughts do not just pop up suddenly. Carrying around guilt, remorse, and shame are oftentimes what leads to suicide. And even if they do not attempt or commit suicide, I certainly don't want any of them to have to wait twenty to thirty years like I did for healing. Talking about traumatic events, indiscretions, or misunderstandings when they are fresh can alleviate that guilt, remorse, and shame and allow them to move past the event with a fresh start and to approach a healthy life. And don't be afraid to seek professional help if talking at home is not enough.

"Forgive us our trespasses as we forgive those who trespass against us." Forgiveness of self, forgiving a perpetrator, and forgiveness from God are all key elements to "letting go" and "moving on." Just talk.

INNOCENCE LOST

I was in my early-thirties, and the words had never been said out loud to a single soul—not to myself, not to my husband, not to my mother, not even to a stranger. Now I sat in a room with fourteen other women who were also trying to win the battle against compulsive overeating and the bulge thereby created.

But no one was talking about food or diets or calories or fat grams or the fat on our bodies. Instead, what I heard was:

"He molested me."

"He fondled my breasts."

"He raped me."

"He put things up inside of me." Adult women recalling their childhood.

I couldn't speak. I had hardly acknowledged my reality to myself, let alone speak about it out loud. I was, after all, a bad person. I had allowed people to do bad things to me. But I wasn't here to talk about those things; I just wanted to lose weight. They didn't seem to be able to focus on the goal at hand. So I left and didn't return.

Six months later, I tried another weight loss therapy group. *Why are they talking about the same thing? Isn't anyone trying to lose weight?* I couldn't stay, I couldn't listen, and I certainly couldn't talk. But at home, this time, I couldn't help but think about it. *Is there a connection?*

I had always assumed my eating was just a lack of self-discipline. Like the molestations, the weight just confirmed that I was a bad person, allowing myself to be unhealthy and unsightly. But now, as I thought back over the years, I began to see a pattern emerge. Molested at ten years old just after a twenty-pound weight loss. Raped just months after losing forty pounds. Molested by a hypnotherapist. Unhappy long enough, I'd forgo safety and lose weight. Feeling threatened, I'd forgo happiness and regain the weight. And on and on it went.

I did not understand what I was doing at the time, of course, but looking back, the pattern was truly clear. Now I had a bit of understanding into why those women in those groups were talking about sexual abuse and not just fat and diets.

Unless someone has survived childhood abuse, there is no way to describe how profoundly one's life is affected. And not just for that day, not just for that year, not just for her childhood, but a lifetime of innocence lost.

For some, the effect of childhood molestation might manifest itself in drug addiction, for others in alcoholism, rage attacks, or being a child abuser themselves. For me, it was a slow suicidal attempt with compulsive overeating.

They said, "Just don't eat so much."
I tried, and the dreams returned.
The article stated that "This diet is guaranteed."
I lost fifty pounds, and the uncontrollable fear returned.
She said, "You look wonderful."
I heard, "Now you are finally acceptable."
Men looked at me admiringly, and
I alternated between feeling afraid or feeling flattered and guilty.
He said, "Wow, that dress looks great on you."
I heard, "You slut, you're asking for it."

The overeating would begin again, the fifty pounds would return, the fears would subside, the guilt would be subdued, and the dreams would go away.

At that point in my journey, I read an article that tried to justify destructive behavior by saying that our genes determine who and what we are, and we have little recourse. Hogwash! I was frustrated with my lack of self-control, but I refused to give in to that kind of thinking. No doubt we are greatly influenced by our genes, but we don't have to be ruled by them. Nor do we have to be ruled by life's circumstances. If that was the case, I might as well give up, accept obesity, and give in to the desire to eat myself into a slow suicide.

I think not. And at that juncture, I began my journey from victim to victor. My innocence was lost, but I did learn to regain power in my life.

Tools employed:

| Fill in the Blanks | Ghost Chair | GOD CAN | God Talk |
| Hurt List | Mirror Talk | Personalize Your Bible | |

"Ask the animals and they will teach you." Job 12:7

Foster Parenting Guide Dog Puppies

Good Boy, Cochise

Understanding

FOSTER PARENTING GUIDE DOG PUPPIES

It is a noble calling that we have answered—rewarding, fun, exasperating, heart wrenching. Eighteen months ago, my family and nine other families each picked up an eight-week-old furry bundle of puppy breath. Our first mission was to just give lots of love and potty training. The loving continued forever, while the potty training, hopefully, took no more than two to four weeks. Then, for the remaining sixteen to eighteen months, we were to teach good house manners and take her out into the world and teach her how to behave in every possible public and home setting.

Most of the puppies are raised in a family atmosphere, but one person in the family generally takes on the role of the primary caretaker. In our family, as in most, it was me, the mom. Our maternal instincts are strong, but we know that we are only foster parents and will, in eighteen months or so, go through the emotional ordeal of giving this furry bundle back to Guide Dogs of America (GDA) in Sylmar, California.

I reminded myself every day to not get too attached. Cheyenne gave me a moist kiss. I reminded myself to keep a distance with my emotions. She nuzzled my hand to be petted. I told others about the program, reminding myself of the inevitable. She behaved perfectly in the presence of the stranger and looked up for approval with a sparkle in her eyes. I smiled and shook my head, knowing that I was losing the battle with emotional distancing. Despite all the efforts and intentions and given the fact that I just couldn't deny my maternal instincts, that bundle of joy crept into my heart, and she endeared herself to me forever.

Each month at our training classes, I noticed that all the other puppy raisers had lost the battle with emotional distancing as well. I took that as a sign of good hearts, not suckers! We all found it was impossible to spend every day with our foster pups and not get emotionally attached.

As we were instructed, and as I chose with pleasure, Cheyenne accompanied me everywhere and was with me in every aspect of my life. She went with me to the bank, grocery store, movies, hairdresser, bowling alley, doctor, dentist, and church. Most of our social outings became dog related, providing new experiences for Cheyenne like riding on an airplane, a boat, the train, rides at Disneyland, day trips to the local snowcapped mountains, and rides on the city bus. I'd never ridden a city bus before and had to figure out the system so she could get some bus experience. Overall, I'm sure that I spent more time in the company of Cheyenne than with my daughter or my husband. I recognized my inability to detach emotionally and accepted the risks of eventual separation anyway.

We were advised of our turn-in date, and each puppy-raising family approached that time frame with guarded emotions. We told family, friends, and others around us when she would be leaving us. Each time we gave the news, we were preparing ourselves for that moment. The last time frame was crucial to allow the reality of what was coming to be acceptable. Some of us spent more time hugging our pup (who by then was an adult but would always be a puppy to us). Some of us seemed to be distancing ourselves in preparation of the detachment. Some suddenly realized all the bad habits that still hadn't been corrected and tried to cram in a course of Puppy Behavior 101. I spent a lot of time on the floor cuddling. Regardless of our method, we all went through a period of preparation.

It wasn't until we neared the turn-in date that I became aware of the attachment to those around us—the grocery clerk who reminded me to bring Cheyenne in for one last visit; the minister who prepared a commissioning service; the church members who, with a tear, brought their children for one last caress and then tried to explain why they wouldn't see Cheyenne at church anymore; the bowlers who brought a farewell cake on Cheyenne's last night at bowling; the neighbors who had a going-away party to tell us, "I couldn't do it, you're a saint."

The day finally arrived. I was sending Cheyenne off to boarding school. We were told we didn't need to bring anything for our puppy. But I gathered shot records and wrote notes about how her ears need to be cleaned often and how she loves to be scratched vigorously. I bagged up the leftover food and brought it along "just in case." I packed her favorite squirrel squeaky toy that was missing one ear and a box of her favorite Paul Newman heart-shaped treats.

My husband held my hand, and I wrapped my arm around my daughter as we arrived at a luncheon. We were thankful to be with so many others who were going through the same gamut of emotions. We asked our anxious questions of the trainers and looked for assurance that they would treat our puppy well. And then we took the longest walk of our puppy-raising career.

Arriving at the kennel run designated for Cheyenne and her kennel mate, Coco, we said a tearful goodbye and walked away. I glanced back to see them romping and playing, paying no attention to the fact that we were leaving. That made me cry even more—with relief that it appeared she was going to be OK and with sadness for missing her already. My husband put one arm around me and hugged our daughter with the other. Some puppy raisers walked away in silence, some found comfort in consoling each other, and all of us felt a heartache that cannot be described.

Now why, you ask, would anyone willingly put themselves through this emotional turmoil? All I can say is to invite you to come to a graduation sometime and see for yourself. Our puppies will have six months of harness training and then another month of training with their blind partner. We are not allowed to see our puppies in that time frame so that they can form a bond with their new partners.

In six to eight months, I will return to the GDA campus for Cheyenne's graduation and to meet her blind partner. From previous experience, I know that at the ceremony there will not be a dry eye as each blind recipient tells how their new canine partner will change their life. It is at that point that my broken heart will be healed, and I will truly understand the meaning of "it is better to give than to receive." In the meantime, I am on my way back to GDA to gather up some more puppy breath and start all over again.

Tools employed:

GOD CAN   Live for Today   WWJD

GOOD BOY, COCHISE

M y husband and I took on the task of training a guide dog for the blind. We faithfully attended obedience classes, guide dog activities, and actively socialized Cochise, a yellow Labrador retriever. He went everywhere with us—to work, church, the grocery store, restaurants, concerts, movies, amusement parks, on the boat, the train, and the plane. Although my husband would occasionally remind me that only about 50 percent of the puppies raised to be guide dogs actually complete the program to become a full-fledged guide dog, I was unfaltering in my single vision of Cochise as a guide dog.

We spent eighteen months training our Cochise. Our loving church congregation had taken an active interest in Cochise's progress and commissioned him in church as God's ambassador to assist the blind. That was, evidently, our plan, but not God's. Eighteen months of training down the drain—all for nothing. Or so it seemed.

As instructed, we had returned Cochise to the guide dog school to get his final harness training, but only a week later, they called to tell us that he was being dropped from the guide dog program. Hip dysplasia. I allowed myself time for self-pity—failure and disappointment are not my strong suits. I was thrilled to have Cochise home, now as a pet, but at the same time, I was devastated.

How could God have allowed us to spend eighteen months of training for nothing? Of course, there was the man who was going blind. He was afraid of the future, and his doctor's recommendation of a guide dog scared him even more. So when his wife saw us with Cochise awaiting our flight at the airport, she brought her husband over to talk to us. He had a lot of fears and questions and a lot of misinformation. We were able to answer his questions and allay his fears, and by the time we were ready to board our flight, he was talking about how anxious he was to get home and get started with a guide dog. Good boy, Cochise, you instilled peace and understanding that day.

But time is precious. I don't have time to spend eighteen months of training for nothing. I felt so betrayed. Of course, there was the young boy at Knott's Berry Farm. Oh, how his face beamed as he stroked Cochise and with unseeing eyes looked up at me and said, "I can't wait until the day I can have one." Good boy, Cochise. You instilled hope and joy that day.

But there is one less blind person who received a guide dog. That little boy and others will have to wait longer—that's just not acceptable. Of course, there are the many people who took literature and business cards, numerous potential puppy raisers and donors. There wasn't a single outing in eighteen months that we didn't educate someone in some form as we talked with people who approached us only because of our special dog with the special jacket. Good boy, Cochise. You enlightened and educated those days.

But he was supposed to be a guide dog. How am I supposed to just let go of that goal? How could we transition Cochise to being just a pet? How can we afford to deal with hip dysplasia? It's not fair! Of course, there was the young girl at our bowling league. She had been traumatized as a toddler by a stray dog, and Cochise's appearance at the bowling alley each week almost caused her parents to quit the league to spare their daughter's fears. We offered to leave Cochise at home, but at the request of the mother, we kept bringing him each week. The girl came a foot closer to Cochise each week until she could finally sit and stroke his back. Her mother's joy was evident as she thanked us for helping her daughter to get past her fears. Good boy, Cochise. You instilled healing and love and acceptance that day.

But I am still having such a hard time letting go of my disappointment. Why can't I just accept? Of course, there was the woman at the car wash who cried as she told me she had just recently learned that her ten-month-old baby was blind. She saw no hope for him to live a normal life in this society. She seemed relieved to just connect with a possible future for her son as she stroked Cochise's head and shared her fears. Good boy, Cochise. You comforted and brought peace that day.

But I had such high hopes for Cochise! Of course, there were the numerous classrooms of students who, because their teacher invited Cochise and me to visit the classroom, now had a better understanding of service dogs and the challenges of the handicapped. Good boy, Cochise. You taught and showed children another part of their world.

High hopes? I can see now that they've been met, just not the way I had envisioned. So we entered a new phase of life with Cochise, confident that God would use us when and where we were needed.

We learned that service comes in many forms. Cochise did require a hip replacement, and God led us to a specialist where Cochise was a part of a study group getting a new type of replacement that ultimately changed the way hips are replaced in humans. Good boy, Cochise. You continue to enlighten and instill hope.

We next discovered the world of therapy dogs. Cochise traded his yellow guide dog jacket for a red one that identifies him as a certified therapy dog. With it, he is visiting hospitals, convalescent homes, homes for abused children, and library programs. He brings cheer, assists in physical and emotional therapy, and helps students to learn to read out loud. Good boy, Cochise. You continue to bring healing and love to everyone you encounter.

As a guide dog, Cochise would have left us to live with someone else. My daughter, from the very beginning, believed that God gave Cochise to *us*. We have the best of both worlds now—the love and companionship of a pet and the continuing satisfaction of service to our community through the therapy dog programs, including READ.[10] Good boy, Cochise. You touch our hearts every day.

We thank God for the opportunity we've had with Cochise to be ambassadors doing His will, not ours. Aren't His ways mysterious? Now, I wonder what He has in store for Zuni, the nine-month-old black Labrador retriever that we're training to be a guide dog?

Note: Cochise was dog #1. Zuni (dog #2) went on to become a guide dog, as did Cheyenne and Kosi (dogs #3 and #6). Denali (dog #4) was not perfectly suited to guide work but transitioned to the Rancho Cucamonga Fire Department in California as an arson investigating dog. And finally, Kiva (dog #5) had a career change as a result of cataracts and became my own service dog to help with my PTSD.

Tools employed:

Bible Reading	Deep Breathing	Ghost Chair
GOD CAN	Prayer and Meditation	

---

[10] READ, for Reading Education Assistance Dogs Program, is the first and foremost program that utilizes therapy animals to help kids improve their reading and communication skills and also teaches them to love books and reading.

UNDERSTANDING

In raising a guide dog for the blind, I thought we were doing a service for others, but as usual, in giving to others, we were the real benefactors. I've heard it said that one can't experience joy without risking a little sorrow. So I would do it all over again. The lessons we learned from Cochise will be with us for the rest of our lives.

Cochise loved people. When we went to the dog park, he was the only dog that didn't play with the other dogs. Cochise went to the dog park to meet people. While other dogs were sniffing and chasing each other, Cochise was making the rounds to the humans. He loved to be petted, scratched, and caressed more than any dog I've ever known. So when hip dysplasia prevented him from pursuing our original goal of being a guide dog for the blind, it should have been obvious to me that therapy dog work was the perfect choice for his career change.

Instead, I dwelled on our failure. As usual, when I'm feeling sorry for myself, God hears all my rage and frustration. For a while, He lets me linger there and then, through Prayer and Meditation, He leads me to understanding.

I came to realize that there had been a purpose all along. I learned that service comes in all forms and that the foundation laid through his guide dog training was a perfect catalyst to therapy dog work. Therapy dog work is quite simple, actually—just take the dog and let him be spoiled, petted, caressed, fed, brushed, and walked in a controlled manner and in a controlled environment. You just never know what door will be opened.

Cochise and I visited four establishments on a regular basis. The first was a school and group home for teenage girls who'd been removed from troubled homes. Three faces stand out from our visits: Heather, Tina, and Theresa. Heather and Tina were shy and didn't quite fit in with the other girls—until Cochise arrived.

These girls had once had dogs in their homes and were quite knowledgeable about the care and handling of dogs. When Cochise arrived, they came and took charge. They walked him, taking him to visit their schoolmates, teachers, and counselors, imparting their knowledge of animals along the way. Cochise gave them an avenue to begin relationships that otherwise would not have existed. They found respect from their schoolmates for their knowledge and abilities. One girl confided in me that Heather and Tina had often talked about their dogs at home, but no one really believed them until they saw how proficiently they handled Cochise.

Theresa, on the other hand, was afraid of Cochise and didn't really want anything to do with him. But as soon as Heather and Tina took off with Cochise, Theresa would come and sit by my side. At first, it was only to tell me that she didn't like dogs, but eventually it turned into profound conversation that astounded the counselors. Theresa, they told me, never warmed up to strangers. But, then again, I wasn't exactly a stranger. I was the dog lady who eventually held the leash tightly so that she could give Cochise a hug before we left each week.

At our local hospital, we worked with many different patients who were in rehabilitation. The most rewarding were the stroke victims. The simple effort of petting helped many to regain the use of their arm. Cochise quickly learned that if he wanted to be petted, he'd have to find a way to help them get their hand up on his back. He'd nuzzle the underside of their hand and then dip and shake in such a way as to get their hand on the top of his head. Oftentimes, the patients were so amused at his approach that they'd suddenly realize they were petting and using their arm more than they had imagined possible. And as many of them learned to walk again, Cochise was the reward at the end of the parallel bars. Cochise waited patiently as they made their way along the bars, and then he'd roll over for a belly scratch as they approached.

At a school for brain-injured children, Troy and Ann were standouts. It was worth the visit every time just to see Troy's face light up. It was a real struggle for Troy to keep his head erect, but not when Cochise was there. As soon as Cochise entered the room, Troy's head came up naturally, his whole face lit up, a smile spread across his face, and his arms came up in excited celebration. Troy would then laugh and laugh as he rocked side to side. We worked on his dexterity by letting him give treats to Cochise. No matter how shaky the hand, Cochise took treats in the most polite, demure fashion, a fact that always amazed the staff.

Ann was never seen with relaxed hands. They were always folded shut so tight that I feared they'd break every time the staff would pry them open to put a treat in her hand. But Cochise still removed that treat with consistent gentleness. One day I was helping Ann stroke Cochise with her clenched hand, and all of a sudden Ann's hand relaxed and outstretched fingers caressed his fur. At first, I didn't realize how remarkable that was until the therapist excitedly called other staff over to witness the miracle of a simple relaxed hand.

And lastly, we participated in a READ program at the public library. The focus was with children who had reading difficulties. These children were afraid to read in public because they stumbled over words and the other kids made fun of them. In our program, I found a corner and laid out a blanket with a large perimeter, and the kids could come and read to Cochise one at a time. Cochise never made fun of them, and their reading skills progressed with the simple act of doing. The children would often caress Cochise as they read, which I noticed improved their reading as they relaxed. I taught Cochise to put his paw on the page of the book whenever I touched the back of his elbow. Wherever his paw landed, I'd tell the child that Cochise wanted to know more about that. It helped with their comprehension, and they were so amazed that Cochise was paying such good attention to what they were reading.

Rita came faithfully every week. After her turn, she'd choose another book and get in line again. After a couple of months, I had a visit from her fourth-grade teacher who had to come see this reading program that had helped Rita to progress so well. She left with a packet full of information and went back to her classroom with the intention of setting up a program at the school.

Without warning, Cochise moved from therapist to patient. At five and half years old, he was diagnosed with cancer. He'd had a break in his therapy dog work once before for a hip replacement, so I was hopeful that with chemotherapy he'd be back to work soon. He sailed through three months of chemo with only two sick days. His energy returned, his eyes brightened, and the tail wag increased in intensity. He was in complete remission! The doctors said we could move on to a maintenance chemo and Cochise could return to work the following month. I enthusiastically wrote letters to the facilities and included a photo of Cochise in his therapy dog jacket. Two weeks later, complications set in faster than we had any control over, and he was gone.

Once again, my rage and frustration were directed to God. Again, He let me linger there for a while. I am so thankful for a God who, instead of rebuking me in my anger, gently holds me and rocks me like a newborn baby. And once again, through Prayer and Meditation, He led me to understanding.

I will forever treasure the lessons learned from Cochise. He was a testimony of all that we can be. He endured three operations, three months of chemotherapy, and, in the end, a broken leg. Never once did he whine or whimper. Never once did he get snippy or bad tempered. He endured all with a smile, a lick, and a wag of the tail. Job 12:7 says to "ask the animals and they will teach you." He taught me to be more loving, kind, and patient and to enjoy the simple things in life. His final act, before breathing his last, was to reach up and give my daughter a kiss. It was a gift that we treasure. He was a gift that we cherish.

I said at the beginning that one cannot fully experience joy without risking a little sorrow. I will always remember Cochise with joy in my heart. But now I just have to wonder what God has in store for our latest guide dog in training, a little four-month-old black Labrador retriever named Kiva.

Tools employed:

Bible Reading	Deep Breathing	Ghost Chair
GOD CAN	Let Yourself Grieve	Live for Today
Prayer and Meditation	WWJD	

PART THREE

TOOLS AND EXERCISES

Tools, Exercises and Suggested Readings to Enrich Daily Life, to Get through Tough Times, and to Reconcile Past Events

At my lowest point, I had spiraled down into the depths of depression, a seemingly impossible crevice from which to emerge. I could see the light, I could feel the light, I could even gain strength from the light, but I couldn't manage to emerge into the light. No matter how much goodness came my way, the negative self-talk kept me bound in that spiral of despair.

I offer the following tools, exercises, and suggested readings as a means for getting in touch with your true feelings, ways to express your anger, how to get to the point of forgiveness, and ways to let go of the baggage that keeps many of us rooted in depression, inappropriate behaviors, or the inability to live productive, happy lives.

For me there wasn't one magic exercise or experience that helped me climb the spiral and feel good about myself. It was a gradual process of counseling, esteem-building exercises, and working the Twelve Steps that took years to accomplish. Nobody had put this book together yet, so I had to build the program and find or make up the exercises by trial and error over those years. My hope is that you can apply these same tools to your life. If one or more of them can be of help to you, my struggle will have been well worth the journey. If pressed to tell, my personal favorites are the GOD CAN, Ghost Chair, and Writing.

Don't try to do all these at the same time, although some do work well in conjunction with others. Some of them are more time-consuming or demanding than others. We're looking for a lasting recovery, not an overwhelming one that could actually make matters worse. Start with one exercise and see where that leads you. At times you will find that one exercise will lead to another. Slow and steady wins the race. You may find that an exercise loses its effectiveness over time, at which time—stop. Choose one of the other exercises to do for a while. Maybe you will return to that one once again, but for now it has outlived its usefulness. The object here is not to shackle you to these but to use these exercises as a means of moving past that which is in the way of a happy life. If you progress to where you are productive and happy and don't need these anymore, I say, praise God.

If you will be working the Biblical Path to Calm the Chaos, a Twelve Step Bible Study presented here in Part Four, many of these exercises can help you to work through the steps. You might even find that if you are seeing a professional, these tools can help you make it from one appointment to the next and can help to facilitate your progress with the professional. I saw counselors with little progress until I combined my sessions with the following tools. Once I started using these tools between counseling sessions and sharing the results with my counselor, my progress was faster and longer lasting.

Whether you are using the tools sporadically to deal with certain issues or using them intensely to work through the Twelve Steps, my suggestion is to precede the use of each tool with a prayer, asking God to direct your recovery and the outcome of your work with these tools.

Tools, Exercises, and Suggested Readings

List of Contents

Tool/Exercise	Purpose	Page #
Bible Reading	Enrich our daily life	122
	Foster a relationship with God	
	Determine God's will for us	
	Direct our path in life	
Block Wall	Facilitate change	123
Boundary Setting—Personal	Facilitate a personal safety net	125
Boundary Setting—Time	Facilitate time management boundaries	128
The Breaststroke	Clear our mind	129
	Allow for God to reveal Himself to us	
Conflict Resolution	Facilitate relationship resolution	130
Deep Breathing	For inner peace and to clear our mind	132
Fill In the Blanks	Resolve past issues	133
Ghost Chair	Anger and forgiveness resolution	134
GOD CAN	Relieve frustration and anger	136
	Facilitate change	
	Let go of control issues	
God Talk	Help foster self-esteem	138
	To see from God's perspective	
Have a Plan	Help with bad habits	139
Hurt List	Facilitate forgiveness	140
	Relationship reconciliation	
Let Yourself Grieve	Facilitate the grief process	141
Live for Today	Improve our daily life	144

Make a Project or Craft	Celebrate turning points and recovery	145
Medical Profession	When to ask for help	146
Mirror Talk	Foster self-esteem	147
Mythical Character	Facilitate change	148
	Help with decision-making	
Personalize Your Bible	Facilitate healing	150
	Foster a personal relationship with God	
	Love ourselves as God loves us	
Prayer and Meditation	Converse with God	151
	Bring our will in line with His will for us	
	Allow for God to reveal Himself to us	
Relationship Affirmations	Improve relationships	154
Relationship Chart	Set boundaries with relationships	155
Self-Affirmations	Foster self-esteem	158
Self-Help Groups or Counseling	How they can help	159
Talk to Someone	As a sounding board	159
	For advice	
Up in Smoke	Release bad feelings and habits	160
	Extend or request forgiveness	
Visualization	Facilitate change	161
WWJD	Facilitate change	161
	Help with decision-making	
Writing	Help in most areas of our life	162
Speed Writing	Determine what we are really thinking	162
	Determine the root of the problem	
	Facilitate problem solving	
Dear John	Resolve feelings, anger, frustration	163
	Resolve issues with deceased	
Journals		165
General Journals	Look back and monitor progress	165
Relationship Journal	Improve relationships	165
Behavior Journal	Facilitate change	166

Biblical Perspectives   167

   Spousal Relationship   Foster a Godly relationship   167

                                       Repair a relationship in peril

   Forgiveness   Make it a part of our daily life   169

Suggested Bible Readings   What to read when you   171

BIBLE READING

- Enrich our daily life
  - Foster a relationship with God
    - Determine God's will for us
      - Direct our path in life

Commit to being in the Word daily or at least regularly, like three to four times a week or some committed schedule. We speak to God through prayer, and God speaks to us through the Bible. If we never read it, how can we expect to know His will for us or experience His peace? If you miss a day here and there, do not beat yourself up for it; life happens, but resolve to make Bible Reading a regular part of your routine.

There are many devotional books that can help you to focus your reading. Many churches have free devotional books available in the narthex or entry way; usually they are for a three-month period. Don't get legalistic about it—if the dates don't match up, just do one a day and ignore the date. Christian bookstores and online sites have many available. If you are feeling guilty, sad, lonely, or a host of other emotions, check the suggested Bible readings at the end of this section.

Of course, you can just pick up your Bible and start reading.

BLOCK WALL

- Facilitate change

First determine what your goal is: to stop biting your nails, to stop eating compulsively, to stop yelling at your children. Now make a list of the things that you feel are standing in the way of achieving those goals. If you really don't know, then using some of the other tools listed can help you to identify what the blocks in your wall are. Writing is a great tool to achieve this list. Once you have determined that list, the tools can help to resolve those issues and start chipping away at that wall. I used children's toy blocks with the reasons taped to each on a small slip of paper. On my desk I made a wall with the blocks stacked on top of each other.

For example: I wanted to stop eating compulsively. My block wall consisted of blocks of sexual abuse, forced dieting as a child, a perfectionistic mother, my father's suicide, guilt over my dysfunctional relationship with my mother, and low self-esteem because of the weight, to name a few. One at a time I resolved those issues. Useful tools included:

Boundary Setting	Ghost Chair	GOD CAN
Prayer and Meditation	Relationship Affirmations	Speed Writing

The culmination of resolution was forgiveness. Useful tools for this process included:

Dear John	GOD CAN	Prayer and Meditation
Up in Smoke		

With each resolved issue, I took that block out of the block wall. It helped me to visualize my progress, and when a block came out of the middle causing other blocks to fall, I left them in that position, realizing that the wall was crumbling. Once that wall came down, I was able, again, with the help of various tools, to restore relationships, work on building my self-esteem, lose weight, and forgive myself. This exercise is helpful in completing Steps Five, Six, and Seven.

Boundary Setting—Personal

- Facilitate a personal safety net

Personal Boundaries are just another way to say "the rules I choose to live by." It is the standard by which you decide how you want to be treated by others and by yourself. It would stand to reason that you would choose to treat others with the same respect you expect from them.

The purpose of Boundary Setting is to protect and take care of ourselves—physically, mentally, and spiritually. Healthy boundaries allow us to take control of our lives, and they protect us from being manipulated or violated by others.

How do we determine and enforce our boundaries? The answer? Become self-ish and self-centered. Well, not exactly. If you have never set healthy personal boundaries for yourself before, you might feel selfish or self-centered at first. Those of us who have not exercised personal boundaries have oftentimes been people pleasers, seeing to the needs of others and ignoring our own needs. The transition to taking care of our needs may make us feel as though we no longer care about the needs of others, but eventually we can get to the point of putting ourselves first without excluding others. If we are always putting the needs of others ahead of our needs, eventually we will be too exhausted mentally and physically to see to the needs of others anyway. Strive for a healthy balance, and never allow yourself to be at the bottom of the list.

But how do we get to that point? By saying no or maybe. That is a concept that people pleasers are not accustomed to. No is a negative, and we only want to please. And if we have set a pattern of always doing what others expect of us, a no response might come as a shock. Try employing the maybe response, which gives you time to determine if it is something you want to do and have time to do, and to see how it will affect your needs and the needs of your family. Read the tool Boundary Setting—Time for how to implement the maybe response.

What are your boundaries? Your rules? Before you can enforce your boundaries, you need to know what they are. What is important to you? What are your values? What determines right and wrong for you? What attributes are important to you? What attitudes are acceptable?

For instance:

Is it OK for someone to touch you without your permission?
Maybe a handshake is OK, but a hug is too much?
You need to decide what your boundaries are.
Is it OK to loan out material items?
Is it OK for your children to sass back at you?
What about your children expressing opposite opinions in a respectful way?
Is it OK for anyone to yell at you?
Are you secure in your values, or do they change according to the group you are with?
How do you feel about nudity, loud music?
Is it OK for others to smoke around you? Do drugs?
Do you feel guilty when you enforce a personal boundary?
Do you feel guilty if you ask someone to not smoke in your car?
Do you speak up when not treated fairly?
Do you expect others to fill your needs?
Are you self-confident when others criticize you?

The list could go on and on and will continue to evolve over your lifetime. You may not have a personal conviction about a certain issue because you have never encountered that issue before. When confronted with that issue at a later time, you will need to decide where you stand on that.

Once you are confident with what your boundaries are, enforce them by sticking to them. Don't enforce them by posting a list of your boundaries on the back of a T–shirt; enforce them by how you live your life. For instance, if you have a belief that others should not take advantage of you, but you never speak up when you are taken advantage of, then you have not enforced that boundary and will continue to be taken advantage of. If you have a belief that it is wrong to do illegal drugs but do not leave the party when others are engaging in the illegal drugs, then you will be perceived as being tolerant of illegal drugs.

Are there consequences with setting our boundaries and enforcing them? Yes. If you leave the party when illegal drugs are being used, you may not be invited back. If you ask the passenger in your car to not smoke, they may not ask for a ride again. If you explain to a coworker that you would prefer they not touch you when they are speaking to you, you may be gossiped about as being a "prude." If you stand up for yourself in the meeting, the boss may realize he has misjudged you and ask for your opinion more often. If you ask someone to help you with a task, you may be surprised at their willingness to do so.

In setting our boundaries and enforcing them, there may arise, from time to time, conflict in relationships—especially if boundaries have not been set in the past. As needed, refer to the tool Conflict Resolution.

How can we tell if a relationship problem is due to a lack of boundary setting or other causes? I would suggest a Boundary Journal.

- When another person does an action or lack of action that pushes your buttons:
  o Go to a private place
  o Write in the journal
    - what they did or didn't do
    - how it made you feel
    - what you would prefer to have taken place
    - how you wish you would have responded
    - do a Speed Writing exercise
  o Evaluate your answers and writing insights to determine if you need to set a boundary or if you need to change some action on your part.

Boundary Setting—Time

- Facilitate time management boundaries

Do you take on too many tasks, leaving no room for yourself? Take an honest assessment of your life and determine what activities and situations get in the way of achieving your goals and peace in your life.

I was guilty of getting too involved—taking on too many tasks. I didn't know how to say no. I said yes to everything, and then I was overcommitted and had no time for myself. Everything I said yes to was a worthy cause—church work, my children's activities, wonderful hobbies. But one person can only take on so much. I didn't want to overreact by saying no to everything, so I found a compromise that worked for me. My new answer for every request became maybe.

When I could give it some time to really think it through, I asked myself four questions:

- Is it something I *want* to do?
- Does it fit into my schedule?
- How will it affect my spouse, my family, and me?
- Does it fall in line with God's will for me?

Then I would call the person and give an informed yes or no.

Sometimes I would give a qualified yes—a yes with boundaries. If they could not accept my qualified yes, then my answer turned to no. Taking on the maybe attitude does come with some responsibility, though, and that is to follow through with a definite answer every time that you have responded with maybe.

THE BREASTSTROKE

- Clear our mind
  - Allow for God to reveal Himself to us

Have you ever been in the water and observed a layer of leaves and dust floating on the surface? If you put your hands together and stretch them forward along the surface and then sweep both hands and arms outward to the right and left, like doing the breaststroke, the debris is pushed aside, and clear, clean water remains in front of you. When I am feeling overwhelmed by thoughts, schedules, and to-do lists clouding my judgment and befuddling my mind, I sit down, close my eyes, and envision myself in the water.

I see that the surface of the water is littered with all the stuff clouding my mind and making it difficult for me to focus and see clearly. I imagine myself dropping down into the water and moving forward with the breaststroke. With each stroke the debris is pushed away, and clear water remains in my central focus. I continue the breaststroke until I feel clarity, and then I emerge from the water onto a white sand beach—an uncluttered, new slate from which to start over and to allow God to reveal Himself to me. I allow myself some time with that clarity and then, with a deep cleansing breath in and out, I return to the chaos in my world.

This is an especially good exercise to do prior to your Prayer and Meditation.

CONFLICT RESOLUTION

- Facilitate relationship resolution

For those of us who have been victims, it can be challenging to start sticking up for ourselves without becoming overly aggressive. Oftentimes when we try to fix something, we go overboard. In taking care of ourselves, it is important to become assertive but not aggressive. Often people don't understand the difference.

An aggressive person would stand up for themselves by being a bully or being demanding. They think of themselves first and quite frankly don't really care how it affects others. An assertive person would stand up for themselves by setting boundaries, by listening and considering, and by caring about others—just not at the expense of their own good. I think you can see that to be aggressive is to put people at arm's length, while being assertive can allow you to embrace others while still taking care of your own needs.

This is seen most vividly in conflict resolution. If you have a conflict with someone, you can see that approaching them in an aggressive manner will only make matters worse. Approaching them in an assertive manner will have a much better chance of a positive outcome. Proverbs 15:1 tells us, "A gentle answer [or response] turns away wrath, but a harsh word stirs up anger."

When you are in a position where you need to iron out some differences with another person, here are some tools to accomplish that in an assertive manner.

1. Pray before the situation or confrontation. Ask God for wisdom and knowledge. Ask Him to help you to listen and comprehend from the other person's perspective. Ask God to give you the words to say and the actions to take.

2. When approaching that person, ask them, "Is this a good time to talk with you?" If the answer is no, then don't even try to start—it will not end well. Ask if there is a better time, and try to get a commitment to getting together later, or just

try back later. If not being able to talk to them at that point makes you agitated or angry or frustrated, use the Writing tool to deal with those feelings and put them in the GOD CAN to see you through until you can talk with them.

3. If it is the behavior of the other person that is the problem, approach the person with the following formula:

- When you _____
- It makes me feel _____
- I would prefer _____

This formula is a nonthreatening way to approach the person and will give you a better chance of success.

An example with a spouse:

- When you pat me on the rear in public
- It makes me feel like a tramp
- I would prefer that you just put your arm around me and leave the rear-patting for at home

A work example:

- When you criticize me in front of the other workers
- It makes me feel like you don't value me as a supervisor and that you are undercutting my authority with my staff
- I would prefer that we talk privately about those matters

4. For those times when you need to resolve a misunderstanding or a differing viewpoint, start by summarizing what you think the other person has said, such as "In other words..." or "What I hear you saying is..."

- This demonstrates that you are listening and care about trying to understand.
- If your summary is incorrect, you may have fixed the problem by just resolving what they are really saying.
- If your summary is correct, you have a starting point for which you may be able to use the "When you" formula above. If that is not appropriate to the situation, then you will need to communicate your need and/or viewpoint and make your request graciously, but firmly.

DEEP BREATHING

- For inner peace and to clear our mind

In goes the good air, out goes the bad air. Take five minutes and sit with your eyes closed. Breathe in deeply and think only good thoughts. Breathe out fully and visualize the "bad" literally leaving your body—specific feelings or generalized frustration, anger, or hurt. Also, try slowly raising your arms on the inhale and slowly bringing your arms back down on the exhale.

This is another good exercise to use prior to your Prayer and Meditation.

FILL IN THE BLANKS

- Resolve past issues

Knowledge is powerful. There may be times in your life or specific events that haunt you no matter how you try to put them to the back burner. For me it was the events surrounding my father's suicide. I was only five, and suicide at that time held such a negative social stigma. Consequently, it was never discussed. I spent my whole life thinking that my father didn't love us enough to stick around. After my mother died of cancer when I was thirty, I found a poem my father had written about me that suggested a different picture. I began questioning my aunt about him, and with all the facts and stories, I was finally able to forgive him.

Look back over your life and Fill in the Blanks. I was initially afraid of talking to my aunt, since the subject had never been discussed openly in our family, but I found that she was relieved to not have to keep the secret anymore. Once it was out in the open, many other stories of my childhood flowed. I was really only looking for my healing, but I believe my aunt experienced a healing as well.

Talk to family members and friends; look through scrapbooks and family mementos. Look up newspaper clippings from the time period. Once you have the information, writing would be a great tool to use to assist you in coming to terms with the circumstances.

Ghost Chair

- Anger and forgiveness resolution

This exercise can help with anger issues and can help to facilitate forgiveness. I tried for years to get the point of forgiving some specific people for their actions. I realized that my attempts had all been done from an intellectual point of view. I needed a more tangible outlet to release the anger. Women especially are not used to being physical, and I had trouble letting myself really let go. Once I did, however, I was amazed at the relief I felt. The exercise is just as effective if there are no anger issues but just issues to be worked out.

This is an exercise that needs to be done when you are completely alone in a controlled environment—typically at home alone with no one expected home. It could also be done in the presence of a professional who can guide you through the process. But I would caution you against doing this with friends or family members for several reasons. First, you are not exactly sure just what is going to come from this exercise. Second, it might scare them. And third, you might feel self-conscious in front of someone and not be able to fully let go.

Place two chairs or benches facing each other. Have a nonlethal "weapon" at hand—like a pillow or a Nerf bat—something that will not do any damage. Sit in one chair and acknowledge who is "sitting" in the other chair. "Hello, Mom," or whoever.

Talk to that person with all honesty and say everything and anything that comes to mind. Be totally, brutally honest. If it leads to you getting up and moving around, go with it. Allow your emotions to be fully vented. If that means yelling, screaming, crying, and beating the chair with the pillow or Nerf bat, go with it. Push yourself to go on until you have fully vented.

Then sit back down and do some deep breathing and allow yourself to come back to rational thinking. Talk to God about what just happened and pray for healing. Writing is a good way to express what just happened and to put it in perspective. Writing a letter of forgiveness can be helpful in resolving the issue. When done, put your writing in your GOD CAN.

I had several people to put in that chair opposite me. Most of the time one or two sessions was enough, but occasionally I had to do several sessions before I really felt that I had let go and was not hanging on to any more baggage.

This exercise can also be done when you don't know who or what you are angry about—you just know you are angry and frustrated. Sit the two chairs as noted above and then just start talking about your anger and frustration. If you are honest and stay with it, eventually the who or what will emerge, and then you can act accordingly from there.

This exercise is especially helpful when the person you need to confront is deceased. You can't talk to them in person, so this is one way to get some resolution. By the time I did this exercise, my mother and father were both gone, but I had a lot of unresolved issues with them. Doing this exercise allowed me to express my anger and frustration. But by the end of the session, it also allowed me to forgive them. I wrote out the issues and the forgiveness and put them in my GOD CAN.

This exercise can be effective for the living as well. If you need to talk to someone with whom you have a lot of pent-up anger, doing this exercise before you meet with them might help to defuse what could have been an explosive meeting. In the case of unresolved issues with a person who will not meet or talk with you, this is one way that you can deal with the issues. Put the results in your GOD CAN and realize that you have done all that you could do. For now, just move on with life without them and let God decide if you will ever meet with that person again.

If you are working on Step Nine or Nine A and the person with whom you need to meet is deceased or will not meet with you, this exercise can allow you to apologize and ask for forgiveness or bring about healing without them actually being there. Again, put the results in your GOD CAN and rest assured that you did the best that you could do.

GOD CAN

- Relieve frustration and anger
  - Facilitate change
    - Let go of control issues

You can order a GOD CAN at www.auntsherrysgodcan.com. Or get yourself a can with a lid, such as a coffee can. Decorate it to match your personality and include the words "GOD CAN" on the outside of the can.

Set it in a prominent spot where you will see it several times a day. You can have more than one if you want in different parts of your house or at additional locations, such as your place of work.

Use the GOD CAN whenever you have a situation that makes you feel angry, frustrated, out of control, or any other negative emotions. In those circumstances, read the Serenity Prayer (see Addendum Three). You are asking God for serenity in the circumstances that you cannot change, courage to change the things you can, and wisdom to know the difference. Now think it through backward. Ask for wisdom to determine if your problem is something you can change or not. If it is something you can change, ask God for the courage to take action. For those items that you cannot change, take a small slip of paper, and write down the circumstance, how it affects you, and how it makes you feel. Go to your GOD CAN and place the slip of paper in the can while saying, "I can't control this, but God can." Over time you will find that you are indeed leaving the frustration or anger there with God, and an inner peace will prevail.

Here is an example: "Dear God, I wish I'd never met that man! But then I wouldn't have my wonderful daughter. But now he will be in life forever and I can't stand him. He pushes all my buttons and goes out of his way to make me angry. I can't change him but You can. I don't seem to be able to change how I react to him, but You can change me." With that written down, put the slip of paper in the GOD CAN while saying, "I can't control this situation, but God can." You could follow up with the Ghost Chair exercise. Write about what came with that exercise and put it in the GOD CAN as well.

About every three to six months, take the slips out and review them. Have you improved since you first started? Are any of those same situations still surfacing? If you find with some of them that the problem is ongoing, say another prayer and put it back in the GOD CAN. If you find with others that the problem has been resolved, say a prayer of thanksgiving. Celebrate the successes and perhaps have a burn party where you burn the slips and actually watch your problems go up in smoke.

God Talk

- Help foster self-esteem
  - To see from God's perspective

Put a tablet and pen at the bedside. Every night before going to sleep (or whatever time frame works better for you), write a note from God to yourself. Write it as if God were writing to you. Include anything that comes to mind, but be sure to include at least these three elements:

1—Something you did that day that God appreciates or is proud of for you.
2—Something that God forgives you for.
3—That God loves you.

So it might read something like this:

Dear Sherry—I am so proud of you for standing up for yourself. They were not treating you right. You had the right to speak up, and I'm proud of how you did it as well. I forgive you for yelling at your husband this morning, and if you ask him, I bet he'll forgive you too. As always, Sherry, I love you yesterday, today, and always. Love, God.

I did this daily for about three months, and it was amazing that I actually started to see the qualities in myself that were loveable. It helped tremendously in restoring my self-esteem.

Have a Plan

- Help with bad habits

Whatever your problem, anticipate it ahead of time and have a plan before you are presented with the situation. Determine ahead of time three or four things you can do before giving in to a behavior.

Sneak-eating and compulsive overeating have been a longtime problem for me. So I made a list of things that I can do when I feel an overwhelming urge to give in to those behaviors. My list included:

1—Call someone
2—Pray and read 1 Corinthians 10:13 and/or Philippians 4:13
3—Deep Breathing: in goes the good; out goes the bad
4—Go shopping (have to be careful of overspending)
5—Take a bubble bath

When you plan ahead, you are setting yourself up for success. For instance, I know that going to a party is always a challenge for me, so before heading to the event, I plan ahead what I will eat there, and I make sure there are safe things for me to have, even if it means bringing those items with me.

HURT LIST

- Facilitate forgiveness
  - Relationship reconciliation

Make an all-inclusive list of anyone and everyone who has ever hurt you in any way. If you are working the Twelve Steps, Step Eight A and Nine A would be the perfect time to work on this.

You could do this in list form and cross them off as completed or in a block wall fashion as in the Block Wall exercise.

Deal with them one at a time. If you have listed some very minor hurts for which you really do not feel that you are harboring any grudge or bad feelings, start with them. You should be able to resolve those quickly, and then it will feel good to mark them off the list. For those minor items, I would suggest that you sit down and write to the person like the Dear John tool. Do not mail it. When done, put it in your God Can.

For those major items, resolve those issues one at a time. Useful Tools and Exercises may include:

Boundary Setting	Ghost Chair	GOD CAN
Medical Profession	Prayer and Meditation	Speed Writing
Relationship Affirmations		

The culmination of each resolution will hopefully be forgiveness. Useful Tools and Exercises may include:

Dear John	GOD CAN	Prayer and Meditation
Speed Writing	Up in Smoke	

LET YOURSELF GRIEVE

- Facilitate the grief process

We tend to think of grieving as applying only to the death of a loved one. Going through the grief process can help tremendously also in the loss of a job, losing a house to bankruptcy, a friend moving away, a divorce, empty nest syndrome, and yes, the death of a loved one.

There is a list of emotions that we go through with a loss—shock, disbelief, anger, depression. No matter what kind of loss you are experiencing, acknowledging these steps and going through them to accept the loss will help you to find a new normal and to be able to move on in life.

When I was in my late forties, a great sadness came over me. Looking back, I realized I had always wanted a second child, but I was talked out of it for intellectual reasons. I did not act from the heart and always regretted that decision. I realized I needed to allow myself to actually grieve the child I never had. Once I accepted that and went through the process, I came to terms with it. Although I still wasn't particularly happy about the decision, I came to accept it, and the sadness went away.

If you have circumstances or events that you need to grieve, I suggest that you use the tool of Writing and other tools listed here with the following Five Stages of Grief in mind. There is no correct order and no right or wrong way to work through the process—acknowledgment is the key and allowing yourself the feelings and the time to heal. As always in recovery, if you get stuck and just can't seem to proceed on your own, there is no disgrace in seeking professional help.

Ideally, we should allow ourselves to move through this process as soon as possible. I do not mean that you should rush, but do not put it off either. Coming to terms with an incident or loss that is relatively fresh has the advantage of clarity. The less time that has passed, the less muddled the facts will be. When one does not deal with the loss for many years, the facts will get lost, unhealthy habits will have developed to keep the feelings at bay, anger may be misdirected, and the why of the circumstances may be an elusive quest.

I did not deal with my father's suicide, childhood molestation, and many other issues for over thirty years. In that time, I tucked away feelings and facts so deeply that I had to work through layers and layers of literal fat to start the healing process. I had developed behaviors such as overeating and binge eating to hide the guilt and shame. The longer one waits to deal with a loss or any circumstance, the harder and longer it will take to deal with them later. My best advice for a child who has been harmed is that therapy be sought right away. The issues can be dealt with immediately, allowing that child to continue on with as near a normal life as possible.

Whether it's a recent or long-ago loss, use the following Five Stages of Grief along with Writing and other appropriate tools to resolve your feelings and develop a new normal. Your job here is not to force these emotions; they have come about naturally or will do so. But you may not have acknowledged the emotions that allow you to be stuck in the process. So acknowledge the feelings, and use tools to help you get to a point of acceptance. We may not like the new normal, but we can get to the point of acceptance so we can move on from there.

Denial—Usually the first stage is that of denial and shock. Putting up a wall to the reality and the feelings is a defense mechanism. It helps us to just get through the initial days until we are able to let our guard down and begin to allow the feelings. Once you allow that wall to come down, Writing is a good tool to help you identify your feelings. That wall most certainly will have affected much of your life and relationships.

Anger—Allow yourself to feel the anger; it is a normal reaction. The more you allow yourself to feel it, the sooner it will begin to dissipate and allow you to heal. We hear a lot today about anger management that could be misunderstood. Just because we need to control how we express our anger doesn't mean we don't have the right to feel the anger. The tools of Writing, Ghost Chair, GOD CAN, and Talk to Someone are all excellent tools to express and release the anger. Sometimes it is hard to release the anger because we don't really know where to place the blame and direct the anger. For instance, the anger may actually be directed at the person who died, but that is a hard reality to accept. These tools can help you to identify where to place the blame and what to do with the anger.

Bargaining—Bargaining is most used before the loss. "God, I will dedicate my life to you if you will just cure her cancer." We are desperate to promise anything to avoid the loss. But even after the loss, bargaining is seen in living the "If only" or "What if" lifestyle of guilt. We would do almost anything to go back to a point in time when we could have effected a different outcome: "If we had found the tumor sooner." Bargaining can also take the path of promising anything to just not have to feel the pain of the loss anymore. Acceptance and forgiveness are the keys to moving on. The tools of Bible Study, GOD CAN, Suggested Readings, Talk to Someone, Up in Smoke, and Writing can be helpful in moving past this stage.

Depression—Forgiveness and letting go is necessary to move beyond the bargaining stage, but it oftentimes ushers in depression. Once we accept the reality, we may feel a profound sadness that we think will never go away. This does not in any way indicate mental illness but a normal and appropriate response to loss. If you did not go through a period of depression, it would be unusual. Some of the tools that can help you through this stage are Bible Study, Deep Breathing, GOD CAN, Suggested Readings, Talk to Someone, Up in Smoke, and Writing.

Acceptance—At this point we still don't like the loss; we will never really be OK with it, but we have accepted the reality of it, putting one foot in front of the other, and carving out a life without that person or thing. Even things that some people might see as a positive can launch us into the grief process. A job promotion is usually seen as a good thing. But if it requires a move to another city, the loss of our comfortable neighborhood, the loss of our church family, and the loss of our friends at school, then even it can trigger grief. Just as we would eventually find a new church family, make new friends at school, and find a new neighborhood, so we will learn to move on in our lives with the loss of a loved one or situation. Some adjustments, such as who is going to take the kids to school now that Mom is gone or who is going to coach the Little League team now that Dad is gone, will need to be made. As each adjustment is made, a new normal will become the routine. It will never be the same, but it can be OK. All the tools that brought you though the denial, anger, bargaining, and depression will bring you to acceptance.

Live for Today

- Improve our daily life

I found this verse in a greeting card with the notation "Author Unknown":

> *First I was dying to finish high school and start college.*
> *And then I was dying to finish college and start working.*
> *And then I was dying to marry and have children.*
> *And then I was dying for my children to be old enough so I could go back to work.*
> *And then I was dying to retire.*
> *And now I am dying...*
> *And suddenly realize that I forgot to live.*

Recovery is hard work. In addition to doing all the other things in our life (like working, cooking, cleaning, taking care of kids, laundry, etc.) we are trying to fix relationships, deal with the effects of PTSD, overcome addictions, and more. In the midst of it all, don't forget to take an occasional day to do nothing or do something fun—anything away from the day-to-day grind.

MAKE A PROJECT OR CRAFT

- Celebrate turning points and recovery

Read my story "Bridging the Gap" in Part Two. This is the story of a doll that I made that represents my recovery. That doll sits in my bedroom every day; she is a reminder of my recovery journey and the "little girl" that I found one day that was a turning point in my recovery.

At some point in your journey, you may encounter a key piece of your story or a turning point of your own. Find some way to commemorate that as a lasting memory of where you've been and who you are. For instance, if finding an old photo of a grandmother sparks a memory that turns out to be a key in your recovery, maybe you should get the photo restored and framed. Or if you find a baby blanket that is tattered and worn but speaks volumes to your heart, perhaps you could use pieces of it in a quilt. Depending on your expertise, you could write a song or a poem or a story, paint a landscape, make a quilt, make a doll, do a needlepoint, or make a photo collage. The list of possibilities is endless. Don't force a project; just stay open to the idea, and one day the perfect project will present itself.

In making our amends in Step Nine and in our healing with Step Nine A, there are times when we cannot fully conclude our amends or healing because of death or refusal of the other party. This tool offers one way to conclude these steps. Find something to do or make that would be symbolic of your amends or healing.

Medical Profession

- When to ask for help

Get a good physical to determine your overall health. If you have some unknown health issues or known issues that you have been ignoring, not addressing them will only hinder your recovery. If there is a history of mental health issues or you are dealing with depression, having that analyzed would also be appropriate.

In a particularly hectic time in my life, I was telling my doctor about my feelings of helplessness and bouts of tears. After some discussion he suggested I try an antidepressant. I cried. I felt that if I had to be medicated, I must be a lost cause, and I didn't have much faith that they would help anyway. He sat down next to me and said, "Sherry, if I told you that you had diabetes, would you refuse the medicine?" So I gave it a try. It took three tries to get the right medicine for me, but then I really did see an improvement in my mood. I did not stay on them forever, but they did see me through a rough patch. I'm not saying this is the path for everyone, but we do need to consider all avenues when approaching recovery.

A psychiatrist for testing and medicine or a psychologist for talk and behavior therapy should also be considered in your battery of tools. Again, this may not be the path for you, but I do suggest that you leave no stone unturned in determining what kind of help you may need.

Mirror Talk

- Foster self-esteem

I encouraged my teenage daughter to do this, and she just laughed and said, "Oh, Mom!" But a few weeks later, she confessed to me that she had been doing it and that it worked. Wow.

- When you are in the bathroom doing your duties at the sink and mirror:
  - Simply stop and look at yourself eye to eye and then say something nice to yourself. You can do it in the first or third person—just be looking at yourself in the mirror when you say it:
    - You really do have nice eyes
    - I am such a nice person and a good friend
    - You are a fantastic singer
    - I have a great smile

There are some days that my makeup just goes on better and my hair turns out the best. On those days I've been known to break into song— "I Feel Pretty" from the play and movie *West Side Story*.

It just takes a few seconds a day and can start your day in a positive way and boost your self-esteem.

MYTHICAL CHARACTER

- Facilitate change
  - Help with decision-making

I personally love the What Would Jesus Do (WWJD) movement, and it works well for me. However, I have heard some people say, "But Jesus was perfect. I can't live up to that." OK—so invent a sidekick. Invent a character that is exactly what you would like to be, who exemplifies the qualities of Jesus. Talk to this person. Ask advice. Give this character a name. It can be just a regular name or a descriptive name like Sober Guy or Self-Control Girl. When presented with a circumstance that is difficult for you, ask your sidekick, "What would you do?"

In the movie *A Beautiful Mind*, when someone new talks to the main character, he has to ask someone else if they see that person too. Because he is subject to delusions, he has created a reality check for himself. By creating a mythical character, you are creating a reality check for yourself. For instance: if you want to stop at a fast-food restaurant and order a meal, first ask your sidekick out loud if that is a logical choice. If it is 12:30 p.m. and you haven't eaten since breakfast, then it is a logical choice. If you had lunch just half an hour ago, then it is not a logical choice. By getting the thought process out of your head and out in front of you, you have created a reality check to help with your decision-making. It makes you look at the situation from another perspective.

Another way to approach the mythical character exercise would be to create shoulder alter egos. Have you ever seen the Goofy cartoon where the angel sits on one shoulder and the devil sits on the other? The shoulder angel is encouraging good behavior while the shoulder devil is encouraging bad. Rather than choosing an angel/devil, choose characters or people who have an emotional attachment for you.

For instance, for your "good" shoulder, you want to choose someone who encourages decisions that are in your best interests such as good health, good relationships, fulfillment, happiness, security. When I did this exercise, I chose my grandmother for my good/right shoulder. She always accepted me the way I was. She wanted what was best for me but encouraged it in a loving, nonjudgmental fashion. For your "bad" shoulder, you want to choose someone or something whose actions and choices are not in your best interests, someone who stands in the way of your progress and happiness. I did not want to choose a single person for this role, but a combination of attributes from persons who had had a negative impact on my life. I took those attributes and rolled them into a troll who sat on my left shoulder. When faced with difficult decisions, such as whether to eat inappropriately, I could feel that left shoulder bouncing up and down with glee at the prospect. And then I'd hear Grandma's German accented "Ach!" as well as a tender touch. Sometimes that stupid troll won, but increasingly Grandma won out. With the drama unfolding outside me, it was easier to see and deal with the choices. When the drama was kept within, it was so much easier to ignore and just give in to the battle.

PERSONALIZE YOUR BIBLE

- Facilitate healing
  - Foster a personal relationship with God
    - Love ourselves as God loves us

As you read and study your Bible, personalize it—this is your book; don't be afraid to write in it. Draw a line through pronouns or circumstances or actions and replace them with your name and an appropriate action that would be helpful to you.

For instance, in I Corinthians 13:11, the Bible reads, "When I was a child, I talked like a child, I thought like a child, I reasoned like a child. When I became a man, I put childish ways behind me." In the margin of my Bible I have written, "When I was a child, I turned to food for comfort. That was the best I could do then. I'm not a child anymore and have access to other means for comfort."

In Psalm 51:1b, the Bible states, "according to your great compassion blot out my transgressions." Next to the word *transgressions*, I added, "and my compulsions, obsessions, and fears," making the generic term *transgressions* more specific to my situation.

Ephesians 2:4–5 states that "because of His great love for us, God, who is rich in mercy, made us alive with Christ even when we were dead in transgressions—it is by grace you have been saved." I put lines through the pronouns and wrote in my name so that it now reads, "because of His great love for Sherry, God, who is rich in mercy, made Sherry alive with Christ even when Sherry was dead in transgressions—it is by grace that Sherry has been saved."

This exercise helps to personalize your relationship with God and helps you to develop a habit of looking to the Bible for advice and strength. It also helped me to learn to love myself as God loves me.

Prayer and Meditation

- Converse with God
    - Bring our will in line with His will for us
        - Allow for God to reveal Himself to us

Some people think that prayer needs to be formal with a bowed head and folded hands. Certainly, we do sometimes pray in that fashion. But most prayer is really just a conversation with God. We should talk to Him in an active relationship, tell Him our feelings, our fears, our concerns. Share with Him our joy, our love, and our victories. Ask for His guidance and healing. Thank Him for blessings and lessons learned.

Look up Matthew 6:5–13 in your Bible. In verses 5–8 Jesus explains how we should pray. In verses 9–13 He gives us the Lord's Prayer, which can be used as written as a memorized prayer, but more importantly it can be used as a model for how to organize our prayer life. See Addendum Three for more about that. My favorite verses are 7 and 8. Jesus tells us that we should not babble on in our prayers just for the sake of making our prayer longer. A sincere prayer will be heard more than a long, babbling prayer. Jesus reminds us that "your Father knows what you need before you ask Him." So some would say, "Then why should we pray if God already knows what we need?" God wants a personal relationship with each and every one of us. Honest, sincere conversation makes for a better relationship than mindless babbling.

In contrast to babbling, the Bible talks about being in persistent prayer. 1 Thessalonians 5:17–18 tells us to "pray continually" and to "give thanks in all circumstances." Instead of one big prayer a day, try to include Him in all areas of your life. I talk to Him while I'm driving, shopping, cooking, cleaning, working, and at my kid's sporting events. One of my favorite times to pray is in line at the store.

Standing in a long line can be very tedious and frustrating for me. So I start at the front of the line and pray for each person ahead of me. I may not know their needs, but God does, and it is amazing what clues we can gather about someone from just observing. An impatient mother, an irate customer, the person pleading on the cell phone for more time to pay his bill. It takes up the time and serves a purpose as well. When I encounter emergency vehicles, I pray for the safety of the responders and those involved in the accident or incident. I invite God into every aspect of my life, and the result is that of an inner peace that comes, as only God can calm the chaos.

For the most part, I like to encourage praying from the heart, not by rote. Memorized prayers are not bad in themselves, but there is a tendency to not even think about what the words mean when we repeat them over and over and over again. Two powerful prayers are the Lord's Prayer and the Serenity Prayer. These are wonderful prayers as well as bedtime and mealtime prayers that many of us say. The only thing I caution is that when you repeat memorized prayers, you should make a conscious effort to concentrate on what you are saying and the meaning of the prayer. Addendum Three presents some of the more common memorized prayers and reasons to incorporate memorized prayer, scripture, and songs into our prayer life. Although memorized prayers have a meaningful place in our lives, they should not be our only prayers. Make sure to just speak from your heart to God.

I have to admit that I have always struggled with the meditation part. Meditation is a time to sit quietly and just listen. This is God's time. God speaks to us through the Bible but can also impart knowledge and His will to us directly—not perhaps in a burning bush or a voice from the heavens—but we need to stop and listen. If we never stop, how can we hear that small, still voice amid all the commotion? My problem with meditation was that I had a hard time just stopping long enough to do it. I have a highly active mind and find it hard to turn it off. If I tried to sit still and just *be*, my mind would wander, or I would drift off to sleep. So I decided to start small—just one or two minutes to begin with. If my mind wandered, I would softly repeat "Jesus" several times or concentrate on my breathing. As time went on, I got better at it and could sit still and allow my mind to be silent for longer periods of time. Sometimes I come away from meditating with just a feeling of refreshment, tranquility, or renewal. Sometimes I come away with an insight or idea or solution to something. I don't usually go into meditation with any agenda—that is God's time, and I allow that time to be His. When I have a need for specific direction in an area of my life, I will present my request at the beginning of my meditation time and then allow the time to proceed as He pleases.

Making time for daily or at least regular Bible Reading and Prayer and Meditation can be challenging, which reminds me of the priority jar filled with rice and walnuts. The walnuts represent our time with God through Bible Reading and Prayer and Meditation. The rice represents all the rest of the activities in our lives—work, kids, school, church, and sports. In filling the jar, if you put the rice in first and then try to put the walnuts in, they will not fit. But if you put the walnuts in first and then pour the rice in, it will all fit nicely. It is a good reminder that if we put God first in our lives, the rest will work itself out. It is a good visual tool—try it out.

Relationship Affirmations

- Improve relationships

Use this for any relationship that needs to be improved. I suggest concentrating on just one relationship at a time.

Make it a point each and every day to say something positive to that person. Find something positive to say every day regardless of how angry or frustrated you are with them that day. Even if the only thing you can manage is "nice haircut," it counts as positive.

As time goes on, it will get easier, and you'll be surprised at how it will improve the relationship. This behavior will help to improve any relationship.

RELATIONSHIP CHART

● Set boundaries with relationships

You've heard the phrase "You can choose your friends, but you can't choose your family." I don't believe that is exactly true. Genetically we can't choose our family, that is true, but we can choose whether we want to have a relationship with them and what the ground rules for that relationship will be. This exercise helped me to put those relationships in perspective and decide just what to do about them.

Why are the people who are in our lives in our lives? The people in our lives are family, friends, coworkers, fellow church members, and acquaintances from organizations, sports teams, school affiliations, and civic activities. Some of these people come with the territory, and some we choose. It is in our best interests to surround ourselves with people who have integrity, good morals and values, positive attitudes, upbeat personalities, and who care about us. Take some time to evaluate who you spend time with. Are they in your best interests? Some you may choose to walk away from if you decide they are not in your best interests. Of course, you should do that in a kind way and not out of anger.

Others you will have to learn how to live with even if you feel they have a negative impact on your life. For instance: your mother, your coworker, the principal at your child's school, a person on your baseball team. These are people who have been put in your life not exactly by your choice. You may want to walk away from some of them, but it may not be practical to do so. If the coworker situation is so negative that you want to leave, you have that choice, but you have to accept the consequences of doing so as well. Figuring out how to live with that person might be the better option. If you feel that the relationship with your mother is so negative, you do have the option to walk away from the relationship. But if you cannot do that with peace of mind, then, again, the better option might be to figure out how to live with that person in your life.

First, make a list of all the people who regularly impact your life primarily in a positive fashion. Say a prayer of thanksgiving to God for putting them in your life.

Second, make a list of all the people who negatively impact your life but with whom it would be difficult to have no relationship. Also include people who have had a negative impact on you in the past only if you have not been able to forgive them or get past the negative impact they made on you. Make four columns across the page. Title the columns Name, Accept, Reject, and Boundaries/Action Items.

After you put the name in column one, in column two list the attributes of that person that are positive. Next list the attributes of that person that you reject. Spend some time evaluating those lists. First, concentrate on the attributes that you accept. In your relationship with that person, try to focus on those positive attributes. Sometimes the negative attributes have overshadowed the relationship to the point that you don't even notice the positive in that person. Now look at the attributes that you reject. Are there some boundaries you can set or exercises you can do (check some of the other Tools and Exercises) that would help you to deal with those attributes? If so, list those in column four.

With this exercise I found that it helped me to let go of current and/or past negative relationships. It allowed me to accept that although all relationships will not be perfect, I don't necessarily have to reject those people from my life totally. I choose to accept the part of them that I like and appreciate and reject the part that has a negative impact and put some tools and boundaries in place to deal with them.

Following is an example of how it would work with these two people:

Name	Accept	Reject	Boundaries/Action Items
Mom	Love Her Faith Involvement Vulnerability	Control Judgmentalism	I will choose what I decide to share with her. She does not need to know everything in my life, and then I will not have to deal with her judgment and control of my actions. I will attend church with her but not her Bible Study.
Hank	Love Fun Loving Tenderness	Unfaithful Angry Unpredictable	I will use the tools of Writing, GOD CAN, and Ghost Chair to release the anger and hurt and to finally forgive and let go but I will have no further contact with him.

SELF-AFFIRMATIONS

- Foster self-esteem

If you have low self-esteem, doing this exercise can help to boost it. I did this exercise for about three months and was quite surprised at the wonderful results. This exercise is a lot like the God Talk exercise, but this exercise is done from *your* perspective instead of God's:

Put a tablet and pen at the bedside.

Every night before going to sleep (or whatever time frame works better for you), write a note to yourself. Just list three things:

1—Something positive that you did that day for yourself.

2—Something positive that you did for someone else.

3—Something that took place that day that you had a part in and feel good about.

So it might read something like this:

I asked my husband to pick up the kids today, and I went and got a manicure. It feels good to do something nice for myself sometimes. I sent Aunt Rose a postcard—I know how much she likes getting mail. That customer at the counter was really upset today, and I felt good that I was able to intervene and bring it to a happy ending for all.

When a child grows up hearing only what they do wrong, a daily list of what we do right can help to undo a lot of damage.

Self-Help Groups or Counseling

- How they can help

Just a word about self-help and counseling programs: choose wisely. Twelve step groups, Bible studies, hospital programs, counseling, group therapy—there are a lot of programs to choose from. I got a lot of help from Overeaters Anonymous, but that was not the end-all for me. I still needed to work my recovery at home with Bible Study and prayer and many of the tools presented here.

And not all groups are the same. As I said, choose wisely. I attended some groups where week after week they just complained about their problems; I did not see any progress. That was very discouraging. I did not want a place to just go complain every week. Choose a group where you hear victories and recovery being discussed.

Talk to Someone

- As a sounding board
  - For advice

Duh—that sounds so simple. Sometimes just talking out loud to someone gets the problem out of your head and out in front where you can see it, and the answer will be so obvious. Or that someone may have had a similar experience and just might have some good advice for you.

As always, when you share with others, choose that person wisely—preferably a Christian and definitely someone with integrity, a proven record of good choices and someone who will keep your confidentiality.

Up in Smoke

- Release bad feelings and habits
  - Extend or request forgiveness

Take paper and pen and go to a peaceful or favorite place of special meaning to you. Perhaps the park or lake or just alone at home. Take with you matches, a container of water, and something suitable in which to burn pieces of paper—metal container, firepit, or BBQ.

This exercise is to help *you* release unhealthy issues affecting your life. It can also be used as a means of asking for or extending forgiveness.

Take slips of paper and write down the particular issue. While talking out loud about the issue and stating that you do not need this in your life any longer, put the slip of paper in the burn container. Set a match to the paper and watch your issue literally go Up in Smoke.

For instance, I wrote things like "I forgive you for abandoning me after my dad died." As I burned the slip of paper, I cried and talked about how the abandonment felt and acknowledged that it was a painful experience but that I needed to let go of the past and move on. I gave the hurt away as I burned the piece of paper and watched it go Up in Smoke.

This is a meaningful way to release your shortcomings to God in Step Seven and as a means of closure for Steps Nine and Nine A.

VISUALIZATION

- Facilitate change

Write down in detail how you would imagine yourself fully recovered. What would your life be like? How would you look—your hair, your clothes? What would you be doing? Who would you be with? Where would you be? What would the weather be? Whenever you have a few minutes, read through that description, and then close your eyes and visualize the whole scene and own it. Make it yours, and eventually it, or some version of it, will be yours.

WWJD

- Facilitate change
  - Help with decision-making

What would Jesus do? When put in a situation where you are tempted to do the wrong thing or take the wrong path, stop and ask, "What would Jesus do?" It is just a way of pulling away from self-centered thinking and literally asking, "What is the right thing, and give me the strength to do it." 1 Peter 2:21 tells us, "To this you were called, because Christ suffered for you, leaving you an example, that you should follow in his steps."

WRITING

- Help in most areas of our life

Writing can be used in various forms to help facilitate healing and/or to help identify our feelings or what is really underlying our feelings or actions. The Writing tools below would be helpful in determining our stumbling blocks and then would be helpful again in coming up with a solution. I believe that in almost all cases, my advice would be to make Writing our first line of defense. Below are several ways that we can use Writing effectively.

SPEED WRITING

- Determine what we are really thinking
  - Determine the root of the problem
    - Facilitate problem solving

Take a tablet of paper and pen in hand. Just start writing as fast as you can. Do not worry about punctuation or proper grammar or complete sentences. Keep writing until you just can't write anymore or until you have an aha moment. Continue writing after the aha moment to see where it leads you. When I have trouble getting started, I just start by writing something like "I'm just writing I don't know what to write but I will just keep writing again and again and I am really mad at my boss about…"

When I started, I might not have even realized I was really mad at my boss, but it just came out. It is pretty amazing the way this style of writing can bring out feelings and issues that you thought you'd long ago buried or forgotten or never even realized existed.

Reread what you have written and take appropriate action. Ask yourself what you have learned from this experience or how this has changed your life. Use the writing to help you move on from the circumstance.

What to do with the writing? My advice is to put it in your GOD CAN or, if the issue is resolved, burn it, and literally watch it go Up in Smoke.

DEAR JOHN

- Resolve feelings, anger, frustration
  - Resolve issues with deceased

This letter is especially useful when the issue involves a person who is dead or unwilling to speak with you. It is similar to the Ghost Chair exercise. This is a letter we write to a person, living or deceased, expressing all our feelings about them or what they have done or not done.

DO NOT MAIL THIS LETTER!

This letter can help you identify issues, settle old issues, or forgive others or yourself, but it is not a letter to be mailed. Depending on what you learn from this letter, you might need to take other action, or you can take this letter and put it in your GOD CAN or burn it.

This form of letter can be helpful in working Steps Nine and Nine A when the person with whom you need to make amends or effect healing is deceased or unwilling to meet with you.

Write this letter in a Speed Writing format. In this format we just let our feelings flow onto the page, letting all the hurt, anger, frustrations, and disappointments express themselves to the fullest. This is a hold-nothing-back letter that is for our eyes only. It is a way to express all our feelings about this person and the relationship.

Once the letter is done, set it aside for some time then go back and read it over and let what came about sink in and then ask God to guide you in determining what to do with that letter.

Some possibilities are:

1—Put it in your GOD CAN and allow God to heal the wounds.
2—Burn the letter along with all the hurts and frustrations.
3—Use the letter to learn how to proceed with the relationship.
4—Rewrite the letter in a form that can be mailed.

Never mail that first letter. But sometimes it is appropriate to now write a letter that can be mailed. Now that we have vented our anger and frustrations, we may be able to write a letter with the issues at hand but without the accusatory tones and angry outbursts. It may require a third or fourth draft even before a mailable letter is achieved. Once that mailable letter is achieved, my advice is to set it aside for a couple of days. Then reread it once again before deciding if it is a mailable version. Once sent, the words cannot be taken back—do not mail in anger!

Journals

- Look back and monitor progress
  - Improve relationships
    - Facilitate change

A journal can be done from several perspectives. It can just be a daily list of things you do each day, or it can focus on particular areas of your life.

The *General Journal* is helpful, especially in retrospect. Looking back can help you to realize your progress or lack thereof. On a daily basis, it can feel like you are making no progress. But if you go back and read something from three months ago, it can be an eye-opener. It can make you realize that you are no longer struggling with that issue and you don't even remember exactly when that happened. Or it can show a lack of progress and inspire you to put forth a better effort.

A *Relationship Journal* can help you to strengthen or repair relationships. Each day note the interactions, positive and negative, that you've had with significant people in your life, or, if you want to work on a single relationship, just note the interactions of that relationship. It is helpful to note the circumstances around the interaction such as the time of day, activities before or after, or location. Just writing it down might make you aware of things that you hadn't noticed before, or you might start to see patterns develop that can give you clues as to how to repair the relationship.

An example is a Relationship Journal I kept about a boss I once had. He was moody and particularly difficult to consult with. After just a week of journaling, I realized that my interactions were generally positive or at least not terribly negative if I approached him in the morning. But if I approached him in the afternoon, especially with more delicate issues, it never ended well. So whenever possible I kept my issues and questions to converse with him in the mornings, and our working relationship improved significantly.

A *Behavior Journal* (with a focus on a single behavior) can help you to realize triggers that lead to the offensive behavior. As you read back over the journal, you might realize that you never noticed before that every time you go to lunch with Jill, it launches you into a three-day binge. Maybe you should drop Jill from your friend list or take the time to determine what it is about Jill that sets you off. Figuring it out would be the better option, since you may encounter another Jill in your life in the future. Or if your issue is anger management, you may look back and realize that after you've been on the phone with your sister, you always go out and get drunk and then get into a fight. Just as with Jill, it would be best to determine the why of the matter.

One example of this was my "I can" discovery. I was a binge eater and could never get a handle on the why of it. I started a Behavior Journal and discovered that every time I binged, it was because "I could." Growing up, I could not. My mother controlled all the food. Not often, but every once in a while, I came home and there was a note that she was running errands and would be home soon. I was delighted and would eat all the forbidden foods as quickly as I could before she got home. Somewhere along the line, "I can" turned into "since I can, I must!" The "I can" moments turned into a challenge to get as much as I could, when I could, since I never knew when the next opportunity would present itself.

When I was a child, this did not create a weight problem, as the opportunities were few. But as an adult, out from under my mother's watchful eye, the opportunities were frequent, and without my understanding, the "I can" behaviors presented themselves in a way that I could not control, and the scale increased significantly.

With the understanding that came about with the Behavior Journal, I realized I needed to find a way to reprogram myself. Paul writes in 1 Corinthians that all things are permissible, but not all things are beneficial. I realized that as an adult, "I can" have those foods anytime I want and in any quantity I want. I have the choice. There is no one there any longer telling me I can't have them.

So now whenever "I can" moments present themselves, I respond with "But do I really want to right now?" I acknowledge that I can whenever I want to, but that I don't have to just because I can.

BIBLICAL PERSPECTIVES—SPOUSAL RELATIONSHIP

- Foster a Godly relationship
  - Repair a relationship in peril

Around the ten-year mark in our marriage, my husband, nearing his fortieth birthday, went through a classic midlife crisis. He had lost his identity as a deputy sheriff through an on-duty injury and subsequent forced disability retirement. He was questioning who he was and what his role was in the next chapter of his life. Instead of bonding us closer, he emotionally distanced himself from me. I made a conscious effort to fight to save our marriage. Talking to him and eventual nagging were only driving a bigger wedge between us, and he would not consider counseling. I turned to the Bible for inspiration, and the following scriptures led me to the principles discussed below. I put these principles into action, and it turned our relationship around. It didn't happen overnight. It took several months of putting my faith to the test, but through the Holy Spirit, I managed to remain constant with these principles and eventually saw the results. Finally seeing results made it easy to continue practicing these principles, which we both now do to this day. We have a healthy, respectful, fun, and loving relationship, and we thank God every day that we were able to make it through that rough patch with His help.

The following principles put into action in a relationship will create a bond of trust, mutual adoration, love, and respect. Read the following scriptures, which support the relationship discussion below:

Ephesians 5:22–33; 6:10–18
Proverbs 18:21; 19:13; 31
1 Peter 3:1–9
Colossians 3:12–21

In relationship with your spouse: first, realize that unconditional acceptance of the spouse and godly submission are based on the belief that God provides what is best. The wife should submit to the husband in the final decision, but that does not mean that she does not have a voice. The husband should take her wishes into consideration as an act of love and godly submission.

In dealing with your spouse:

- Listen.
- Believe in your spouse.
- Let the husband make the final decision after consideration of both opinions.
- Build your spouse up—don't put each other down. Sow words of praise, not negative speech.
- Applaud your spouse for good choices.
- Forgive and do not throw the past back in each other's faces. Do not pry for details of past indiscretions. To bring up the past is not moving past it and only keeps the wound festering (for more on forgiveness, see the forgiveness topic following this discussion).
- Each should live life obedient to God—be a good example to each other.
- Determine the other's needs.
- Pray for your spouse. If change is needed, pray for that change, but don't nag or manipulate or try to control. Pray and then let God be in charge. Don't expect overnight results, and don't set unrealistic expectations (the GOD CAN is helpful here).
- Advise and then let go.
- Accept your spouse unconditionally.
- If serious talk is needed, first ask if it is a good time to talk. If the other responds in the negative, then let it go—nothing good would be accomplished at that moment.
- If you have to put off the talk, what to do with your emotions at that point? Go do some Speed Writing and get your feelings out of your head. Put that writing in your GOD CAN and leave it with God until you can find the right time to talk. You might even find that the writing will help you clarify some issues and find a better approach in the end.

- Learn when to be silent and when to speak. Ask God to guide your words and your actions.
- Give your spouse the freedom to fail.
- Focus on pleasing your spouse.
- Keep life manageable.
- Be slow to anger/slow to speak.
- Do not go to bed or part for the day with unresolved anger at your spouse.
- Pray for Christians who can give sound advice to be placed in each other's lives.
- Develop close Christian friendships—individuals and couples.
- Be strong in the Lord with the full armor of God, for Satan lurks and watches for the unexpected.

That is a long list, and it can feel overwhelming to approach. Don't try to do them all at once. Focus on two or three, and when those become second nature, include two or three more.

If your spouse will not or cannot practice these principles, do your best to be faithful to them on your side. If *you* remain faithful to these principles, the chances are good that your spouse will come around. However, there are no guarantees. But if he never comes around, you will know that you did everything you could from your side and will not have to live with regret for what you could have or should have done.

BIBLICAL PERSPECTIVES—FORGIVENESS

- Make it a part of our daily life

Forgiveness is an issue of the heart between you and God. Make forgiveness a daily lifestyle. Let go of resentments and bitterness. Seek God's will instead of reacting to those who sin against you. Even if the sinner is not repentant, still forgive. Trust is another issue—they may need to earn your trust, but do not allow that to build a wall between you and them. Do not treat others as they treat you—be willing to be God's channel to that person. Forgive others, yourself, and even God. Yes, God. I used to feel guilty about getting mad at God. But I came to realize that it is OK to get mad at

God, just like we do with our parents. It is a natural feeling when we don't get what we want. But eventually we will need to forgive Him as well as ask for His forgiveness.

This pathway to forgiveness along with the previous discussion on spousal relationship can even heal a marriage from infidelity *if* both parties want to work it out and if the transgressor is repentant. In my first marriage, I wanted to work past his affair, but he was not repentant and wanted out of the marriage. No amount of work or good faith on my part could have brought that marriage back together. In my second marriage, he lost himself after an injury that prompted a midlife crisis for him, and he emotionally walked away from the marriage. I employed all the suggestions below and from the spousal relationship list above on a daily basis, and he eventually came to his senses and realized how he had essentially abandoned the marriage. He was repentant and wanted the marriage to heal. At that point we both empowered our marriage with the principles listed below and have a stronger marriage than ever. We both appreciate what we almost lost and cherish what we regained. It would be virtually impossible for a marriage to heal without forgiveness. The following is a recipe for when anyone has sinned against you or hurt you in any way.

Read Matthew 18:15–17 and Philippians 4:6–8, which support the following:

1—Forgive them.

2—Do not remind them of the sin again.

3—Tell no one else but God.

(This is biblical but hard to do. I think in practice the general idea is to not be spreading the word to everyone and anyone. If you need to confide in someone, you should be discrete and choose someone who will keep your confidence. Also, a trained counselor or therapist could be beneficial.)

4—Do not dwell on the incident/sin.

5—Give over to God any bitterness, resentment, and anger.

6—Commit the sin/person over to God.

7—Fix your mind on thoughts of good, not the negative.

8—Claim God's peace.

Easier said than done? When you've been hurt deeply, truly forgiving is not all that easy. It will take time and persistence. Use the Tools and Exercises to help you achieve this list. Sound impossible? Through Christ, all things are possible.

Suggested Bible Readings

What to read when you:

Are struggling with **addiction**—Isaiah 26:3–4; Luke 9:23; Romans 6:1–23; Romans 12:1–2; 1 Corinthians 6:12–20; 1 Corinthians 10:13; Philippians 3:17–4:1; James 4:7–8; 1 John 1:8–9

Are **afraid**—Psalm 9:9; Psalm 23; Psalm 27:1; Isaiah 41:10; Romans 8:37–39; 2 Corinthians 1:10; Ephesians 6:10–18; 2 Timothy 1:7; Hebrews 13:6

Are **angry**—Proverbs 29:11; Matthew 5:21–22; Matthew 18:21–35; Ephesians 4:25–5:2; James 1:19–21

Are **anxious**—Psalm 42:5; Proverbs 12:25; Matthew 6:25; Matthew 11:28–30; Philippians 4:6–7; 1 Peter 5:7

Are struggling with **apathy**—Matthew 25:1–13; Luke 12:35–48; Philippians 4:6–7; 1 Thessalonians 5:1–11; Revelation 3:1–6,14–22

Feel things are going from **bad to worse**—Proverbs 3:5–6; John 16:33; 1 Corinthians 10:13; 2 Corinthians 4:8–9; 2 Timothy 3; 1 Peter 2:23

Are tempted to be **bitter**—Matthew 6:14–15; 1 Corinthians 13; Ephesians 4:29–5:2; Hebrews 12:14–15

Need **blessings**—John 1:16; John 10:10; Romans 8:16–17, 28; Ephesians 1:3; 1 Peter 1:3–5; 1 John 3:1–3

Need **comfort**—Psalm 34:19; Isaiah 49:13; Lamentations 3:9–26; John 16:33; 1 Corinthians 10:13; 2 Corinthians 1:3–7, 7:6–13; Hebrews 4:16

Are **confused**—John 8:12, 14:27; Romans 7:18, 23–25; 1 Corinthians 2:15–16; Hebrews 11:6; James 1:5–8

Need **courage**—Joshua 1:1–9; Psalm 27; Psalm 46; Romans 1:14–17; Romans 8:35–37; Philippians 2:14–16; 1 Peter 4:12–13

Are challenged by **dark forces**—Romans 6:14; Romans 8:38–39; 2 Corinthians 4:7–18; Ephesians 6:10–18; 2 Timothy 4:6–7

Need guidance in **decision-making**—Psalm 25; Proverbs 3:5–6; Proverbs 16:3; Proverbs 23:20–21; Matthew 6:33–34; James 1:5–6

Feel **dejected**—Psalm 43; Lamentations 3:31–33; Matthew 11:28–30; Romans 8:26–27; Hebrews 4:16; James 4:8, 10

Are **disappointed**—Matthew 19:25–26; Mark 9:21–24; John 15:7; Ephesians 3:20

Feel **discouraged**—Psalm 23, 34, 43; Lamentations 3:55–58; Romans 8:38–39; Philippians 4:11–13; Hebrews 4:14–16; Hebrews 13:5–6

Are **doubting**—John 3:18; John 11:25–26; Romans 4:5; 1 John 4:15–16

Need **encouragement**—Psalm 37; Philippians 3:13–14; Philippians 4:11–13; 1 Thessalonians 5:23; 2 Thessalonians 2:16–17; Hebrews 6:10; 1 Peter 2:9

Need reassurance of **everlasting life**—John 3:16; John 6:40; John 10:28; 1 Corinthians 15:51–52; 1 Thessalonians 4:17

Are **failing**—Psalm 37:39–40; Romans 3:23–24; Romans 5:8; Hebrews 10:36; 1 John 1:8–9

Are **fearful or lonely**—Psalm 23; Psalm 27; Isaiah 41:10; Isaiah 58:9; Matthew 11:28–30; Matthew 28:20; Hebrews 13:5–6; 2 Timothy 1:7

Need **forgiveness**—Matthew 6:14–15; Mark 11:25; Luke 15:3–7; Acts 10:43; 2 Corinthians 2:5–11; Ephesians 1:7; 1 John 1:9; 1 John 3:1–21

Need to **forgive others**—Matthew 6:14–15; Matthew 18:21–35; Mark 11:25; Luke 15:20–24; Ephesians 4:31–32; Colossians 3:12–14.

Need to **get along with others**—Proverbs 13:20; Proverbs 22:24; Matthew 7:12; Romans 12; 1 Corinthians 13:4–5; Colossians 3

Need **God's direction**—Proverbs 3:1–6; Romans 8:26–27, 34b; Romans 12:1–3; Ephesians 5:15–17; Colossians 1:9–14; James 1:5–8; 1 John 5:14–15

Are **greedy**—Luke 12:13–21; 1 Corinthians 10:24; 2 Corinthians 9:6–15; Ephesians 5:3–7; 1 John 3:16–18; James 3:14–16

Need **guidelines** for living—Joshua 24:14–15; Psalm 25:8–11; Psalm 37:3–5; Matthew 5–7; Romans 12; Philippians 4:6–7; 1 Thessalonians 5:17–18; James 1:22

Feel **guilty**—Matthew 6:12; Matthew 11:28–30; Luke 7:47–50; Romans 7:18–25; Romans 8:1–2; 1 Corinthians 6:11; Ephesians 3:12; Philippians 3:13–14; Hebrews 10:22–23

Are **grieving**—Psalm 23; Psalm 55:22; Matthew 5:4; Luke 23:46; John 14:1–3; John 16:20–22; Romans 8:38–39; 2 Corinthians 1:3–4; 1 Thessalonians 4:13; 1 Peter 1:3–5; Revelation 21:3–4

Feel **hopeless**—Psalm 50:15; Psalm 57:1–2; Isaiah 41:10; Matthew 6:25–34; 1 Corinthians 15:20–28; 1 Peter 1:1–9, 5:10–11; Revelation 11:15–19

Are **impatient**—Psalm 37:7; Romans 2:7; 1 Corinthians 13:4–5; 1 Timothy 1:6; Hebrews 6:12; James 5:7–11; 1 Peter 3:9

Are **jealous**—Exodus 20:17; Proverbs 14:30; Matthew 6:19–24; Galatians 5:13–15, 19–21; 1 Timothy 6:7–10; Hebrews 13:5; James 3:13–18

Need **joy**—Psalm 33:1–5; Psalm 92:1–4; Proverbs 15:30; John 15:10–11, 16:22; Romans 16:13; Galatians 5:16–25; 1 Thessalonians 5:16–18; 1 Peter 1:8; Colossians 3

Are **lazy**—Proverbs 6:6–11; Proverbs 14:23; Matthew 25:14–30; Ephesians 5:15–16; Philippians 2:12–13; 1 Thessalonians 4:1–12; 2 Thessalonians 3:6–15

Need **love**—Matthew 10:30–31; John 3:16; John 15:9, 13; 1 Corinthians 13; Ephesians 2:4–7; 1 Peter 4:8; 1 John 3:1; 1 John 4:9–16

Are struggling with **lust**—Exodus 20:17; Matthew 5:27–30; Romans 7:7–25; Romans 13:8–14; Galatians 5:16; Titus 2:11–12; James 1:13–18

Feel **needy**—John 6:35; 2 Corinthians 9:10–11; Ephesians 3:20–21; Philippians 4:19

Need **peace**—Psalm 23; Matthew 11:28–30; John 14:27; Romans 5:1–2; Galatians 5:22–23; Ephesians 2:14; 2 Thessalonians 3:16; Philippians 4:6–8

Are **persecuted**—Psalm 34:7; Psalm 121:7–8; Matthew 5:10–12; 2 Corinthians 4:8–12; 2 Timothy 1:11–12; 1 Peter 3:13–14

Are feeling **proud**—Proverbs 13:10; Proverbs 16:18; Matthew 25:34–40; Mark 10:35–45; Romans 12:3; Philippians 2:1–11

Are **quarreling**—1 Corinthians 3; Ephesians 4:1–6; Ephesians 4:15–5:2; 2 Timothy 2:14–26; James 4:1–12

Want to seek **revenge**—Leviticus 19:17; Proverbs 29:11; Matthew 5:38–42; Matthew 6:14–15; Romans 12:17–21; Galatians 5:15; 1Thessalonians 5:12–22; 1 Peter 3:8–14; 1 John 2:9–11

Need **self-control**—Proverbs 25:28; Galatians 5:22–23; 2 Timothy 1:7; 2 Peter 1:13; I Corinthians 4:13; 1 Thessalonians 5:4–8

Need to bolster your **self-esteem or self-love**—Genesis 1:27, 31; Isaiah 43:46, 49:5; Jeremiah 1:5, 31:36; Psalm 100:3, 119:73 & 139:13–14, 147:10; Ecclesiastes 3:11a; Malachi 1:2a; Matthew 6:25–34, 22:37–39; John 17:20–26; Romans 143:9–10; Colossians 3:12; Hebrews 13:5b; 1 Peter 5:7; 1 John 4:4, 19

Are **sick**—Psalm 41; Matthew 8:16–17; John 16:33; Romans 8:37–39: James 5:14–15

Feel that others have **sinned against you**—Isaiah 54:17; Matthew 6:14–15; Matthew 18:15–17; Matthew 18:21–35; Romans 12:14–19; 2 Corinthians 2:7–8; Colossians 3:12–14; Galatians 6:1; James 2:12–13

Have **sinned**—Psalm 32:1–5; Psalm 51:1; Romans 3:22–24; Romans 6:11–14; 1 John 1:7–10; 1 John 2:1–2

Need **strength**—Psalm 18:2; Psalm 28:7; Psalm 37:39; Psalm 46:1–3; Psalm 73:26; Romans 8:26; 1 Corinthians 1:7–9; 2 Corinthians 4:7–9; 2 Corinthians 12:9–10; Ephesians 3:20; 2 Thessalonians 3:3; 1 Peter 5:10

Need to **submit**—Proverbs 16:3; Romans 12:1–2; Ephesians 5:21; Hebrews 12:9–11; James 4:7–10

Are **suffering**—Psalm 23; Psalm 32:7; Psalm 138:7; Matthew 11:28; John 14:1; John 16:33; Romans 8:16–17; 1 Peter 2:20–21; 1 Peter 4:12–13

Are **tempted**—Matthew 4:1–11; Romans 8:26; 1 Corinthians 10:13; Galatians 5:16–17; Hebrews 2:18, 4:15–16; James 1:12; 1 Peter 5:8–10

Are **thankful**—Psalm 21; Psalm 33; Psalm 105; Philippians 4:4–7; I Thessalonians 5:16–18

Are **weary**—Isaiah 40:28–31; Matthew 11:25–30; Romans 8:31–39; Galatians 6:9; Hebrews 12:1–3

Worry—Psalm 37:3–7; Psalm 46:1–3; Proverbs 12:25; Matthew 6:19–34; Philippians 4:6–7; 1 Peter 5:6–7

PART FOUR

A BIBLICAL PATH
TO CALM THE CHAOS

A Biblical Path to Calm the Chaos

The Twelve Steps of Alcoholics Anonymous have been the basis of recovery for millions since it was introduced in 1935 by Bill W. and Bill S. With a proven history, it is no wonder that the steps have been adapted to many other addictions and obsessions. I have adapted the Twelve Steps to be more generic for use with any disorder, dysfunction, obsession, or addiction and to heal relationships, to revive spiritual life, or for anything just haywire in our lives. They are written to be used from a Christian point of view with biblical references.

Step One—We admitted we were powerless over compulsive and/or unhealthy behaviors—that our lives had become unmanageable.

Step Two—Came to believe that a Power greater than ourselves (God) could restore us to sanity.

Step Three—Made a decision to turn our will and our lives over to the care of God.

Step Four—Made a searching and fearless moral inventory of ourselves.

Step Five—Admitted to God, to ourselves, and to another human being the exact nature of our wrongs (in Christian terms, confessed our sins).

Step Six—Were entirely ready to have God remove all these defects of character.

Step Seven—Humbly asked God to remove our shortcomings (in Christian terms, humbly asked God to forgive our sins).

Step Eight—Made a list of all persons we had harmed and became willing to make amends to them all.

Step Eight A*—Made a list of all persons who had harmed us and became willing to release all anger and resentment and to forgive them.

Step Nine—Made direct amends to such people whenever and wherever possible, except when to do so would injure them or others.

Step Nine A*—Resolved pent-up anger and resentment toward those who had harmed us.

Step Ten—Continued to take personal inventory, and when we were wrong, promptly admitted it.

Step Ten A*—Continued to take personal inventory, and when we found ourselves vulnerable, took appropriate action to avoid being a victim again.

Step Eleven—Sought through scripture, prayer, and meditation to improve our conscious contact with God, praying only for the knowledge of His will for us and the power to carry that out.

Step Twelve—Having had a spiritual awakening as the result of these steps, we tried to carry this message to others and to practice these principles in all our affairs.

* Disclaimer

I believe the Twelve Step Program is God-centered, and I find it to be totally in line with scripture. As I worked the program, however, I found that it was lacking in one area. In the Twelve Step Program, we reconcile ourselves with God. We reconcile ourselves with those we have harmed. We resolve to continue living a life worthy of God and others. But I found no place to release the anger and resentment I held inside for those who had victimized me. So I have incorporated Steps 8A, 9A, and 10A to address that portion of many of our lives. If those areas do not pertain to you, just skip right over them. For those of us who have been victims, I hope you will find these additions helpful.

For reference, these are:

The Twelve Steps of Alcoholics Anonymous

1. We admitted we were powerless over alcohol—that our lives had become unmanageable.
2. Came to believe that a Power greater than ourselves could restore us to sanity.
3. Made a decision to turn our will and our lives over to the care of God as we understood Him.
4. Made a searching and fearless moral inventory of ourselves.
5. Admitted to God, to ourselves, and to another human being the exact nature of our wrongs.
6. Were entirely ready to have God remove all these defects of character.
7. Humbly asked Him to remove our shortcomings.
8. Made a list of all persons we had harmed and became willing to make amends to them all.
9. Made direct amends to such people wherever possible, except when to do so would injure them or others.
10. Continued to take personal inventory and when we were wrong, promptly admitted it.
11. Sought through prayer and meditation to improve our conscious contact with God, as we understood Him, praying only for knowledge of His will for us and the power to carry that out.
12. Having had a spiritual awakening as the result of these steps, we tried to carry this message to alcoholics, and to practice these principles in all our affairs.

Copyright c A.A. World Services, Inc.

The Twelve Steps of Alcoholics Anonymous reprinted and adapted with biblical scriptures with permission of Alcoholics Anonymous World Services, Inc. ("AAWS"). Permission to reprint this adaptation of the Twelve Steps does not mean that AAWS has reviewed or approved the contents of this publication, or that AAWS necessarily agrees with the views expressed herein. A.A. is a program of recovery from alcoholism only—use of the Twelve Steps in connection with programs and activities which are patterned after A.A., but which address other problems, or in any other non-A.A. context, does not imply otherwise. Additionally, while A.A. is a spiritual program, A.A. is not a religious program. Thus, A.A. is not affiliated or allied with any sect, denomination, or specific religious belief.

INTRODUCTION

A Biblical Path to Calm the Chaos with a Bible Study for working
the Twelve Steps from a Christian perspective

What does our life ultimately consist of?

- Our relationship with God
- Our view of ourselves
- Our relationships with our spouse, family, and friends
- Our attitude

This Bible Study, worked properly, will bring those four things into harmony and will ultimately allow God to calm our chaos. It is a process that sets us free of unhealthy behaviors and the low self-esteem and shame that accompanies them. The steps are presented in a "we" format. That is intentional. It reminds us that we are not alone in this process. Many have gone before us who have experienced the same range of emotions and difficulties in life. When we feel overwhelmed with the process, we step back, take a deep breath, and realize that millions have made it through the Twelve Steps, and so can we.

Why should we work this program?

- Because it is difficult to get on with the present until we resolve the past.
- Because it will enhance or begin healthy relationships with God and the people in our lives.
- Because we deserve to move forward in life without the yoke of guilt.

Who can benefit from this program?

Certainly, if you identify with any of the following list, you could benefit from this program:

- Victim of abuse
- Dealing with anger, grief, guilt, depression, eating disorders, PTSD
- Addiction to alcohol, drugs, sex, power, or any substance or behavior
- Relationship problems
- Low self-esteem
- Lack of a healthy spiritual life
- Issues around forgiveness—forgiving and being forgiven
- A sense of abandonment—by people or God
- A general sense of unhappiness or discontent
- A general feeling of being "out of sorts" with life

We tend to think that Twelve Step programs are only for people with really messed up childhoods or alcoholics or addicts. But the reality is that all of us have been harmed by someone along the way in life. Many of us have developed coping mechanisms that perhaps helped at one time but are no longer appropriate. Most of us have unresolved anger or hurt that we'd like to get past. Maybe you had a perfect childhood and can't figure out what went wrong in adulthood. Who among us wouldn't like more peace in our lives? How many of us would like to repair relationships and develop a closer relationship with God? We can all benefit from a Twelve Step program.

I heard a sermon one time that cautioned against being a "Cafeteria Christian." The pastor defined Cafeteria Christians as those people who go through the Bible picking and choosing what they will incorporate into their lives or not. The same can be said of the steps here. If you are not sure that you really need all of the Twelve Steps but do have a couple of relationships that need to be repaired, you might be tempted to page through to steps eight and nine. I would ask you to start with Step One and go through them chronologically even if all you do is read through them. They are not long reads.

A LITTLE BACKGROUND

We live in a chaotic world, a fact that I doubt anyone would contest. On the global level, we deal with pandemics, terrorists, wars, famine, earthquakes, tornados, and flooding. On the local level, we have politics, street gangs, schoolyard bullies, and petty neighborhood disturbances. On the personal level, we have addictions, disease, and broken relationships. And all these feed off of each other, only complicating the chaos in our world and in our personal lives.

Just when we think we've gotten past one crisis and can return to *normal*, another situation arises. No matter how much we try to control the circumstances, we soon learn that we have no real control. I doubt that we will ever achieve resolution of these issues to the point of world or even national peace. But each of us *can* achieve personal peace even in the midst of chaos in our lives. God can calm the chaos.

One evening, I bundled up against the evening chill, got a folding lawn chair, and walked to the end of our road. I set the chair at the edge of a meadow, sat down, and waited. The deer started to appear about fifteen minutes later—first one doe, then another, and then four more with their spotted fawns. It was magical to just sit in awe of God's magnificent creatures. There was no rush. They leisurely appeared and slowly moved along as they grazed. Every now and then, one would stop and look at me. I sat still, breathing at an easy, hypnotic pace. Then she'd go back to her leisurely pace of grazing. Every now and then, the fawns would frisk and frolic, and I'd be reminded of the carefree days of childhood. Then the song "As the Deer," based on Psalm 42:1, entered my conscious mind:

> *As the deer panteth for the water*
> *So my soul longeth after Thee*
> *You alone are my heart's desire*
> *And I long to worship Thee.*

You alone are my strength, my shield
To You alone may my spirit yield
You alone are my heart's desire
And I long to worship Thee.

How is it that the deer, and all of nature in fact, manages such a serene existence? Serene? Well, they do have to deal with weather, hunters, predators, drought, and famine. But don't we deal with all that too? They don't sit and fret, turn to drugs or alcohol, or commit suicide. I found myself wishing I could be like them.

But do I really want to be like them? In all of creation, except for man, God has preordained their nature, their habits, and their instincts. But with humans, God decided to give us free will. He also offered us a relationship with Him. We are free to choose, to accept that gift of love, or we can choose to go it alone and miss out on our heart's desire. Our rebellious nature creates broken relationships and daily struggles.

In 2 Corinthians 12:10b, Paul tells us, "When I am weak, I am strong." Indeed, Christ had told Paul in 2 Corinthians 12:9, "My grace is sufficient for you for my power is made perfect in weakness." It seems a contradiction of terms, and yet it works. The more I relinquish to God, the more I am at peace, the better I am able to deal with life's difficulties, and the more I experience clarity of thought for decision-making. When I am weak, I am strong!

I suppose some people can just make the decision to relinquish their will over to God and stick to it. But for most of us, we try to relinquish and then take it back over and over again. I have encountered some churches that told me that my faith was just not strong enough, and that was why I failed and struggled. Each person has to answer that claim for themselves. But when I heard those words, I knew that was not the case. In my heart, my faith was strong, steady, and sure, but my ability to relinquish was consistently weak.

The only *real* peace I have achieved in my life has been from God; through His Son, Jesus Christ; and the indwelling of His Holy Spirit. It is a simple concept in words, but it is not always so easy to surrender our will over to God and let go of our control. But wait a minute. Didn't we just agree that we don't really have any real control anyway? Yes, but it seems to be in our nature to keep trying to maintain control anyway.

Through Overeaters Anonymous (OA), I encountered the Twelve Steps and was finally able to relinquish my control, my will. I discovered freedom, strength, and peace in the midst of chaos. I encountered the steps through OA, but the same steps are beneficial to alcoholics, the hard-hearted, drug addicts, overeaters, people with relationship failures, sex addicts, etc. The principles learned through the steps are a guide to putting our affairs in order—accounting for our actions, repairing relationships, and relinquishing ourselves to God.

If you have a particular addiction, I encourage you to attend meetings that target your addiction. But you do not need to have an addiction to benefit from the steps. Everyone can benefit from working the Twelve Steps.

I have organized the steps in this book as a Bible Study and from a Christian perspective. Nothing about the Twelve Steps is in conflict with the Bible; in fact, for each step, I have referenced Bible verses that support the incorporation of each step into our lives. It is a biblical path to calm the chaos.

Now you may be thinking, "But I don't want to work the steps. It's too much work, too much time. I just want to stop drinking, or dwelling on the past, or overeating, or obsessing. I just need to put the horrors of war, or my childhood, or failed relationships behind me." If you can pray for God to just come in and fix you with positive results, so be it. I can't tell you how many times I prayed for that. I didn't want to do the work either, but evidently God did. Unless God grants you an instant miracle, my advice is to pray to God for Him to help make you willing, willing to do the work. Recovery involves peeling the onion—one layer at a time until we get to the core—dealing with the layers one at a time. The steps put our whole life in balance. It is not a bandage to put over the hurt. Eventually, the bandage will fall away, and unless the whole wound was treated, it will fester again. This is a program to put an end to unhealthy behaviors and attitudes once and for all.

Committing yourself to a recovery program is a big deal, and you need to be able to put your focus there. You probably already have plenty of competition for your time with your job and home life. I would encourage you to not take on any additional activities while working your recovery program. Please include child abuse in your prayers and perhaps in your finances but put the bulk of your extra time into yourself for now. So, no more bellyaching—let's just get started.

How to Proceed

This is not a program in which you can hole up in your bedroom and do it all by yourself. Certainly, you will need some time like that to reflect and contemplate. But ultimately, you need a partner with whom to share your findings. This is a biblical principle. James 5:16a tell us to "Confess your sins to each other and pray for each other so that you may be healed." And Ephesians 5:21 tells us, "Submit to one another out of reverence for Christ."

A. Find one person with whom you can share your work for each step. We will call this person your Accountability Partner (AP).
   1. This needs to be someone you can be completely honest with and who will be trustworthy to keep your information confidential.
   2. This also needs to be someone you believe to have good integrity and good values, preferably a Christian, and someone whose opinion you value.
   3. This can be a professional such as a counselor/therapist or minister or a close friend or fellow church member.
      a. It may not be necessary to incur the cost of a professional if you can find someone who possesses the qualities noted above.
      b. If you have complex issues such as abuse, incest, or other such issues, you might want to consider working through the steps with a professional or at least connecting with a professional at some point in the process.
      c. Generally, I would stay away from family members, especially if any of your issues involve family members.
   4. The person you choose should be willing to read through this book in order to understand how they are assisting you.
   5. Someone who meets all the qualities listed and has previously worked the Twelve Steps themselves would be a great choice.
   6. If you truly have no one, you might consider joining one of the Twelve Step groups. You can attend any of the Twelve Step programs available—you can find meeting locations, time, and the focus of the group (alcohol, eating, drugs, codependency) on the internet. There is also a Christian recovery

group called Celebrate Recovery,[11] which is open to people of all faiths and all dysfunctions. Their program is also based on the Twelve Steps, and meetings are held at churches across the country. You can just type in "Celebrate Recovery" on your computer and find the meeting closest to you.

7. All these Twelve Step groups have sponsors (they call them sponsors—I call them accountability partners) who are available for the asking. Generally, you would attend several meetings and listen to people as they share until you find one who seems to share your values and experiences. When people share at these meetings, if they are an available sponsor, they will usually announce that. Or you can ask the group's leader to introduce you to the available sponsors. Simply ask if they will be your sponsor—usually they would want to meet and talk with you and lay out their ground rules to see if it seems that the two of you can work together. Make sure to share the following information with your AP or sponsor, asking them to please commit to adhering to the following principles:

a. In sharing, each of you should focus on your thoughts, feelings, and actions. Use words like "I" and "me."

b. Do not try to *fix* your partner or *tell* them what to do—the AP can suggest and discuss, but ultimately the decision is yours. The purpose of the AP is to act as a sounding board, to help you be truthful in everything, and to pray together about what the next action should be.

c. Confidentiality is crucial. Nothing said in partnership should *ever* be shared with anyone else (unless there is concern for the partner's physical safety or the safety of others).

8. Do not be alarmed if your AP does not make it through all Twelve Steps with you.

a. Working through all the steps can take a long time, especially if you have a busy life and if your issues are complicated. It took me one year. In the course of that time frame, people change, they move away, circumstances change, so a change in AP is quite possible and probably inevitable. I had three APs in my process.

---

[11] Celebrate Recovery, www.celebraterecovery.com

B. Set aside regular time to work on the steps as outlined in this book. Don't try to do too much at one time, or you will likely not get the full benefit. Two or three dedicated sessions per step should work pretty well to obtain the full benefit yet move along at a reasonable pace.

1. Some steps (such as the fourth and fifth steps) are more involved and will take additional sessions to adequately complete.

2. There is no exact time required—it takes what it takes. Just don't fall into shortcutting.

3. Once or twice a week for one or two hours each time is a fairly good pace. It keeps you progressing forward but allows time between sessions to reflect.

4. Remember that you need to be brutally honest with yourself. As the angels from the TV show *Touched by an Angel* used to say, "The truth will set you free."

C. What should you do in your sessions?

1. The steps are laid out as a Bible Study workbook. Start at Step One, read, reply, write, reflect, meet with your AP, and then move on to the next step.

a. Some additional materials you might want on hand with each session are your Bible and a journal or notebook for answering questions posed with each step.

D. When should you meet with your AP?

1. You should meet before you start and discuss the nature of your relationship and establish ground rules. Discuss the suggestions in section A.7. above. Also establish guidelines for your relationship such as times to call or not call, what your relationship will be outside the program, what you expect of each other, and so on. Make sure the relationship rules are clear before you proceed.

2. You may get together or talk on the phone if you feel you need guidance while working the step. Once you have completed the step, you should schedule a meeting with your AP. You should allow at least one hour or possibly a second meeting, depending on the complexity of each step. Set this meeting at a location and time where you will have privacy and will not be interrupted.

3. Go over the step—read your answers—discuss the material—resolve any remaining questions about that step in discussion with your AP.

4. If both you and your AP agree that you have adequately completed that step, conclude your meeting with a prayer and move on to the next step.

5. If, however, you and/or your AP feel that you have not fully completed that step, you will need to discuss how to proceed.

a. You may need to redo a particular section of that step.

b. Refer to Part Three—Tools and Exercises. One or more of these tools may help you complete your step. Also, near the beginning of each step, I have described how I worked through the step and discussed some pitfalls to watch for. You and your AP should read through the step's introduction and go through Tools and Exercises to see if there are helpful hints to completing your step.

c. Conclude your meeting with a prayer asking for God's guidance with whatever plan or goals you have adopted in this meeting.

d. Take at least two sessions on your own to rework the step and then reschedule with your AP to conclude your step.

6. Once you and your AP agree that you are ready to move on, you may begin working your next step.

7. Complete each step as described above.

Note: Don't let it stop you, but be aware that often as you work the steps, issues may surface that you were not even aware of or whose significance you were not aware. Things might surface that you'd rather not deal with. You have two choices—work through it and get past it or ignore it and let it continue to fester. Shoving it back inside has never been a good solution. It is work that you sometimes may not want to do. But you also don't want to stay stuck where you are. So…say a prayer for guidance and then step forward in faith. And, yes, talk to your AP, and if your AP agrees, perhaps talk with a professional.

E. What to do after you have completed Step 12? Are you ever completely done?

1. You can set your workbook aside and do your best to incorporate all the principles you have learned into your daily life.

2. Retain your workbook, however, because I've never known anyone who hasn't had to revisit one step or another.

a. You may encounter things like the death of a loved one, loss of a job, physical injury, or broken relationship. In these or other circumstances, if you find yourself backpedaling:

1) Go back through the steps and see where you have reverted.

2) Reconnect with your AP or choose a new one.

3) Work through the relevant steps just as before. Then just keep moving forward—one day at a time.

F. How to keep from backpedaling?

1. On a daily basis, keep in mind the basic principles of the Twelve Step Program and live them daily. If needed, post the steps where you can see them regularly.

2. Stay in touch with other Twelve Steppers and/or your AP.

a. Have monthly meetings to discuss step-related issues as a support to each other and as a social get-together.

b. If you do not know other Twelve Steppers, you could start a group at your church or place of employment as a support group. But remember that any group needs to understand the responsibility of confidentiality.

c. You could attend any twelve step meetings. Even if you are not an alcoholic or overeater, etc., you can attend those meetings just to keep the principles alive for you. Call before going to a meeting—most are open to anyone, but some are closed to those not sharing their particular issue. You can find meeting places, time, and contact names on the internet. Just type in "twelve step meetings," and you will find more than you ever imagined to choose from.

3. Stay in prayer. Feel free to present prayers of a request nature, but remember to not neglect prayers of praise and thanksgiving as well.

4. Implementing daily Bible time and quiet time help to keep you focused and connected. You can approach that in several ways.

a. The internet has twelve-step-focused devotion books that you can read daily.

b. Christian bookstores have many daily devotional books—some of a general nature and others with specific themes.

c. Many churches offer free daily devotional booklets.

d. Join a Bible Study. Of course, most churches offer Bible Study groups, but you might be surprised to know that many Christians gather at work or school for lunchtime Bible Study, prayer, and support. Bible studies can also be found at senior centers.

Once you have found your AP, let's get started with Step One.

STEP ONE

We admitted we were powerless over compulsive and/or unhealthy behaviors—that our lives had become unmanageable.

The principle behind Step One is **honesty**. If we cannot be honest with ourselves, honest about the scope of our behavior or circumstances, honest about a sincere desire to change, then we will not succeed.

Romans 7:15 and 18, Paul writes, "I do not understand what I do. For what I want to do I do not do, but what I hate, I do. I know that nothing good lives in me, that is, in my sinful nature. For I have the desire to do what is good, but I cannot carry it out."

For many years, I was the exact model of what Paul speaks of in that Romans Bible verse. I was a good person, but I did bad things that I could not control. I was good to others but not to myself. I had no idea why I ate the way I did. I was a binge eater and a compulsive overeater. I knew I should stop, but I couldn't. And therein lay the insanity. I spent countless years dieting, failing at dieting, feeling guilty and shameful, hating myself, losing weight, gaining weight, and ultimately feeling worthless.

Through a series of attempts to lose weight, I finally landed in psychological counseling. There, I learned the why of my behavior and why the bizarre eating had started in the first place. Now I had others to blame. Indeed, there were many legitimate mitigating circumstances that led to those behaviors, such as my father's suicide, a childhood molestation, and a rape, to name a few. So I spent many years blaming others for my behaviors and my overweight condition, but the eating didn't change, and neither did the weight, and neither did my self-image.

After one more successful weight loss and yet one more failure to maintain the weight loss, I found myself contemplating suicide. I eventually realized that, regardless of how I had gotten to this point—who had done what to me, what my past indiscretions had been, who hurt me—I had to finally stop playing the blame game and accept responsibility for who I was and what my actions were *now*. I had to choose to accept responsibility for myself *today*. I had over thirty years of bad habits, and although there may have been good reasons for them at some time, it was time to let them go. After I came to that awareness, it seemed that changes in my behavior would be inevitable. But it was not. Awareness and knowledge are one thing, but action is another, and I could not do it on my own. I needed help. I was at the point of Step One—admitting I was powerless over my behavior and that my life had become unmanageable. And with that decision, I felt a heavy yoke fall off my shoulders, and I physically slumped to the ground, exhausted and weary but breathing freely for the first time in an awfully long time.

I found the following Tools and Exercises most helpful:

Bible Reading	Deep Breathing	Personalize Your Bible
Prayer and Meditation	Talk to Someone	Visualization
Writing		

Spend some time in reflection with the following Bible verses that were helpful for me in coming to acceptance of Step One. Write your answers and thoughts in your journal or notebook and use any of the Tools and Exercises to help you further explore your feelings and thoughts. You may be tempted to just answer some of the questions in your head, but I suggest that you write out *all* your answers in your journal. Writing them makes a bigger impact than just saying them in your head and can sometimes lead to other thoughts that can be helpful as well.

Romans 7:15 and 18—"I do not understand what I do. For what I want to do I do not do, but what I hate, I do. I know that nothing good lives in me, that is, in my sinful nature. For I have the desire to do what is good, but I cannot carry it out."

What are some examples of how and when you have felt this way about yourself? How did it make you feel? Did you think you were the only one who felt this way? How long have you had these feelings? Are the feelings continual, or do they come and go?

2 Peter 2:19—"For a man is a slave to whatever has mastered him."

Do you feel like a slave to anything? Is there anything in your life that takes preference over your own health and needs? Is there anything in your life that takes preference over God and your family?

Psalm 6:2–3—"Be merciful to me, Lord, for I am faint; O Lord, heal me, for my bones are in agony. My soul is in anguish. How long, O Lord, how long?"

Psalm 6:6—"I am worn out from groaning; all night long I flood my bed with weeping and drench my couch with tears."

Psalm 22:1—"My God, my God, why have you forsaken me? Why are you so far from saving me, so far from the words of my groaning?"

Psalm 69:1–3—"Save me, O God, for the waters have come up to my neck. I sink in the miry depths, where there is no foothold. I have come into the deep waters; the floods engulf me. I am worn out calling for help; my throat is parched. My eyes fail, looking for my God."

Do you believe that God will or can or cares enough to listen? Have you felt like He has not responded to your cries in the past? Did He not respond, or were you not willing to accept His answer? I considered listing only one or two of these passages from Psalms but then decided to leave the list intact for this reason: the psalms were written by David, who was close to God's heart and had God's favor. But even David was close to despair over and over again. It is in our human nature to ask for help and then try to do it on our own. David knew that God heard, and that God responded, but David also knew that he did not always heed God's response. Yet when he did, things always worked out for the better. In Step One, we are admitting that we cannot do it on our own—that our way has not been working. We admit that we need to relinquish completely. Are you at that point? What are some examples of how your life has not been working to the fullest?

Psalm 102:1–5—"Hear my prayer, O Lord; let my cry for help come to you. Do not hide your face from me when I am in distress. Turn your ear to me; when I call, answer me quickly. For my days vanish like smoke; my bones burn like glowing embers. My heart is blighted and withered like grass; I forget to eat my food. Because of my loud groaning I am reduced to skin and bones."

Have you ever felt this overwhelmed with sadness and helplessness? Have you ignored it so long that it is festering inside of you? For how long? What is contributing to those feelings? Do you feel like God has turned his back on you? Rewrite this psalm in your own words using your own circumstances. Then ask yourself if you want to stop feeling this way. Write about why or why not.

Psalm 55:4–8—"My heart is in anguish within me; the terrors of death assail me. Fear and trembling have beset me; horror has overwhelmed me. I said, 'Oh, that I had the wings of a dove! I would fly away and be at rest—I would flee far away and stay in the desert; I would hurry to my place of shelter, far from the tempest and storm.'"

Have you ever wanted to just fly away? Sounds lovely, doesn't it? And an occasional getaway is sometimes acceptable and great medicine—but then we have to come back to reality. Have you ever considered suicide? Attempted suicide? That is the ultimate "flying away." Despair can lead to those feelings, but we do not have to act on those feelings. Write in your journal about times you have felt this way. It is normal to feel this way on occasion, but if you are seriously considering suicide, you should seek professional help right away.

Proverbs 26:12—"Do you see a man wise in his own eyes? There is more hope for a fool than for him."

Solomon, here in his wisdom, tells us that if we see ourselves as wise and try to live life on our own, we are more the fool. Have you ever put yourself above God? In what ways? Have you been foolishly trying to handle life on your own? Do you think you have all the answers? Are you in control? How is that working for you?

We only think we know what is best for us. How many times have you looked back in your life and been grateful that things worked out the way they did? Can you think of any times or circumstances when you thought you knew what you wanted, but it turned out that you were wrong? God will always direct us in the right path, but we have to relinquish our will to Him for that to happen. What is holding you back from relinquishing your will?

2 Kings 5:1–15—[paraphrased] Naaman was commander of the army of the king of Aram. He was a valiant soldier, but he had leprosy. A young captive girl from Israel said that if he would go see the prophet Elisha, he would be cured. So Naaman went to Elisha's house. Elisha sent a messenger to tell him to go and wash himself seven times in the Jordan, and he would be cured. But Naaman went away angry, thinking that Elisha had been dismissive to him, saying, "I thought that he would surely come out to me and stand and call on the name of the Lord his God, wave his hand over the spot, and cure me of my leprosy." But he finally went down and dipped himself in the Jordan seven times, and his flesh was restored and became clean like that of a young boy. (For full story, read 2 Kings 5:1–15.)

Naaman went expecting to be healed, but he had preconceived notions as to how that should be done. When the cure was presented to him, devoid of the pomp and circumstance he had expected, he rejected the cure. In what ways have you rejected God's attempts to help you? Do you have preconceived ideas of how God can help you? I knew that I just needed God to make me thin and all my troubles would be gone. God knew better. Can you see that your preconceived notions have not worked for you?

Acts 9:1,3–9—"Saul was still breathing out murderous threats against the Lord's disciples. As he neared Damascus on his journey, suddenly a light from heaven flashed around him. He fell to the ground and heard a voice say to him, 'Saul, Saul, why do you persecute me?' 'Who are you, Lord?' Saul asked. 'I am Jesus, whom you are persecuting,' he replied. 'Now get up and go into the city, and you will be told what you must do.' The men traveling with Saul stood there speechless; they heard the sound but did not see anyone. Saul got up from the ground, but when he opened his eyes, he could see nothing. So they led him by the hand into Damascus. For three days he was blind." (For the full account, read Acts 9:1–31.)

This was what it took for God to get to Saul's heart, to convince him that Jesus was the Son of God. Saul became Paul and traveled the regions proclaiming the Good News of Jesus Christ. What will it take for God to reach your heart? Are you willing to admit that your way has not been working for you?

2 Corinthians 12:9–10—"But he said to me, 'My grace is sufficient for you, for my power is made perfect in weakness.' Therefore I will boast all the more gladly

about my weaknesses, so that Christ's power may rest on me. That is why, for Christ's sake, I delight in weaknesses, in insults, in hardships, in persecutions, in difficulties. For when I am weak, then I am strong."

How well have you done on your own? I was *happy* to admit to my weakness and to be made strong through Christ. It lifted such a burden from my shoulders to say, "Here, God—you take it, I can't carry it any longer." His grace is sufficient for me. Might it be for you? Can you envision life with that burden lifted? How does that look and feel to you? Do you recognize your weaknesses?

Luke 15:17—"When he came to his senses, he said, 'How many of my father's hired men have food to spare, and here I am starving to death!'" (For the entire prodigal son story, read Luke 15:11–32.)

Just because the prodigal son chose a path of destruction didn't mean he had to stay there. Returning to his father was another choice available to him. We can continue to live on our own as well or ask our Heavenly Father to take us by the hand and direct our paths. Which choice seems better to you? Before he could return home, though, he had to humble himself and admit that his life had become unmanageable. Are you at that point? Can you admit to being powerless?

Step One Resolution

We admitted we were powerless over compulsive and/or unhealthy behaviors—that our lives had become unmanageable.

Read over the instructions for Speed Writing in Part Three. In Speed Writing style, answer the following questions in your journal.

- What are some examples of your unhealthy behaviors?
- What have you experienced as the consequences of those behaviors?
- In what ways has your life become unmanageable?

- In what ways has that affected your relationships?
  - Your work?
  - Your home life?
  - Your relationship with God?
  - Your self-esteem?

Keep in mind that at this point, you do not need to know the why of your life. You do not need to have any answers. Those will be explored in some of the other steps. At this point, we are only concerned about where you are right now.

If you have not accepted Step One, discuss with your AP and consider the Tools and Exercises to see if one or more can help you get to that point.

Date you accepted Step One: _____

Date you shared that decision with your AP: _____

STEP TWO

C ame to believe that a Power greater than ourselves (God) could restore us to sanity.

The principle behind Step Two is **hope**. In order to be successful, there must be hope—otherwise there is no reason to even try. Many of us have had enough failure in our lives to be afraid of even trying. But in many cases, we were, most likely, depending on ourselves. We now understand that we have a greater power in God with this program—not only are we not going it alone, but the greatest force in the universe is at our side. Additionally, we can feel hopeful due to the proven history of the Twelve Step program that has brought relief to millions of people. It is our hope that if they can do it, and with God at our side, we can too.

Isaiah 41:9b–10 and 13—"God spoke through the prophet Isaiah saying, 'I have chosen you and have not rejected you. So do not fear, for I am with you; do not be dismayed, for I am your God. I will strengthen you and help you; I will uphold you with my righteous right hand. For I am the Lord, your God, who takes hold of your right hand and says to you, Do not fear; I will help you.'"

In Part One, I gave a detailed account of my loss of faith. When I entered a Twelve Step program, I had no problem acknowledging in Step One that I was powerless, but I was in no frame of mind with Step Two to accept God as my power. As far as I was concerned, God had let me down on every front. I broke down and cried, acknowledging that there was, therefore, no hope for me. I had tried every program in existence, I had tried my own will power, and now I had entered a program that was my last chance, and Step Two was to be my undoing. I felt like all my bones had turned to mush as I slumped to the floor in defeat.

At that moment, I had no faith that this program could work for me, but, for the moment anyway, there were no other options. Someone suggested for me to act as if I believed God could restore me to sanity. Or in other words, *fake it until you can make it*. So that was how I proceeded. I moved forward working this step, reading the literature, reading Bible passages, and acting as if I believed. Just simply reading and thinking was not enough—I had to reach into my bag of tricks (Tools and Exercises) for help. I had developed many of these tools in the years prior as I worked with therapists, and I continued to add to them as I worked through the Twelve Steps. Putting the two together, the tools and the Twelve Steps, was the catalyst needed for forward progression with the steps and meaningful recovery.

I picked up my Bible and reread all the places where I had Personalized it. It touched my heart to read the passages in that personalized fashion. In John 5:6, I read, "Sherry do you want to get well?" Yes, I did. I began to use my GOD CAN again.

As I read scripture, I wrote down all my doubts and put them in the GOD CAN. I did a lot of Speed Writing that helped me identify some of what had led to my loss of faith and my nervous breakdown. I used the Ghost Chair exercise to express and vent my anger and the God Talk tool to help me reestablish my relationship with God.

It was an agonizing process, but I kept one Bible verse at the forefront that kept me going. Paul wrote in Philippians 3:13b–14: "Forgetting what is behind and straining toward what is ahead, I press on toward the goal to win the prize for which God has called me heavenward in Christ Jesus." Make a note of this verse in your journal and refer to it as you work through each step.

It reminded me every day that I don't have to do it perfectly—I just have to keep trying. It took quite some time for me to accept this step, but when I finally did, that "peace that passes all understanding" that we are promised in Philippians 4:7 became mine, and as my friend Ellie had once advised me, I stopped struggling and started snuggling. That peace and the snuggling (visualizing myself on God's lap in the rocking chair) saw me through the rest of the steps and continues to this day.

Remember to not get too far ahead of yourself. In Step Two, you are only acknowledging that God *can* restore us to sanity. Don't look too far downstream and get overwhelmed with all that is to come. Focus only on the belief that God *can*.

Spend some time in reflection with the following Bible verses. Remember to use your journal and *write out* (don't just work in your head) your answers to the following questions. If you cannot resolve any questions, try going through the Tools and Exercises for suggestions to help you get past the impasse. And don't forget to include your AP if you get stuck in the process.

Isaiah 41:9b–10 and 13—"God spoke through the prophet Isaiah saying, 'I have chosen you and have not rejected you. So do not fear, for I am with you; do not be dismayed, for I am your God. I will strengthen you and help you; I will uphold you with my righteous right hand. For I am the Lord, your God, who takes hold of your right hand and says to you, Do not fear; I will help you.'"

What I really like about this Isaiah passage is that God says He has chosen me and has not rejected me. Even if I have rejected Him, He has not rejected me. Nothing that I can do will separate God from me. Being a mother, I understand that. I will never, nor could I ever, reject my daughter. I am not a perfect mother by any means, but I would use all the means at my disposal to protect, help, and instruct her. God will do the same for us, and His ways are perfect. When He says we do not need to fear, that is a fact. When He says He will help and strengthen us, that is a fact as well. When He says he will take hold of our right hand, you can believe that the fear will melt away as He does.

Psalm 46:1—"God is our refuge and strength, an ever-present help in trouble."

One way for us to come to the belief and understanding that God can restore us to sanity is to see Him through the eyes of His followers. Here, David describes God as our refuge and strength—a statement of fact. It is a statement that David believes with his whole heart because God had proven to him over and over again to be just that. David, the disciples, and Paul in his letters to the churches describe God in the following verses as a God who is trustworthy, supportive, loving, compassionate, powerful, and all knowing. All of these people's opinions help to shape our opinions. If someone is known to have a stellar reputation, it is a lot easier to trust that person. All of these people's opinions absolutely tell us that God can be trusted to do as He says and to be constant in His support of us.

The prophet Isaiah confirms God's support
Isaiah 40:28–31—"Do you not know? Have you not heard? The Lord is the everlasting God, the Creator of the ends of the earth. He will not grow tired or weary, and His understanding no one can fathom. He gives strength to the weary and increases the power of the weak. Even youths grow tired and weary, and young men stumble and fall; but those who hope in the Lord will renew their strength. They will soar on wings like eagles; they will run and not grow weary, they will walk and not be faint."

Mark confirms God's support through His Son Jesus Christ
Mark 1:40–42—"A man with leprosy came to him and begged him on his knees, 'If you are willing, you can make me clean.' Filled with compassion, Jesus reached out his hand and touched the man. 'I am willing,' he said. 'Be clean!' Immediately the leprosy left him and he was cured."

Luke confirms God's support through His Son Jesus Christ
Luke 8:43–45a and 47–48—"And a woman was there who had been subject to bleeding for twelve years, but no one could heal her. She came up behind Him and touched the edge of His cloak, and immediately her bleeding stopped. 'Who touched me?' Jesus asked. Then the woman, seeing that she could not go unnoticed, came trembling and fell at his feet. In the presence of all the people, she told why she had touched him and how she had been instantly healed. Then he said to her, 'Daughter, your faith has healed you. Go in peace.'"

John 20:30–31—"Jesus did many other miraculous signs in the presence of his disciples, which are not recorded in this book. But these are written that you may believe that Jesus is the Christ, the Son of God, and that by believing you may have life in his name."

As John tells us, there are many more witness accounts attesting to the compassion, the power, the trustworthiness, and the love of our God for us, His children. He will be there for us when we call upon His name and even when we do not. Do you believe that? If not, why? What would it take for you to believe? Present that to God.

I have heard people say of the miracles in the Bible that they believe the accounts, but that God does not do miracles anymore today. I believe that God does indeed perform miracles every day. Every day, there are stories of people who against all odds perform some feat or beat the odds with a disease. And there are the miracles that go unseen—like a near-miss accident or a second-chance opportunity. Do you believe in miracles? Do you believe in them for yourself or just for other people? Why?

God, through His Son Jesus Christ, healed the sick and raised the dead. Surely, He can restore us to sanity. What is required of us? Faith—to believe that it is possible. Step Two only asks that we believe.

Ephesians 2:8–9a—"For it is by grace you have been saved, through faith—and this not from yourselves, it is the gift of God—not by works."

Paul tells the Ephesians that they are saved not by doing good works but by simply accepting the gift from God—the gift of His Son Jesus Christ. We are saved by grace through faith. What does it mean to be "saved?" God ordained that His Son, Jesus Christ, would die on the cross as a sacrificial lamb on our behalf. The shedding of His blood guarantees the forgiveness of our sins. We have simply to believe, repent, and accept the gift of forgiveness that is offered to us. What other benefits are offered? Eternal life! Jesus died on the cross and arose from the grave. We are promised the same future—we will die one day, but we will arise, as did Christ, and spend eternity in heaven. John 3:16, perhaps the most quoted piece of scripture, promises, "For God so loved the world that he gave his one and only Son, that whoever believes in him shall not perish but have eternal life." Not only will we have eternal life, but we will have a home in heaven as Christ promises in John 14:1–4: "Do not let your hearts be troubled. Trust in God; trust also in me. In my Father's house are many rooms; if it were not so, I would have told you. I am going there to prepare a place for you. And if I go and prepare a place for you, I will come back and take you to be with me that you also may be where I am. You know the way to the place where I am going." If you do not know the way, continue to read this passage in your Bible reading, adding verses 5–21 also.

The gift is presented. It is our choice to accept or reject it. When you have been presented gifts at your birthday or at Christmas, have you ever refused one? Have you ever opened all the gifts except one? I can't even imagine having a wrapped gift in my lap that I set aside and dismiss as unimportant. Have you accepted God's gift? Have you not accepted God's gift because you feel that you have not earned it? We are not asked to earn it—just accept it. At Christmas, children are often reminded that if they are not good, Santa might not bring them presents. Our God is not Santa Claus—God offers the gift regardless of our behavior. He does expect repentance and a sincere desire and effort to be our best. But if we fail, not only do we retain the gift, but we are also given forgiveness for our failures and continued love and support.

John 15:1–2—"I am the true vine, and my Father is the gardener. He cuts off every branch in me that bears no fruit, while every branch that does bear fruit He prunes so that it will be even more fruitful."

Anybody can prune a tree, but not just anybody can prune a tree with the desired outcome. An arborist is a specialist in the care and maintenance of trees. He can prune a tree to grow to its fullest and healthiest. You and I can prune a tree as well, but without the right cuts, we may stunt its growth or induce growth in the wrong direction. Let God be your arborist and shape you as He knows what is best for you. Can you relinquish the pruning of your life to God? In what ways?

Hebrews 7:24–25—"But because Jesus lives forever, he has a permanent priesthood. Therefore he is able to save completely those who come to God through him, because he always lives to intercede for them."

If you are having trouble reaching out and simply accepting God's gift, can you pray for Christ to intercede for you? Jesus will act on your behalf for God to soften your heart or heal your wounds so that you can accept the gift.

Matthew 11:28–30—"Come to me, all you who are weary and burdened, and I will give you rest. Take my yoke upon you and learn from me, for I am gentle and humble in heart, and you will find rest for your souls. For my yoke is easy and my burden is light."

By not accepting God's gift and by trying to handle life all on our own, we truly burden our lives and become very weary. If we choose unforgiveness, we are, in essence, choosing to keep our problems. Jesus tells us that His yoke is easy and the burden light. What a weight off our shoulders when we relinquish control to God. Do you believe that by relinquishing control our burden can be lifted? If you have a huge project to complete, will the burden be lighter by asking others to help? Write about a time that a project went better because of the support.

Step Two Resolution

Came to believe that a Power greater than ourselves (God) could restore us to sanity.

Do some Speed Writing about the following:

- Have you, like me, experienced a loss of faith?
- What were the circumstances?
- Is that still standing in the way of your acceptance of Step Two?
- If you have not experienced a loss of faith or have never had a faith in God, what is standing in the way of accepting the philosophy presented here in Step Two?

Remember, all you have to do at this point is believe that God *can*.

If you have not accepted Step Two, discuss with your AP and consider the Tools and Exercises to see if one or more can help you get to that point.

Date you accepted Step Two: _____

Date you shared that decision with your AP: _____

STEP THREE

M ade a decision to turn our will and our lives over to the care of God.
The principle behind Step Three is **faith**. In making the Step Three decision, we are stepping out in faith. We are acting as if this will work. Through faith, we are relinquishing our will over to God. And if we fully allow that to take hold, we can take a deep sigh of relief and relax.

Proverbs 3:5–6—"Trust in the Lord with all your heart and lean not on your own understanding; in all your ways acknowledge him, and he will make your paths straight."

This Step, for me, was actually the easiest. But no two journeys through the steps are the same. In Step One, we admitted we were powerless; our lives had become unmanageable. That was so evident in the way my life was going, in my behavior, and my relationships. In Step Two, we accepted that God could restore us to sanity. That was a rough one for me. I had been convinced that God had abandoned me, so it took a lot of work and a lot of time for me to accept that. But by the time I did fully believe that God could restore me, I was ready to fully relinquish myself to Him as well. So I had pretty much taken care of Step Three with Step Two. Therefore, I was tempted to just skim over this step and move on.

I was feeling pretty motivated and wanted to shortcut the system. And that is one reason we have accountability partners. She wanted to see my work before she'd sign off on me moving on to Step Four. I simply assured her I had turned my will and my life over to God, and she said, "I'll believe it when I see the work." I felt like I was in kindergarten—*who the heck is she to tell me what to do*—*I'm an adult; I'll do as I darn well please*—oops—There I was taking control back. Doing life my way had not turned out so well, so I decided I'd take the program as it was intended to be.

I decided to start each of my sessions with the Breaststroke exercise to clear my mind. I reviewed my journal to get a sense of all the ways I had tried to take care of myself in the past. Failed diets, pills, laxatives, bingeing, purging—oh yeah, I'd done a great job. I made a list of other people in whose care I had been in the past—parents, teachers, doctors—and wrote Dear John letters as a means of forgiving and releasing. I sat down with the Ghost Chair and talked, yelled, hit, and forgave all those who should have protected me in the past. I came to the understanding that they were, after all, human. Most of their actions were misdirected but not intentional. Turning my life over to God would be different, as His will and His actions are above reproach.

Using Speed Writing, I wrote about all the attempts I'd made in the past to put myself in God's care and realized that all I had ever done was tell God to "fix me" or "make me thin." I never asked Him to help me with the underlying causes. I had discussions with my AP about my misconceptions of love and acceptance. With an open and frank discussion, I realized that I had always viewed myself as unloved and did bizarre things for acceptance to feel love, which never turned out to really be love after all. And finally, I used small slips of paper and listed the many times and circumstances in which I had been in despair. I put them in my GOD CAN and gave them to God to deal with.

Spend some time in reflection with the following Bible verses. Remember to use your journal and *write out* (don't just work in your head) your answers to the following questions. If you cannot resolve any questions, try going through the Tools and Exercises for suggestions to help you get past the impasse. And don't forget to include your AP if you get stuck in the process.

Proverbs 3:5–6—"Trust in the Lord with all your heart and lean not on your own understanding; in all your ways acknowledge him, and he will make your paths straight."

Has anyone in your life proven to be untrustworthy? How did that make you feel? Do you have trust issues with others in your life? Do you believe that God can be trusted? If not, use some of the Tools and Exercises to resolve the trust issues. That alone might help you to be able to trust God. In your Bible Reading, focus on finding passages about trusting God and put it to prayer.

John 5:6–8a—[At the Sheep Gate pool near Jerusalem the blind, the lame, and the paralyzed used to lie there waiting to enter the healing pool.] "When Jesus saw him lying there and learned that he had been in this condition for a long time, he asked him, 'Do you want to get well?' 'Sir,' the invalid replied, 'I have no one to help me into the pool when the water is stirred. While I am trying to get in, someone else goes down ahead of me.' Then Jesus said to him, 'Get up! Pick up your mat and walk.' At once the man was cured; he picked up his mat and walked."

The key in these verses is the phrase "Do you want to get well?" So I ask you: Do you want to get well? It seems like the answer should be an automatic yes. But I wanted to get thin; I didn't want to do what it was going to take to get thin. I just wanted God to wave a magic wand and *poof.* So I guess the question should be, are you willing to do whatever God asks of you to get well? Are you willing to give up your wants and desires and accept God's will for you? Write God a letter about that.

John 16:33—"Jesus said, 'I have told you these things, so that in me you may have peace. In this world you will have trouble. But take heart! I have overcome the world.'"

It would also seem that accepting His peace would be a slam dunk. After all, who wouldn't want their life to have peace? But I know people who—and I was there once myself—thrive on the unrest in their lives. Moving from one panic to the other gives purpose to their lives—they are needed or get to play the hero. I'm sure it is a different reason in each person's life, but for many, there is something that they crave from the chaos. Are you hanging on to the chaos? In what ways? What do you get from that? Are you ready to give it up? Realize that even if you achieve His peace, there will still be chaos in your life, but God will give you the tools to deal with it in a healthy way instead of the destructive ways we often find.

Matthew 6:31–34—"So do not worry, saying, 'What shall we eat?' or 'What shall we drink?' or 'What shall we wear?' For the pagans run after all these things, and your heavenly Father knows that you need them. But seek first His kingdom and

His righteousness, and all these things will be given to you as well. Therefore, do not worry about tomorrow, for tomorrow will worry about itself. Each day has enough trouble of its own."

Are you a worry wart? Are you constantly looking downstream to the problems that might come? Do you find yourself living in the future instead of in the present? The best way that I have found to deal with worry and anxiety is to make lists. Making a list takes it out of my head and puts it down on paper instead. Once it's on paper, I put it in my GOD CAN and say, "OK, God—these are in your hands now. I can't deal with them, but God can." Billy Graham stated, "Anxiety is the natural result when our hopes are centered on anything short of God and His will for us."[12] Let's not try to do it on our own. What stands in the way of you living in the present? What can you do about that?

1 Corinthians 6:12, 10:23—"Everything is permissible for me—but not everything is beneficial. Everything is permissible for me—but I will not be mastered by anything. Everything is permissible for me—but not everything is constructive."

Determining God's will for us can seem elusive at times. Should we take that job or this one? That can be a difficult decision. But in much of life, common sense and the knowledge of good and bad should suffice. Everything is permissible—but is it beneficial? Is it constructive? Is it taking control of us? I had lived with a life of rules about food—"no" to everything that most children want. Thus, I rebelled and wanted everything that was prohibited. When I stumbled upon this Bible verse, it gave me the freedom I needed. Instead of a list of rules, I was given the authority to decide for myself. Instead of saying no to a second piece of cake because I had to, I now said no to the second piece of cake because it was not beneficial. Some people might not understand the difference, but it was a huge revelation to me. Do you have areas of your life in which you are not choosing what is beneficial or constructive? Do you have areas of your life that you have allowed to control your actions? Are you willing to turn those over to the will of God?

---

[12] Billy Graham, "The Cure for Anxiety," *Decision Magazine*, July/Aug 2004, accessed 2017.

Psalm 23—"The Lord is my shepherd, I shall not be in want. He makes me lie down in green pastures, He leads me beside quiet waters, He restores my soul. He guides me in paths of righteousness for His name's sake. Even though I walk through the valley of the shadow of death, I will fear no evil, for you are with me; your rod and your staff, they comfort me. You prepare a table before me in the presence of my enemies. You anoint my head with oil; my cup overflows. Surely goodness and love will follow me all the days of my life, and I will dwell in the house of the Lord forever."

Have you experienced the valley of the shadow of death? Have you felt surrounded by enemies? Write these experiences down on a piece of paper. Then sit down in a quiet place and close your eyes and visualize the green pastures. See yourself strolling through the pastoral scene. Now, interject the experiences you have written down. See them dissipate in God's presence. See yourself with God, dining and talking and laughing. Spend as much time there as you would like. When you leave, put the paper describing the bad experiences in your GOD CAN. Keep this as a mental image of what it will be like to turn your will over to the care of God.

Psalm 147:11—"The Lord delights in those who fear Him, who put their hope in His unfailing love."

Do you have any memories of your parents being excited and overjoyed with something you did? Or have you felt that way with something your children did? Bask in the glow of those memories and then imagine God standing on the sidelines excitedly cheering you on.

Romans 3:22–24—"This righteousness from God comes through faith in Jesus Christ to all who believe. There is no difference, for all have sinned and fall short of the glory of God, and are justified freely by his grace through the redemption that came by Christ Jesus."

Are you in that category? Do you believe that faith in Jesus Christ will redeem you? That is at the center of Christianity and what sets us apart from all other people. There is no doubt that if you believe, you will be redeemed. My problem was that I couldn't forgive myself, and if I couldn't forgive myself, then it was hard to accept His forgiveness. I did not feel worthy. I believed in my head, but I don't think I believed it in my heart. What helped me significantly was the God Talk exercise. That exercise helped me to see myself through God's eyes and to begin the process of loving, accepting, and forgiving myself, which then helped me to be receptive to God's love and His gifts. At that point, I could truly turn my will and my life over to the care of God.

Philippians 4:11–13, 19—"I am not saying this because I am in need, for I have learned to be content whatever the circumstances. I know what it is to be in need, and I know what it is to have plenty. I have learned the secret of being content in any and every situation, whether well fed or hungry, whether living in plenty or in want. I can do everything through him who gives me strength. And my God will meet all your needs according to his glorious riches in Christ Jesus."

These verses were fundamental in helping me to truly turn my life over to the care of God. I decided I wanted what Paul describes here. I could no longer fool myself with thoughts like "I'll be happy when I get a better job" or "My life will be wonderful when we get past these legal problems" or "Everything will fall in place once I get this loan paid off." I wanted to feel contentment every day, no matter what was going on around me. I could not even fathom that kind of contentment, but I knew I wanted it. Are you content in your life right now? What changes could make it better? And then what?

Psalm 40:1–2, 7–8—"I waited patiently for the Lord; He turned to me and heard my cry. He lifted me out of the slimy pit, out of the mud and mire; He set my feet on a rock and gave me a firm place to stand. Then I said, 'Here I am, I have come— it is written about me in the scroll. I desire to do your will, O my God; your law is within my heart.'"

Where we have been (a slimy pit), where we are now (on firm ground), and where we want to go (within God's will for us). Have you decided where you want to be? If not, do some Speed Writing to see if you can identify what is blocking your path. Look through the Tools and Exercises to see if there is something else that might help you past this roadblock.

Step Three Resolution

Made a decision to turn our will and our lives over to the care of God.

If you have not accepted Step Three, discuss with your AP and consider the Tools and Exercises to see if one or more can help you get to that point.

Date you accepted Step Three: _____

Date you shared that decision with your AP: _____

Some folks like to do something to commemorate the completion of these first three steps. We have turned our will and our life over to the care of God. It is a monumental step. I know of one person who made and framed a needlepoint lighthouse scene and hung it in her bedroom to be seen every day when she awoke. I went to the Christian bookstore and purchased a plaque that states, "Christ is head of this house." It hangs in my entryway where I see it coming and going every day. Others have knitted blankets with which to snuggle, made a photo collage to frame, painted a picture...the list can be endless. Use your imagination to make or find something that will have a value to you representing this decision.

STEP FOUR

Made a searching and fearless moral inventory of ourselves.

The principle behind Step Four is **courage**. Making a full disclosure inventory with brutal honesty takes courage. This courage will reveal the reasons behind much of our behavior.

Lamentations 3:40—"Let us examine our ways and test them, and let us return to the Lord."

Why, you may ask, is this necessary? Many of our destructive behaviors are rooted in our past. Until we reveal them and discover their hold on us, it is nearly impossible to just brush them aside and make a new life for ourselves. We cannot go back and change the things that have happened to us or change the things that we have done. But we can forgive and be forgiven. We can refuse to let our past define the rest of our lives. One by one, we need to recall our past and say, "Yep, that happened to me" or "I did those destructive things to others, but it doesn't have to define who I am any longer."

This inventory needs to be done in writing and is probably best in a narrative form. Just tell your story. This is for your eyes only and to share only with your AP. You can share it with others if you want, but it is not necessary, and keeping it private allows you to be brutally honest with yourself, not having to worry about what anyone else will think of you. The directions are to write a fearless (meaning to be brutally honest) moral inventory. So the focus is on your moral history—that area of your life concerning right and wrong behaviors, based on what most people would agree as right or wrong standards of behavior.

That said, it should not be just a list of what you did good and bad. Tell your story—about your parents and siblings, your childhood, school experiences, home life, friends, and relationships. Anything that you feel describes your life and, if known, the why of certain behaviors. Include any and all of your negative and destructive behaviors and actions. Also include incidents in which you were the victim, because oftentimes our destructive behavior develops as a result of that abuse. When I wrote my inventory, I literally started with "I was born," and then I told my life story chronologically. There is no right or wrong way, but I will share how I did mine, and you can adjust from there.

For most of us, this is not a project that can be done in one sitting—it took me a couple of weeks on and off. Before each Writing session, I did some Bible Reading and Prayer and Meditation. In my prayers, I asked God to help me to complete this Writing assignment completely and accurately so that I could receive the maximum benefit from it.

Shortcutting this work will not be of any benefit. When I was working the Twelve Steps, I heard many people speak about Step Four and how they had not taken it seriously and eventually had to return to Step Four and do it all over again in order to receive the full benefit. Plus, this inventory will be used as a guide in completing some of the remaining steps, so shortcutting at this point can impede progress with those steps as well.

The idea is not to just put a checkmark next to Step Four but to fearlessly bring to the surface any and all events and incidents in your life that you need to deal with. Some of the items might be lighthearted memories of your childhood, which will be wonderful to recall, but others may be painful memories that you need to deal with. You'll notice I said *need* to deal with, not *want* to deal with. We need to bring all these incidents to the piece of paper so that we do not keep them locked up inside any longer. Keeping those feelings locked inside only allows them to fester and fuel our shame. We need to deal with them in one way or another. With some of them, you may need to ask God and other people for forgiveness, which you will deal with in Steps Five, Eight, and Nine. Some may require you to extend forgiveness to others—either face-to-face or just in your heart. Some may be so deep seated that you will need to spend extra time with some of the Tools and Exercises to be able to get to the point of releasing the anger or hurt. We will discuss that process at the appropriate time with the appropriate steps.

As I was writing my inventory, I would sometimes get stuck and wonder if I should include an incident or not. I finally decided that if it came to mind, it probably had some relevance, so I included most anything that came to mind. It was, after all, for my eyes and my AP's eyes only. If a particular event or incident came to mind with confusing details or concerns about what that meant in my life or why it had even come to mind, I would separately Speed Write about that incident or event to gain a further perspective.

Once my inventory was complete, I shared it with my AP. She was not the least bit shocked, and she was not judgmental, but she didn't coddle me and say "Poor Sherry" either. She asked how I felt about the process and if I had ever shared some of those incidents with anybody before. Some I had not, and I admitted to her how difficult it was to share with her. We prayed at the end of our session and thanked God for the process and for seeing me through it. We asked that He continue to see me through the steps and give me the words to say and the actions to take at the appropriate time. We prayed for knowledge of how to proceed with resolving some of the issues and feelings that had surfaced with this inventory.

Spend some time in reflection with the following Bible verses before you write your inventory, as they are designed to help prepare you for that Writing. Remember to use your journal and *write out* (don't just work in your head) your answers to the following questions. If you cannot resolve any questions, try going through the Tools and Exercises for suggestions to help you get past the impasse. And don't forget to include your AP if you get stuck in the process.

Proverbs 16:3—"Commit to the Lord whatever you do, and your plans will succeed."

Before every Writing session, commit your work to God, and He will bless your work and give you the fortitude and honesty and knowledge to see it through to the end. It would be a good idea to write this scripture passage in your journal for reference in working all the steps.

Lamentations 3:40—"Let us examine our ways and test them, and let us return to the Lord."

God will love us and accept us just the way we are. But if we want forgiveness and if we want to be able to hear His voice and discern His will for us, we need to first examine our lives and make things right and then return to Him with a repentant heart. Christ forgave many sinners in the New Testament, and He was known to conclude with the phrase, "Go and sin no more." Are you ready and willing to make permanent changes in your life? If not, what is holding you back?

Proverbs 18:12—"Before his downfall a man's heart is proud, but humility comes before honor."

Can you recall times when you allowed your pride to get in the way? Doing this inventory could temporarily hurt your pride—it is hard to admit our failures, but this verse tells us that humility brings honor. Would you rather be filled with pride or honor?

Luke 9:23–24—"If anyone would come after me, he must deny himself and take up his cross daily and follow me. For whoever wants to save his life will lose it, but whoever loses his life for me will save it."

With the Twelve Steps, we are saving our lives by losing our old way of life. Write about some old ways that you need to change. These can be incorporated into your Step Four inventory.

Romans 6:11–12—"Count yourselves dead to sin but alive to God in Christ Jesus. Therefore, do not let sin reign in your mortal body so that you obey its evil desires."

List some sins that you would like to put to death. How would their demise make you feel alive? These too can be incorporated into your Step Four inventory.

Romans 6:20–23—"When you were slaves to sin, you were free from the control of righteousness. What benefit did you reap at that time from the things you are now ashamed of? Those things result in death! But now that you have been set free from sin and have become slaves to God, the benefit you reap leads to holiness, and the result is eternal life. For the wages of sin is death, but the gift of God is eternal life in Christ Jesus our Lord."

We are promised forgiveness from God, but we still need to ask for that forgiveness with a repentant heart. Without making our moral inventory, what would we ask forgiveness for? In order to wipe the slate clean, we need to be honest about the nature of our lives. We will ask God for that forgiveness in Step Seven, but for now we just need to put it out there in black and white.

The passage asks, "What benefit did you reap from your former ways?" We may be inclined to say that there were no benefits—after all, it was all from a negative perspective and created problems in our lives. For me, although I hated being overweight and the way I looked, in all honesty, I had to admit that the benefit of remaining fat was that it kept me safe from sexual predators. Was that a reason to stay fat and lose my health? No, and now I know that I have other resources to avoid sexual predators, but at that time it did serve a purpose. You may find that there were benefits to some of your former ways. So what benefits *did* you reap from your destructive ways? Include them in your inventory.

Psalm 130:3—"If you, O Lord, kept a record of sins, O Lord, who could stand?"

God will forgive—we just have to ask, and the record is scrubbed clean. He does not want to hold any sin over our head. If He did, He never would have sent His Son as a sacrificial lamb to atone for our sins. Is there any sin that you have committed that you believe God will not forgive you for? Even if you believe God will forgive you, can you forgive yourself? Make sure to include these in your inventory.

John 8:32, 34—"Jesus said, 'Then you will know the truth, and the truth will set you free...I tell you the truth, everyone who sins is a slave to sin.'"

This inventory is going to lay the truth out in front of you so that you can be set free. We have been slaves to our sin, to our misperceptions, and to the shame. Let's get that inventory done and be set free of the past.

As you move forward now to begin work on your Step Four inventory, keep in mind that the Ten Commandments and 1 Corinthians should serve as a moral compass.

Exodus 20:1–5a, 7–8, 12–17—

And God spoke all these words:

"I am the Lord your God, who brought you out of Egypt, out of the land of slavery. You shall have no other gods before me."

"You shall not make for yourself an idol in the form of anything in heaven above or on the earth beneath or in the waters below. You shall not bow down to them or worship them."

"You shall not misuse the name of the Lord your God, for the Lord will not hold anyone guiltless who misuses his name."

"Remember the Sabbath day by keeping it holy."

"Honor your father and your mother, so that you may live long in the land the Lord your God is giving you."

"You shall not murder."

"You shall not commit adultery."

"You shall not steal."

"You shall not give false testimony against your neighbor."

"You shall not covet your neighbor's house. You shall not covet your neighbor's wife, or his manservant or maidservant, his ox or donkey, or anything that belongs to your neighbor."

1 Corinthians 6:18–20—"Flee from sexual immorality. All other sins a man commits are outside his body, but he who sins sexually sins against his own body. Do you not know that your body is a temple of the Holy Spirit, who is in you, whom you have received from God? You are not your own; you were bought at a price. Therefore, honor God with your body."

Step Four Resolution

Made a searching and fearless moral inventory of ourselves.

Date you committed to making a searching and fearless moral inventory of yourself: _____

What is your target date for completion? _____

Now go write your inventory and return here when completed. If you are unsure how to start, refer back to the opening paragraphs of Step Four.

If you have not completed your inventory, discuss with your AP and consider the Tools and Exercises to see if one or more can help you get motivated.

Date you completed your searching and fearless moral inventory of yourself: _____

Date you shared your inventory with your AP: _____

Evaluating the right and wrong of your actions described in your inventory will be handled in Step Five. Here in Step Four, you are sharing your work with your AP strictly for the purpose of determining that you have done a thorough job. If the AP feels that you might have done a less-than-thorough job, it is the job of the AP to ask questions in an effort to help you determine if you are being honest with yourself. Your AP may then suggest revisions or rewrites. For instance, if your Step Four inventory consists of one handwritten page only, or if you don't have a single character defect or sin exposed, or you have written only those things done to you and not anything you've done to others, your AP might question whether you've done an honest and thorough job. Once you both feel that an honest and thorough job has been completed, then you can move on to Step Five.

Are there any revisions or rewrites to be done? _____

If so, what is your target date for completion? _____

Date revisions/rewrites completed and shared with AP: _____

STEP FIVE

A dmitted to God, to ourselves, and to another human being the exact nature of our wrongs (in Christian terms, confessed our sins).

The principle behind Step Five is **integrity**. Now that we have made a fearless and honest inventory of our lives, are we willing to really own up to it? Are we willing to accept responsibility for our actions? By admitting the nature of our wrongs to God, to ourselves, and to our AP, the answer to those questions is yes. Not for the faint of heart, doing so tells us a great deal about our character, our integrity, and our ability to be fair and honest.

James 5:16a—"Confess your sins to each other and pray for each other so that you may be healed."

In Step Four, we wrote our moral inventory—our life history. That was all we had to do in Step Four—just write it all down. Now we need to look over that inventory and look at the ramifications of our actions. Step Five tells us to admit the "exact nature of our wrongs." Not just a list of the wrongs, but the nature of them as well. Identify those character defects that were present in our actions, why we did what we did, and how they affected all aspects of our lives and our relationships.

I read through my inventory and pulled out the incidents or events in which I was responsible for causing harm or hurt feelings. I wrote each on a separate piece of paper. Then, one at a time, I did a Speed Writing exercise for each one. In that way, I was able to gain an understanding of why I did certain things, what the underlying causes were, and what defect in my character I needed to fix. In some cases, I had to investigate the circumstances surrounding the incident in order to gain understanding. This involved talking to other family members or friends to get their insight and using the tool of Fill in the Blanks to fill in my memory bank.

In many cases, I wanted to point the finger at someone else as the cause of the incident, but generally that did not excuse my actions. I'm reminded of the analogy I've heard that when you point your finger, there are three fingers pointing back at you. Try it—point your finger—now look at your hand—see the three fingers pointing right back at you? Seldom is only one side to be blamed, and in this evaluation of our inventory, we are looking only at that for which we are responsible: our behavior.

If you have been a victim of incest, molestation, rape, or any violent crime, that is a totally different story. I had been the victim of date rape in the days before that term existed. I never told anyone because I was convinced that it was my fault. I felt as though I shouldn't have let myself get into a situation where it was even possible. Many victims of rape have been made to feel that it was their fault. Even children who are victims often feel that they did something wrong. Those situations need an entirely different approach to reconciliation, which we will discuss in Steps Eight A and Nine A. The only thing we might need to look at within the confines of this step are any actions that were taken after being victimized. For instance, in my case, I needed to look at the fact that I never told anyone as a character defect exposing my lack of self-esteem. Another example would be if the victim took retaliatory action that ended up harming someone other than just the perpetrator. We are responsible for our actions to others but not for their actions to us.

Once I had completed the Writing exercise of each of my character defects, I made a list of them and the underlying causes and effects. Keep this list to use with Step Seven. Some of my defects (that I'm willing to admit to the world) included low self-esteem, perfectionism, gluttony, and anger (and that last one was a total surprise to me). Again, don't worry about perfection—all of us have missed one here or there and had to revisit Steps Four and Five on occasion. It's just all part of the ongoing process.

My AP and I went over the list and mapped out some strategies for change, which included the use of the Tools and Exercises.

Spend some time in reflection with the following Bible verses. Remember to use your journal and *write out* (don't just work in your head) your answers to the following questions. If you cannot resolve any questions, try going through the

Tools and Exercises for suggestions to help you get past the impasse. And don't forget to include your AP if you get stuck in the process.

James 5:16—"Confess your sins to each other and pray for each other so that you may be healed. The prayer of a righteous man is powerful and effective."

We are told not only to confess our sins but also why we should confess them—so that we may be healed. I have said it several times in this book, but here we go again: keeping sin bottled up inside only allows it to fester and grow "bigger and badder." Can you think of some examples where you have tried to ignore a sin in your life and doing so only created more problems? How did that manifest itself? Then the verse goes on to tell us the other reason to confess—because the prayer of that person to whom we confess will be powerful and effective in bringing about that healing. Prayer is an action verb and is immensely powerful. Can you recall any time in your life when you felt the power of prayer?

Psalm 25:4,5a,7—"Show me your ways, O Lord, teach me your paths; guide me in your truth and teach me. Remember not the sins of my youth and my rebellious ways; according to your love remember me, for you are good, O Lord."

We come to the Lord here with a repentant heart, asking forgiveness and asking Him to teach us a better way to live. Are you teachable? Make a list of areas in your life in which you have learned new skills (at work, as a parent, at school). Do you see that you can change and learn new ways?

1 John 1:8—"If we claim to be without sin, we deceive ourselves and the truth is not in us."

There is no shame in admitting our sin. The shame would be in not admitting our sin. How does keeping the sin within ourselves keep us a slave to sin?

Psalm 32:3–5b—"When I kept silent, [about my sins] my bones wasted away through my groaning all day long. For day and night your hand was heavy upon me; my strength was sapped as in the heat of summer. Then I said, 'I will confess my transgressions to the Lord'—and you forgave the guilt of my sin."

When we do not admit our sin, this passage describes how it makes us feel—sapped of our strength, groaning all day, and feeling as if our bones are wasted away. Is that how we want to feel? But if we confess our sin, not only are we forgiven for the sin itself, but we are forgiven the guilt of our sin. Even after our sin is forgiven, many of us cannot forgive ourselves, and that guilt can eat away at us for years. Let God remove it all.

1 Peter 5:6—"Humble yourselves, therefore, under God's mighty hand, that He may lift you up in due time."

We are, generally, a people of action. We see something that needs doing, and we do it. This verse is telling us that sometimes we need to wait. We need to humble ourselves—admit that we don't have all the answers. We need to wait for God to lead us in the correct action at the correct time. Waiting is oftentimes not our strong suit. We often try too hard, thinking that some action is better than no action. Can you recall some incidents in which the harder you tried, the worse it got? Make a list. God does expect us to take action but at the appropriate time and of the appropriate nature.

Matthew 5:23–25a—"Therefore, if you are offering your gift at the altar and there remember that your brother has something against you, leave your gift there in front of the altar. First go and be reconciled to your brother; then come and offer your gift. Settle matters quickly with your adversary."

Jesus tells us here of the importance of admitting our wrongs. We are told that it takes preference even to spending time with God. He wants us to spend time with Him, of course, but not with an unrepentant heart. This passage emphasizes the importance of expediency—not only should we reconcile, but it should be done quickly. Have you ever held a grudge against someone, and the longer you held it, the harder it was to admit you were wrong? Think of those examples and consider the consequences of not acting in a timely manner.

Matthew 18:21–22—"Then Peter came to Jesus and asked, 'Lord, how many times shall I forgive my brother when he sins against me? Up to seven times?' Jesus answered, 'I tell you, not seven times, but seventy-seven times.'"

The point here is that God has no limit on the number of times that He forgives us; therefore, why should there be a limit on how many times we forgive others? The Lord's Prayer says, "Forgive us our trespasses as we forgive those who trespass against us." If we want to set a limit on how many times we need to extend forgiveness, then we risk having that same limit imposed on us. Where should the limit be placed on God's forgiveness of us?

Here is what the Bible has to say about some of our character defects:

James 1:19–20—"My dear brothers, take note of this: Everyone should be quick to listen, slow to speak and slow to become angry, for man's anger does not bring about the righteous life that God desires."

Think before you speak. How many times have you been guilty of breaking that sage advice? What were the consequences? It is pretty clear that anger is a character defect.

Ephesians 4:28–29, 31–32—"He who has been stealing must steal no longer, but must work, doing something useful with his own hands, that he may have something to share with those in need. Do not let any unwholesome talk come out of your mouths, but only what is helpful for building others up according to their needs, that it may benefit those who listen. Get rid of all bitterness, rage and anger, brawling and slander, along with every form of malice. Be kind and compassionate to one another, forgiving each other, just as in Christ God forgave you."

Look at the patterns of your life—do you tend to resolve issues or avoid them? We are advised to stop lying, release anger, bitterness, and rage and to stop stealing. It is interesting here that the stealing is not just in the context of taking things from others but in stealing from them by not being a productive member of society. Not only should we work and provide for ourselves, but we are told that our proper role in society is also to share with those in need. Are you a productive member of society? This passage must be where the phrase "If you can't say something nice, don't say anything at all" came from. Are you guilty of unwholesome talk? Gossip, slander, cursing—they are all in the *don't* column. What is listed in the *do* column? Love, compassion, forgiveness. Do you see yourself in the *do* column?

Step Five Resolution

Admitted to God, to ourselves, and to another human being the exact nature of our wrongs (in Christian terms, confessed our sins).

How to proceed:
Read through your inventory and pull out the incidents or events you were responsible for that caused harm or hurt feelings or where you exhibited character defects.

- Write each on a separate piece of paper.
- For each one, do a Speed Writing exercise.
- At the conclusion of each page, read and reread until you can determine what you believe to be the underlying cause and effect for each one and the exact nature of your wrongs.

Date you completed this project: _____

If you have not completed this project, discuss with your AP and consider the Tools and Exercises to see if one or more can help you get you motivated.

Date you confessed your sins to yourself and to God: _____

James 5:16a—"Confess your sins to each other and pray for each other so that you may be healed."

Date you shared your confession with your AP and prayed together for release from your sins and for healing: _____

STEP SIX

Were entirely ready to have God remove all these defects of character.

The principle behind Step Six is **willingness**. Are we willing to give up our defects of character? A yes answer might seem obvious, but we have hung on to a lot of those defects for one reason or another, so it might be more difficult than one might imagine. We may not be able to give up those defects on our own, but notice that the step says "to have God remove them." At this point, we just need to be willing.

James 4:10—"Humble yourselves before the Lord, and he will lift you up."

We have written our inventory and taken the time to evaluate it. We made a list of the character defects that we found in that inventory. We admitted to ourselves, to God, and to our AP the exact nature of our wrongs. We laid ourselves bare and naked with nothing to hide us from our shame. We admitted our failures. Now we need to move past them. We have had so much emphasis on defects of character that it would be easy to mistake those words as the important part of this step. However, the key words in this step are "ready" and "to have God remove."

What is it to be "ready?" If you are ready to go on a trip, it means that you've already done the hard work. You've made the reservations, packed your bags, made provisions for the pets and mail, and are ready to head out the door. There is a lot to do to get ready.

I have found that it is easier to *do* than to *be*—and what I discovered about this step is that it is not a step of action but a step of being. We did the hard work in Steps Four and Five, now it is time to let God work on our hearts Being ready is simply being prepared. In this case, being prepared means we need to take quiet time to be with God, to help us to just be willing.

Willing to do what? To have God remove our character defects. We do not have to effect the change ourselves. We just have to be ready and then let God do it. This now is spiritual work. I simply spent time with the following scriptures until I felt the spirit remove my fear of change. The very word "change" brings an element of fear of the unknown. Change to what? We know what we want to get rid of, but what will be the result? Who will we be? What will we be? Even good change is scary. So this is where faith enters our lives. We move forward in faith that God is in control of the change. As I read on a poster one time, "God don't make no junk." If God will be happy with the change, then I will be as well.

I know that in my heart I didn't really want to give up gluttony. The gluttonous habits had been ingrained as a part of me, and the result of gluttony kept me free from sexual predators. But at the same time, I wanted to be obedient to God, and I did not want to remain fat, undesirable, and unhealthy. So I finally got to the point of welcoming a changed attitude and behavior, ready to have God bring about that change. And, in faith, I trusted that God would give me the right tools at the right time.

As you spend some time in reflection with the following Bible verses, ask God to prepare your heart to be willing for Him to change you. Remember to use your journal and *write out* (don't just work in your head) your answers to the following questions. If you cannot resolve any questions, try going through the Tools and Exercises for suggestions to help you get past the impasse. And don't forget to include your AP if you get stuck in the process.

James 4:10—"Humble yourselves before the Lord, and He will lift you up."

If you hadn't realized it before, you might be getting the drift by now that, biblically, less is more and the weak are strong. In our society, I think the word "humble" takes on a sort of weak position. We are typically proud people, bragging about our accomplishments and sometimes letting power go to our head. The dictionary definition of humble says "that our actions will show that we do not think of ourselves as better than other people." Being humble does not mean that we think less of ourselves; we just don't place ourselves above others and certainly not above God. When we try to live life on our own terms, we are actually putting ourselves above God—putting our needs, our opinions, and our will over His. We are asked to present ourselves to God in a humble fashion, and He will provide for us and give us the desires of our heart.

In your life, have you seen yourself as a humble person? Or do you brag about your accomplishments and hold power over others just for the sake of power? If someone is in a position of authority, is it possible for them to accomplish their tasks in a humble fashion? I believe they can. You can be a humble person but still exercise the authority of your job. For example, my husband was a deputy sheriff with the Los Angeles County Sheriff's Department. Off-duty one day, we were at a hamburger stand, and an attractive, young woman came running across the parking lot to say hi to my husband. They talked like old friends. After she left, of course, I had many questions. My husband explained that he had arrested her several times for solicitation. I did not understand her friendliness to him, but he explained that, although he had arrested her, he always treated her with respect. He did not look down his nose at her but did perform the duties of his job. She knew he was within his rights to arrest her and appreciated him allowing her some dignity. I would say that he was a humble man but certainly nobody's fool. If you are not exercising your authority with humility, what are some ways that you could start?

Romans 12:2—"Do not conform any longer to the pattern of this world, but be transformed by the renewing of your mind. Then you will be able to test and approve what God's will is—His good, pleasing, and perfect will."

In Step Six, we are saying that we are ready to have God remove our character defects—our defect of "having conformed to the pattern of this world." Doing so will clear our mind of old ideas, old ways of thinking, and misperceptions. Once we let God take control of our character defects, we will be in a better position to discern God's will for us as we asked in Step Three. Do you have any concerns about leaving the patterns of this world behind? What and why?

Psalm 119:30–35—"My soul is weary with sorrow; strengthen me according to your word. Keep me from deceitful ways; be gracious to me through your law. I have chosen the way of truth; I have set my heart on your laws. I hold fast to your statutes, O Lord; do not let me be put to shame. I run in the path of your commands, for you have set my heart free. Teach me, O Lord, to follow your decrees; then I will keep them to the end. Give me understanding, and I will keep your law and obey it with all my heart. Direct me in the path of your commands, for there I find delight."

In this passage, we are saying that we have chosen the way of truth in God and that in that truth, we have felt our heart set free and found delight in His presence. But we fear our own humanity sliding us back down the path to our old ways. We ask God to teach and direct us so that we may remain strong in our resolve. In Step Six, we are saying that we are ready to have God remove our character defects, but we oftentimes fear our resolve slipping. What can we do if we take this step and then find ourselves slipping? Indeed, we are human, so it will happen. In this Bible passage, we find the answer—to ask God to teach and direct us. When our resolve fails, we have only to return to this verse and ask again…and again…and again. And each time, our resolve will be firmer until it becomes a natural part of our being, until it finally sticks. Think back to a time when you learned to do something new—riding a bike, learning to skate, first time sitting down at a computer. Did you learn it perfectly overnight?

Matthew 5:3—"Blessed are the poor in spirit, for theirs is the kingdom of heaven."

Poor in spirit means lacking in that force that gives the body life, energy, and power. As I have said before, biblically speaking, less is more, and the weak are strong. God takes us at our weakest and makes us our strongest. We come to him with all our defects, and He gives us the kingdom of heaven. Have you ever been given a gift or a promotion that you felt you did not deserve? Recall that experience—how did it make you feel? Did it inspire you to do better?

Matthew 7:24–26—"Therefore everyone who hears these words of mine and puts them into practice is like a wise man who built his house on the rock. The rain came down, the streams rose, and the winds blew and beat against that house; yet it did not fall, because it had its foundation on the rock. But everyone who hears these words of mine and does not put them into practice is like a foolish man who built his house on sand."

In adversity, the house on the sand comes crashing down. Perhaps that is where we have been, but we have the opportunity to build again. In Step Three, we made the decision to turn our will and our life over to the care of God. This time, we have chosen a path that addresses rebuilding our whole life on the foundation of God. No matter what adversity comes our way, we will withstand the storm, maintain our resolve, and continue to seek God's will in our life. We are ready to let the waves wash away the remains of that house on the sand, as we are now ready to give our remaining character defects to God and begin our new project on His foundation. Letting go of the old and starting a new building is work. Are you willing to do the work to start the new? What might be standing in the way?

Romans 6:11b—"Count yourselves dead to sin but alive to God in Christ Jesus."

Colossians 3:5—"Put to death, therefore, whatever belongs to your earthly nature: sexual immorality, impurity, lust, evil desires and greed, which is idolatry."

Dead is a strong word—it means to be no more, to cease in existence. We are assured that if we give our character defects to God, they will cease to exist any longer, they will be dead, but we will find new life. Is there anything scary in that proposition? Write about anything you really do not want to give up.

2 Corinthians 5:17—"If anyone is in Christ, he is a new creation; the old has gone, the new has come!"

Are you looking forward to a new you, or are you scared and uneasy about what is to come? Write about what you think that new you will look like and feel like.

Galatians 5:24—"Those who belong to Christ Jesus have crucified the sinful nature with its passions and desires."

The very nature of sin brings with it uncontrolled passions and desires. We have to resist that sinful nature, and the best way to do that is to give ourselves over to Christ Jesus, who was crucified for our sins. Does that mean that we will never sin again if we give ourselves to Christ? No, but our past sins are forgiven, crucified, dead, and buried. We are resurrected as a new being with a clean slate and the opportunity to keep that slate clean by relying on Christ to lead us in a new life. We will falter, but we know a new way now, and if we fall, we will get up, ask forgiveness, ask for help, and move forward in the new life. Do you belong to Christ Jesus?

Ephesians 5:8—"For you were once darkness, but now you are light in the Lord. Live as children of light."

Walking down a dark alley at night can be a scary place. Every shadow brings fear, the unknown is unsettling, and your footsteps are unsure. But walking that same alley during the day is a completely different experience. Your footsteps are sure because you can see your way. There are no shadows to fear, for you can see what is ahead and what is behind. That is what it is like to live in the light, to live in Christ. When we give up our character defects, there are no longer any dark shadows engulfing us. We step out into the light and breathe easy. Do some Deep Breathing exercises and Visualization to see what that looks like and how it feels.

Ephesians 4:22–23—"You were taught, with regard to your former way of life, to put off your old self, which is being corrupted by its deceitful desires; to be made new in the attitude of your minds."

It is easy for us to focus on our actions and forget about the attitude of the mind. In considering your character defects, are any of them of the mind? Do you have unwholesome thoughts? Write down some ways that your thoughts may lead to negative actions. Can just the thoughts themselves affect your mood? Write about that and include these thoughts and attitudes in your list of character defects.

1 Corinthians 15:56–57—"The sting of death is sin, and the power of sin is the law. But thanks be to God! He gives us the victory through our Lord Jesus Christ."

We are reminded in this passage that it is not by our power that we are willing to give up our character defects but by the power of God. By the victory of Jesus over death, our sins are washed away. Do you have any doubts?

Revelation 3:20—"Here I am! I stand at the door and knock. If anyone hears my voice and opens the door, I will come in and eat with him, and he with me."

In relinquishing our character defects, we are in effect opening the door and inviting Christ into our home, into our lives. Someone who comes into our home and shares a meal with us is an honored guest for whom we usually prepare a special meal. This meal is special in that it will be prepared without our character defects in the most honest and humble manner. Are you ready to share a meal with your Savior?

Step Six Resolution

Were entirely ready to have God remove all these defects of character.

If there are any defects that you are reluctant to release, discuss with your AP and consider the Tools and Exercises to see if one or more can help you get to that point. Consider the following:

Bible Reading	Block Wall	Mythical Character
Prayer and Meditation	Visualization	WWJD

Remember with this step we are only acknowledging that we are ready to have God remove the defects of character. Do not burden yourself with how that will come about at this point.

Date you accepted Step Six: _____

Date you shared that decision with your AP: _____

STEP SEVEN

H umbly asked God to remove our shortcomings. (In Christian terms, humbly asked God to forgive our sins.)

The principle behind Step Seven is **humility**. In the previous steps, we have admitted our defects and then became willing to let them go. Now we are humbly asking God to help us move past willingness and to let Him remove our shortcomings, to forgive our sins.

Psalm 51:1–2—"Have mercy on me, O God, according to your unfailing love; according to your great compassion blot out my transgressions. Wash away all my iniquity and cleanse me from my sin."

This is an action step. It requires more than just thinking and reflecting. When you give something away, it requires action. For instance, if you are giving away old clothes to the Goodwill, you sort through the clothes and decide which to keep and which to give away. You box or bag the discards and drive to a donation center and physically give them to the people in charge. There are quite a few steps required in giving stuff away.

In this step, we are giving away our character defects. In Steps Four and Five, we sorted through our habits and actions to decide which to keep and which to give away. In Step Six, we boxed or bagged the discards with the decision of being ready to have God remove our discard pile (our character defects). Now in Step Seven, it is time to physically give them away and to ask God for forgiveness.

There is no store that I know of with a donation center for discarded character defects. So we need to create one. Some people simply say a humble prayer, write about their decision in their journal, and list the defects of character that they are giving away. This method will suffice, but I personally believe that the act of giving the defects away is more meaningful if done with some significant ceremony. I have listed a couple of ways at the end of this step, and I did use a balloon release myself. Put on your thinking cap, and you may create another significant way to give your shortcomings to God.

As I said, I chose to use the balloon release as my means of asking God for forgiveness and to remove my shortcomings. As in the Goodwill example, it required several steps. First, I ordered the same number of helium balloons with ribbons as corresponded to the number of character defects on my list. Next, I cut up small slips of paper and on each one wrote a character defect that I was giving to God. I invited my AP and set a date with her. On that day, I picked up my balloons, picked up my AP, and went to a secluded park that was a significantly special place to me. One by one, I tied each character defect slip to a balloon. For each one, I spoke out loud, asking God to forgive my sin and to remove that defect from me. With some, I talked about how that defect had affected my life and why I wanted God to release me from that defect. And then I let the balloon go. The significance of the balloons floating up into the heavens and away from me gave me a sense of fulfillment. When they had all been released, my AP and I concluded with a prayer and went out to lunch.

Disclaimer—When I did the balloon release, we as a society had not yet realized the effect it had on the environment. So while it is an effective tool for recovery, it is no longer a valid tool to use. So then I thought about the candle lanterns—in the sky or on the water. Although popular a few years ago, we are more aware of the danger of fire and to our wildlife, so that is no longer a valid release as well. As an alternative, I offer the tool I call Up in Smoke. Make the same slips of paper and then conduct a burning ceremony where you burn the slips of paper and watch the character defects literally go Up in Smoke. For more details, see the Up in Smoke exercise in Part Three.

I cannot say that I was immediately released of all those defects of character, but I did walk with a lighter step and a sense of breathing deeper. If I did repeat a character defect from that point on, it was not without consequence—I was aware. Sometimes that awareness kept me from repeating the defect; other times my stubborn will pushed through that awareness with childlike stubbornness. But I found that those stubborn moments became less over time and that Bible Study, Prayer and Meditation, and continuing with the Twelve Steps gave me better defenses.

As you spend some time in reflection with the following Bible verses, ask God to prepare your heart and to give you inspiration for how to complete this step. Remember to use your journal and *write out* (don't just work in your head) your answers to the following questions. If you cannot resolve any questions, try going through the Tools and Exercises for suggestions to help you get past the impasse. And don't forget to include your AP if you get stuck in the process.

Psalm 51:1–2, 10–12—"Have mercy on me, O God, according to your unfailing love; according to your great compassion blot out my transgressions. Wash away all my iniquity and cleanse me from my sin. Create in me a pure heart, O God, and renew a steadfast spirit within me. Do not cast me from your presence or take your Holy Spirit from me. Restore to me the joy of your salvation and grant me a willing spirit, to sustain me."

The account of David and Bathsheba can be found in 2 Samuel 11. First David committed adultery with Bathsheba, and then he had her husband, Uriah, placed in battle in a way that would assure his death. And then he took her as his wife. Adultery and murder! The prophet Nathan confronted David with his sin, and this passage from Psalm 51 is David's response. There have been times when I felt my sins were so appalling that I did not deserve forgiveness, no matter how contrite I might present myself. God forgave David, and He forgives me—and you.

Do you have anything in your past or present that you are not sure is forgivable? Anything for which you've asked forgiveness but feel sure that forgiveness has not been granted? Anything for which you cannot forgive yourself?

Psalm 25:8–11—"Good and upright is the Lord; therefore, He instructs sinners in His ways. He guides the humble in what is right and teaches them His way. All the ways of the Lord are loving and faithful for those who keep the demands of His covenant. For the sake of your name, O Lord, forgive my iniquity, though it is great."

In this step, we are asking God to remove our shortcomings. In Christian terms—we are asking God to forgive our sins. In this passage, David asks forgiveness but also asks God for guidance. Forgiveness is for the past; guidance is for the future. With this step, we are putting our past to rest by asking forgiveness and by asking God to remove our shortcomings. Now we need guidance for how to move on with our life as a new person. God speaks to us through the Bible. Are you willing to commit to regular Bible Reading to stay in touch with God? What are some stumbling blocks for you in doing that? And how might you resolve those stumbling blocks?

Psalm 34:4–6—"I sought the Lord, and He answered me; He delivered me from all my fears. Those who look to Him are radiant; their faces are never covered with shame. This poor man called, and the Lord heard him; He saved him out of all his troubles."

What I like about this passage is that David does not ask you to just take his word for what the Lord can do but uses other people as examples. As evidence of how other people's experiences have been with God, David says, in essence, just look at their faces—they are radiant. We often hear the word *radiant* used when describing a bride on her wedding day or an expectant mother. Those are special people and special circumstances. Wouldn't you like to feel and look radiant all the time? But it is not just the outward appearance that is important. David follows that statement with "their faces are never covered with shame." Shame is a devastating place to be and takes us hostage. In this step, asking forgiveness can put all that behind us. Do you have any shame holding you back? Write about that.

Psalm 37:4–6—"Delight yourself in the Lord and He will give you the desires of your heart. Commit your way to the Lord; trust in Him and He will do this: He will make your righteousness shine like the dawn, the justice of your cause like the noonday sun."

If there was any doubt as to the result of completing Step Seven, this is it. We need to delight, commit, and trust, and God will give us the desires of our hearts. Does that mean that if we delight, commit, and trust, God will see to it that we win the lottery? I wish, but no. When we delight in the things of God, our desires and wants will begin to fall in line with what God wants for us. Unlike those who delight in material possessions and are never truly satisfied, God wants us to delight in Him, which will result in satisfaction and joy. In what ways do you think your desires fall in line with what God wants for you? In what ways do you think they are not in line with what God wants for you?

Psalm 37:23–24—"If the Lord delights in a man's way, He makes his steps firm; though he stumble, he will not fall, for the Lord upholds him with His hand."

You may have heard this verse summed up as "God promised us a safe landing, not smooth sailing." We will stumble at times, and we will suffer afflictions in this world, but the point is that we don't have to worry. The love of God will get us through. The promise with God is that He will always be there for us and with us.

Psalm 39:8—"Save me from all my transgressions; do not make me the scorn of fools."

This could be the Step Seven prayer. We are asking God to save us—not only from the scorn of fools, but also all too often from ourselves. I know that I can point fingers at some who created many of my problems, but that doesn't fix anything. As an adult, I am responsible for my actions, regardless of who or what was done to me. But making the change is hard, so it is at this point that we simply pray for God to save us from ourselves. Do you recognize that your problems are *your* problems to resolve?

Psalm 119:133—"Direct my footsteps according to your word; let no sin rule over me."

In Step Seven, we are confessing our sins and asking forgiveness so that no sin may control us. We are asking God to guide us in a new path, to direct our footsteps but—the next part of the sentence is important—according to His word. We are saying that we want what He wants for us. What are some things that you think God wants for you? Do you want those for yourself?

Galatians 5:22–23—"The fruit of the Spirit is love, joy, peace, patience, kindness, goodness, faithfulness, gentleness, and self-control."

Once we have confessed our sin, what next? How do we move forward in life as a new person? First, we need to acknowledge that we have one God who comes to us in three forms, also called the Triune God. He is our creator and our loving, compassionate, unchanging, and forgiving Heavenly Father. He is our Savior, friend, and teacher as God's Son, Jesus Christ. And when Jesus left this earth for His heavenly home, His Father sent His Holy Spirit to indwell in each of us as our guide, comforter, counselor, and advocate. Once we ask forgiveness and begin our walk with the Lord, this verse describes the attributes we are promised through the Holy Spirit. If we pray in the Spirit, ask Him to indwell in us and pray for these gifts, through Him we will be able to leave our sins behind and move forward in His will for us as led by the Spirit.

Luke 18:9b–14—Jesus told this parable: "Two men went up to the temple to pray, one a Pharisee and the other a tax collector. The Pharisee stood up and prayed about himself: 'God, I thank you that I am not like other men—robbers, evildoers, adulterers—or even like this tax collector. I fast twice a week and give a tenth of all I get.' But the tax collector stood at a distance. He would not even look up to heaven, but beat his breast and said, 'God, have mercy on me, a sinner.' I tell you that this man, rather than the other, went home justified before God. For everyone who exalts himself will be humbled, and he who humbles himself will be exalted."

Humbly is the first word in Step Seven. We are not coming to God with a proud heart full of excuses for our past behavior. We are to approach God with a humble heart, taking full responsibility for our actions and asking His mercy to forgive our sins and move us gently to the right path. Have you experienced "pride goes before a fall?" Have you witnessed "pride goes before a fall" in others? Not a pretty sight, is it? Write about the circumstances.

Acts 3:19—"Repent, then, and turn to God, so that your sins may be wiped out, that times of refreshing may come from the Lord."

Do you see the order of things? First, repent. Second, God will wipe away your sins. Third, God will refresh you. When I think of the word *refresh*, I think of jumping in the swimming pool on a hot day or sitting down to a cold soda after finishing my chores. Those are rejuvenating actions and feelings. That is what God promises when we do our part, which is simply to repent. Many are too proud to do that simple action. What about you?

1 John 1:9—"If we confess our sins, he is faithful and just and will forgive us our sins and purify us from all unrighteousness."

Some may wonder at our reasons for stirring the pot and revisiting past indiscretions. Any guilt left from those actions eats at our soul and does not allow us to be totally free. To deny them is to deceive ourselves. But if we confess our sins, this passage assures us that we will be forgiven. We are further assured that He will purify us from all unrighteousness. In other words, not only are the individual sins forgiven, but the slate is wiped clean. We get a do-over. Where else in life is that granted? Even if our boss or spouse or friend forgives us, the consequences are still there hanging over our head. This gift from God is truly a *gift*. As you go on now to complete your Step Seven, keep that gift in mind as you present your shortcomings and request forgiveness in a humble fashion, but at the same time be confident in God's reaction to your request. If we have been out working or playing hard and getting dirty and stinky, doesn't it feel wonderful at the end of the day to shower and get squeaky clean again? It is a breath of fresh air. That is how confession and absolution feel to me; how about you?

Step Seven Resolution

Humbly asked God to remove our shortcomings (in Christian terms, humbly asked God to forgive our sins).

Check out the following Tools and Exercises. Some or all of them might be helpful to prepare for approaching God with your request for forgiveness.

Bible Reading	Block Wall	Mythical Character
Prayer and Meditation	Up in Smoke	Visualization
WWJD		

When ready, find a way to formally ask God for forgiveness of your sins and to remove all your defects of character. Have your list from Step Five available. My favorite suggestion is as follows. You can choose to do the activity alone (just you and God) or invite your AP to join you.

- GOD CAN: Write each character defect on a separate slip of paper. Go to a special quiet place such as the park or beach or mountains. Read each slip of paper, ask God to forgive your sin, follow that by saying, "I cannot remove this character defect, but God can," and place it in the GOD CAN. I particularly like this method because in a few months, you can bring those slips back out and see if any or all of them have been removed. If you can see progress but not complete removal of the defect, repeat your prayer and put it back in the GOD CAN. If you see significant or total improvement, consider saying a prayer of thanksgiving and destroying the paper just as the behavior has been destroyed. Perhaps you could have a burn party and send them on their way, Up in Smoke.
- Personally, I think this release of your character defects and asking for forgiveness should be done with significant ceremony as described above or by any other creative method you can concoct. But a simple, humble prayer will suffice, as well as Writing in your journal.

If you are having difficulty completing this action, discuss with your AP and consider the Tools and Exercises to see if one or more can help you get to that point.

What action method did you choose for asking forgiveness and to release your character defects?_____

Date you completed your action requesting forgiveness and release: _____

Date you shared that decision and action with your AP: _____

STEP EIGHT

M ade a list of all persons we had harmed and became willing to make amends to them all.

The principles behind Step Eight are **reflection and commitment**. It is not easy to look back on our lives and admit when we were wrong. But we know that by committing to this action, we will be removing barriers that stand in the way of full recovery.

Luke 6:31—"Do to others as you would have them do to you."

In making this list of all persons we have harmed, we need to make sure to stay on task with *our* behavior, not the behavior of others. In making our list, we want to consider only our side of the street, and discipline will be required to not slip to the other side of the street—the other person's actions that perhaps led up to our transgression or their retaliation to our actions. We are making a list based only on *our* actions. If you recall the hurtful actions of others toward you, write them down and set them aside—we will deal with those in Step Eight A.

I started with my Step Four inventory and then my character defects list from Step 5. From those, I was able to make a pretty comprehensive list. I let a few days pass and spent time in Prayer and Meditation seeking God's intervention in this process. In doing so, I discovered a couple of incidents that I had missed in my inventory and added those to my list as well.

There is a worksheet at the end of this step study. I developed it as I worked through my amends. For this step, I filled out just the top and first column; the other columns will be filled out with Step Nine. I listed each person with whom

I needed to make amends and then the reason that the amends were needed—in other words, what I had done to create a bad situation.

We do need to be brutally honest with ourselves at this point but not to the point of being ridiculous. For instance, I know of a person who thought back to the third grade and a time when she thinks she might have hurt the teacher's feelings, but she's not sure. Now if that incident weighs heavy on her conscience, she should consider including it on her list. But something like that could just as easily be dismissed if doing so will not leave her feeling guilty. If her story had been more serious, such as if she had been a bully in the third grade and caused physical and emotional harm, then it definitely should be included on the list.

I had a few of those where I couldn't decide if I really needed to make amends or if I was just being too hard on myself. I put those on a separate list and talked to my AP about them before finishing my amends list. She asked me questions about the incidents to help me determine if I had actually done harm to someone or if I just had not forgiven myself for something stupid. One incident I asked her about involved a prank I pulled with another student. As we talked about it, I realized that all I had been guilty of was being stupid, and it had done no real harm except to make me look foolish. In my memory of that incident, I was embarrassed by my stupidity and had not been able to forgive myself. I decided to put it on my list, noting that the person with whom to make amends was myself.

And that brings us to another point. The primary purpose of this step is to make amends to those we have harmed, and we need to also forgive ourselves. We will talk more about that in Step Nine, but I mention it here because we may need to consider areas of our lives where we need to make amends with ourselves, and those should be included on our list as well.

In the end, I had two incidents that my AP agreed with me did not need to be included, but I am glad that I discussed them with her so that I had a clear conscience in making that decision. I had two others that could have gone either way, so I erred on the side of caution and included them.

At this point, we may be tempted to make our decisions on what to include based on the possibility of actually being able to make the amends with that person. Perhaps they are dead, or we do not know where they are, or seeing them would be too uncomfortable for all concerned. Try not to concern yourself with how or if it is practical to actually make the amends. Right now, just focus on making the list. There are other ways to make amends in those circumstances, which we will explore in Step Nine.

Once the list is made, it may be tempting to think we are done. After all, we will do the actual amends in Step Nine. But take note that the other half of this step is to be willing to make the amends. There may be some on our lists with whom we do not want to make amends. Perhaps we have listed them because we know we should, but we don't really want to follow through with the amends. It was at this point that I spent time in Prayer and Meditation. I focused strictly on being willing. I tried not to think about how I would make the amends or if I could actually follow through and do it. I just focused on being willing, and I did get to that point eventually. Willingness may seem like a small part of the step, but I found that the follow-through in Step Nine was much easier than I had expected, and I believe that was because I first became willing.

As you spend some time in reflection with the following Bible verses, ask God to help you to be honest with yourself. Remember to use your journal and *write out* (don't just work in your head) your answers to the following questions. If you cannot resolve any questions, try going through the Tools and Exercises for suggestions to help you get past the impasse. And don't forget to include your AP if you get stuck in the process.

Luke 6:31—"Do to others as you would have them do to you."

If someone hurts our feelings or hurts us in some other way, we would like an apology and whatever else the situation calls for in their making amends to us. Why should we do any less for them? If everyone could live their lives by this short little passage, how much better the world would be.

Luke 19:8—"But Zacchaeus stood up and said to the Lord, 'Look, Lord! Here and now I give half of my possessions to the poor, and if I have cheated anybody out of anything, I will pay back four times the amount.'"

Zacchaeus was not only a tax collector but a Jew taxing his fellow Jews. He was quite despised. For the full account of Zacchaeus, see Luke 19:1–10. Jesus never asked him to make amends, but his response to being treated with respect and kindness by Jesus was to make full restitution and then some. Men might not have treated him with respect, but Jesus did, just as He does with us. Let Zacchaeus's reaction be an example in making our amends.

John 13:34–35—"A new command I give you: Love one another. As I have loved you, so you must love one another. By this all men will know that you are my disciples, if you love one another."

How do we treat those we love? 1 Corinthians 13:4–8a tells us that "Love is patient, love is kind. It does not envy, it does not boast, it is not proud. It is not rude, it is not self-seeking, it is not easily angered, and it keeps no record of wrongs. Love does not delight in evil but rejoices with the truth. It always protects, always trusts, always hopes, always perseveres. Love never fails." Can you honestly say that you treat your loved ones so? If not, what changes do you need to make, and what amends do you need to address?

James 4:11–12—"Brothers, do not slander one another. Anyone who speaks against his brother or judges him speaks against the law and judges it. When you judge the law, you are not keeping it, but sitting in judgment on it. There is only one Lawgiver and Judge, the one who is able to save and destroy. But you—who are you to judge your neighbor?"

In Step Eight, we are making a list of those we have harmed. It will be tempting to make excuses for our actions, placing blame on the other party or parties involved. We may have been provoked, but if we lashed out and hurt someone, we are accountable for our actions regardless of the other person's actions.

Titus 3:9—"But avoid foolish controversies and genealogies and arguments and quarrels about the law, because they are unprofitable and useless."

The famous feud between the Hatfields and McCoys went on for so long that the families had nothing in their hearts but hate and discord, and in the end, most couldn't even remember exactly what had started the feud in the first place. What a shame. Have you been involved in petty quarrels? Are you alienated from someone because of quarrels? Write about those and put them on your list.

Note: not all genealogy is prohibited, but in this verse, Paul is writing to Titus warning about the use of genealogies because the Jewish congregation, in particular, loved to draw reference to their tribal ancestry as their qualification for acceptance into the kingdom. Therefore, the use of genealogies in this way could lead to quarrels about whose lineage is better than someone else's and thus should be avoided.

2 Timothy 1:7—"For God did not give us a spirit of timidity, but a spirit of power, of love and of self-discipline."

On our own, working the Twelve Steps would be exceedingly difficult. Making lists of our mistakes in life and getting ready to face those we have hurt is not easy. This passage explains how we are able to face these tasks. God gave us a spirit of power, of love, and of self-discipline. If we include Him in the process, His support along with those gifts will see us through. Write in your journal a prayer to God thanking him for these gifts. Tell Him any fears and anxiety you may have going into this process and ask for His support.

1 John 2:9–11—"Anyone who claims to be in the light but hates his brother is still in the darkness. Whoever loves his brother lives in the light, and there is nothing in him to make him stumble. But whoever hates his brother is in the darkness and walks around in the darkness; he does not know where he is going, because the darkness has blinded him."

If we do not take this step and make our list of those we have harmed, we are choosing to live in darkness—stumbling around, choosing wrong paths, making bad choices. We can keep our life stumble free by completing these tasks and living in the light, which is the truth.

Proverbs 14:9—"Fools mock at making amends for sin, but goodwill is found among the upright."

Making amends is the right thing to do. Write about a time you felt relief after confessing.

Step Eight Resolution

Made a list of all persons we had harmed and became willing to make amends to them all.

Using the form provided, make a list of all persons you have harmed, including financial or other restitution if needed. Be sure to include ways that you might have harmed yourself and areas where others may have forgiven you, but you have not forgiven yourself. Remember to take care of your side of the street only. Make copies of the form as needed, and I suggest that you use one full page for each person. Fill in the name of the person(s) with whom to make amends and the first column—reason amends are needed.

If you have not made your list, discuss with your AP and consider the Tools and Exercises to see if one or more can help you get to that point.

Date you made your list of all persons you have harmed: _____

Keep this list for use with Step Nine.

Date you became *willing* to make amends to those persons: _____

Date you shared your list and your decision with your AP: _____

Amends List

Make several copies and allow one whole page for each person.
For Step Eight, fill in the person's name and just the first column.
Save and fill in the rest of the columns with Step Nine.

Person with whom to make amends:_____

Reason amends needed	Planned approach	Date amends made	Results Follow-up needed?	Date shared with AP	Date forgave self

Amends List—Example

For the sake of space, I've listed three persons on one page.
But for the sake of clarity and enough writing space, I recommend each
to be on a separate page.
For Step Eight, fill in the person's name and just the first column.
Save and fill in the rest of the columns with Step Nine.

Person with whom to make amends:
1. Grandma Kelly 2. Friend, Kathy 3. Sister Sally

Reason amends needed	Planned approach	Date amends made	Results Follow-up needed?	Date shared with AP	Date forgave self
1. I wrote her a hurtful letter					
2. She moved away before I was able to resolve dispute					
3. Dispute over inheritance					

STEP EIGHT A

Made a list of all persons who had harmed us and became willing to release all anger and resentment and to forgive them.

The principle behind Step Eight A is **resolution**. Resolution is defined as the act of answering or solving. We are committed to resolving any and all issues that surfaced in our Step Four inventory in which we were victims. We are not looking for retribution; rather, we are resolving the anger and resentment that came as a result of the actions of others and forgiving them in our hearts.

Matthew 6:14–15—"For if you forgive men when they sin against you, your heavenly Father will also forgive you. But if you do not forgive men their sins, your Father will not forgive your sins."

In Step Eight, we identified those persons with whom we needed to make amends because of *our* actions. Now, in Step Eight A, we will identify those people with whom we have leftover anger and resentment as a result of *their* actions. The first step, as in Step Eight, is to make a list. Here in Step Eight A, we will complete a healing list, a list we will use to extend forgiveness.

Just saying that I was molested out loud in my Step Four inventory did not make the pain or the anger go away or restore my self-esteem. There is no one to whom I need to make amends, and we've been told to not get stuck in the blame game, but what do we do with our residual anger and self-esteem issues? That is why I developed these "A steps" for Steps Eight, Nine, and Ten. They are not part of the original Twelve Step Program, but I felt they were needed to address these issues in order to complete our transformation or recovery. If you are one of the lucky ones who truly have nothing in this category, feel free to skip these "A steps," but give serious and honest consideration to these steps before making that decision. If you are experiencing uncontrolled anger or bitterness, you may need to look deeply within yourself to find the source. Bitterness often presents as being resentful, cynical, harsh, cold, and unpleasant to be around. It can also present in self-loathing.

As in Step Eight, we are only making the list at this point. Do not concern yourself with how you will resolve the anger and frustration or regain your self-esteem; just make the list. We have pulled from inside of us all the ugliness that was caused by our actions. We are now going to complete our cleansing by pulling all the ugliness from within that was caused by the actions of others.

I used my Step Four inventory as a starting point for my list and then spent time in Prayer and Meditation, asking God to reveal any additional incidents that should be included. After several days in reflection, my list included my father's suicide, a childhood molestation, the way I was treated during my teen pregnancy, a date rape, the child I never had (as explained in the tool "Let Yourself Grieve"), and my first husband's infidelity and abandonment.

Some of these types of incidents caused by others might have been the cause of some of our character defects, but we are only dealing with the action of what the other person did to us. Any behaviors that we developed that in turn hurt others should be dealt with in Step Eight. For instance, my father's suicide and the childhood molestation led to my eating disorder. My eating disorder caused much distress for myself, my husband, and my daughter. In Step Eight A, I would deal only with the suicide and the molestation. In Step Eight, I would deal with my actions and behaviors that came about thereafter—my eating disorder and its consequences to myself and my loved ones.

There is a worksheet at the end of this step that can help you facilitate the objective here. Fill in the persons involved at the top and complete just the first column—the situation needing healing. Spend some time in reflection with the following Bible verses. Remember to use your journal and *write out* (don't just work in your head) your answers to the following questions. If you cannot resolve any questions, try going through the Tools and Exercises for suggestions to help you get past the impasse. And don't forget to include your AP if you get stuck in the process.

Matthew 6:14–15—"For if you forgive men when they sin against you, your heavenly Father will also forgive you. But if you do not forgive men their sins, your Father will not forgive your sins."

Some people feel that if they forgive someone, it is the same as saying that what that person did is OK. Not at all. We forgive others because God forgives us. Do you think that God condones every negative thing we've done just because He has forgiven us? Do you have children? When they hit or bite or say mean words, we forgive them, but that does not mean we appreciate their behavior. We forgive others for two reasons. First: to be obedient to God. He has said that He will forgive us, but He expects us to extend that forgiveness to others as well. Second: to rid our soul of the anger, bitterness, and rage inside of us. Do you have people whom you need to forgive even if you don't want to? Do you think you can get to the point of forgiveness, not for their sake particularly, but in obedience to God and for your sake?

Matthew 18:23–35—

Therefore, the kingdom of heaven is like a king who wanted to settle accounts with his servants. As he began the settlement, a man who owed him ten thousand talents was brought to him. Since he was not able to pay, the master ordered that he and his wife and his children and all that he had be sold to repay the debt. The servant fell on his knees before him. "Be patient with me," he begged, "and I will pay back everything." The servant's master took pity on him, canceled the debt, and let him go. But when that servant went out, he found one of his fellow servants who owed him a hundred denarii. He grabbed him and began to choke him. "Pay back what you owe me!" he demanded. His fellow servant fell to his knees and begged him, "Be patient with me, and I will pay you back." But he refused. Instead, he went off and had the man thrown into prison until he could pay the debt. When the other servants saw what had happened, they were greatly distressed and went and told their master everything that had happened. Then the master called the servant in. "You wicked servant," he said, "I canceled all that debt of yours because you begged me to. Shouldn't you have had mercy on your fellow servant just as I had on you?" In anger his master turned him over to the jailers to be tortured, until he should pay back all he owed. This is how my heavenly Father will treat each of you unless you forgive your brother from your heart.

Without forgiveness, we would all be walking around with hateful hearts. Just as the master forgave his servant, he expected his servant to extend that same forgiveness to others. God has set the example by forgiving us and expects the same from us, even if the offender does not "deserve" forgiveness. Forgiving others frees our heart. Is expecting mercy for yourself but then not extending mercy to others a character defect? Make a list of the character defects involved in that action. Are you guilty of any of those defects?

Colossians 3:8—"You must rid yourselves of all such things as these: anger, rage, malice, slander, and filthy language from your lips."

When we harbor the emotions and actions listed here, we keep hate in our heart. It is almost impossible to communicate with God with such in our heart. Sometimes it is hard to determine God's will for us, but I can say with certainty that retaining those qualities is not in His will for us. Also, it is difficult to forgive when we harbor those qualities. Which of those qualities are you guilty of harboring? Were they included in your list of character defects with Steps Five, Six, and Seven? If not, you should return to those steps and humbly ask God to remove those shortcomings. It will be hard to enter this phase of forgiveness if you are harboring those qualities.

Romans 12:19—"Do not take revenge, my friends, but leave room for God's wrath, for it is written: 'It is mine to avenge; I will repay,' says the Lord."

Our task in making our list here in Step Eight A is not for the purpose of revenge or retribution. God will take care of them in His own way. We need to clear our heart so that our lives are not governed by the anger and resentment that came as a result of the actions of others. Our forgiveness of them does not absolve them of their sin in God's eyes, but it does keep us from hardening ourselves against God. Do you have grievances against others that are so horrendous that you don't think you could ever forgive them? If so, just put it on the list and deal with the "how" in Step Nine A.

Proverbs 20:22—"Do not say, 'I'll pay you back for this wrong!' Wait for the Lord, and He will deliver you."

As in the previous passage, God will take care of them in His own way. If we try to "pay them back," in all likelihood, that will involve sin. If what they have done is a crime, you can and should certainly report it to the police, but if you take the law into your own hands, that is not only against the law but against God. Remember that we are not making this healing list for the purpose of revenge but for the purpose of healing.

Ephesians 4:31–32—"Get rid of all bitterness, rage and anger, brawling and slander, along with every form of malice. Be kind and compassionate to one another, forgiving each other, just as in Christ God forgave you."

How can our anger make us sin? Mostly in the way we treat others. There are many times in our lives when we are not treated fairly, and that makes us angry. In many of those situations, there is nowhere to vent that anger, and so we oftentimes allow our anger to be misplaced and then take it out on the wrong people. For instance, you get a speeding ticket on the way home. You are angry, but there is nothing you can do about it. If you rant and rave at the policeman, you risk getting arrested, so you hold it in until you get home. When you finally get home, your wife is running late, dinner is not ready, and she questions you about coming home late. Get the picture? You start the ranting and raving that you wanted to give the policeman. Fair? No. Sinful? Yes, but human. We've all done it at one time or another. But that does not mean that we don't need to apologize for it.

If we do not apologize for it, then we will feel guilty, and the devil just loves it when we harbor anger and guilt in our heart, for he sees it as a way into our soul. Instead, the passage tells us to get rid of all bitterness, rage, anger, brawling, slander, and all forms of malice so that the devil cannot have a foothold in our life. What does this have to do with making our list of persons who have harmed us? If we keep the anger and hurt of those experiences in our heart, the devil has a foothold in our life, and we are vulnerable to his schemes. But what are we supposed to do with that anger? We will talk about that in Step Nine A; for now, just make your list and make sure it is complete so that you will get rid of all those unsavory qualities once and for all.

Psalm 23:4—"Even though I walk through the valley of the shadow of death, I will fear no evil, for you are with me; your rod and your staff, they comfort me."

Depending on the offenses of others to us, it can be very scary to face reliving the experience. We may be tempted to not put something on our list because we just don't want to face it. I would urge you to put it on the list anyway. For now, it is just a list. In Step Nine A, we will deal with it, but we will do so when the time is right. Verse 4 tells us that even if we are facing death that God will be there to comfort us, and there is nothing to fear. Read again through the entire Twenty-Third Psalm, and allow God's comfort to be with you.

1 Corinthians 10:13—"No temptation has seized you except what is common to man. And God is faithful; He will not let you be tempted beyond what you can bear. But when you are tempted, He will also provide a way out so that you can stand up under it."

My girlfriend Linda was dying of cancer when she told me about this passage. She said she did believe what 1 Corinthians said but then said, "I just wish He didn't have such a high opinion of me." We laughed, but there was seriousness and truth in her statement. It is a sentiment that we have all shared from time to time. Do not be afraid to include God as someone you need to forgive, especially if you have been harboring anger directed at Him or have been directing anger at others instead of at Him.

In making your healing list, do not be tempted to shortcut your work. Although some items may be painful to deal with, "He will provide a way out so that you can stand up under it." He will support you through the process. Trust that He will be there for you. Write about any concerns you have in this regard.

Matthew 5:4—"Blessed are those who mourn, for they will be comforted."

When we think of mourning, we generally think of mourning a death. But there are many other things that we mourn. The loss of a job, the loss of a marriage, the loss of a friendship, a lost opportunity, and more. Whatever we have on our list, whenever we lost something or someone as a result of others, we are assured that we will be comforted. Close your eyes and sit for a few minutes. Breathe deep, and then feel God's hug.

Step Eight A Resolution

Made a list of all persons who had harmed us and became willing to release all anger and resentment and to forgive them.

Using the form provided, make a list of all persons who have harmed you. Make copies of the form as needed, and I suggest using one whole page for each healing. Fill in the name of the person(s) at the top and complete the first column—the situation needing healing.

If you have not made your list, discuss with your AP and consider the Tools and Exercises to see if one or more can help you get to that point.

Date you made your list of those who have harmed you: _____

Keep this list for use with Step Nine A.

Date you became *willing* to forgive those persons: _____

As you prepare to share your list with your AP, focus on the reasons for sharing. One reason is for accountability. And then, since we are victims on this healing list, the other reason to share is to make sure that we are presenting our list with the intent of receiving support and not fueling any resentment.

Date you shared your list and your decision with your AP: _____

Healing List

Make several copies and then use one whole page for each healing.
For Step Eight A, fill in the name of the person(s) involved and
just the first column.
Save and fill in the rest of the columns with Step Nine A.

Person(s) Involved _____

Situation needing healing	Planned approach	Date of healing action	Results	Date shared with AP	Follow up? Forgive self?

Healing List—Example

For the sake of space, I've listed three persons on one page.
But for the sake of clarity and enough writing space, I recommend each to be on a separate page.
For Step Eight A, fill in the name of the person(s) involved and just the first column.
Save and fill in the rest of the columns with Step Nine A.

Person(s) Involved 1. Neighbor Man 2. Guy from party 3. Myself

Situation needing healing	Planned approach	Date of healing action	Results	Date shared with AP	Follow up? Forgive self?
1. Childhood molestation					
2. Date Rape					
3. Child I never had					

STEP NINE

M ade direct amends to such people whenever and wherever possible, except when to do so would injure them or others.

The principle behind Step Nine is **discipline**. It is not easy to admit when we are wrong, so it will require a lot of discipline to fully complete these tasks. In making our amends, we are concentrating on our actions, and discipline will be required to not slip to the other person's actions that perhaps led up to our transgression or their retaliation to our actions. We are only asking forgiveness for *our* actions. It will require discipline to stay on task and not fall into the blame game.

Matthew 5:9—"Blessed are the peacemakers, for they will be called Sons of God."

In Step Eight, we identified those people with whom we felt we needed to make amends. It is time now to take action and complete the amends list started in Step Eight. Remember that we are asking forgiveness for *our* actions. We cannot allow ourselves to get sidetracked by placing blame on the other person as we are making our amends.

What about that part of the step that states, "Except when to do so would injure them or others?" What exactly does that mean? I think I can explain that best with an example. Let's say you had an affair with the husband of your best friend, but she does not know about it. You certainly sinned against her and probably hurt her marriage in many ways. She may not know that you were the cause of those problems, but she surely knows that the problems existed. Going to her and apologizing for your actions would certainly take care of your side of the street, but what kind of upheaval are you throwing into her life? This would be a situation in which you should prayerfully consider how to make those amends. You should discuss it with your AP for advice as well. It is important to complete all the amends, but you need to be sensitive to the person on the other side. Do not inflict pain on them just to clear your conscience. If, in the end, you and your AP decide that you should not approach your friend, there are other ways that you can make amends. For instance, you could write a letter of apology and then prayerfully put it in your GOD CAN acknowledging your sin and asking God for forgiveness. You could also write out a prayer for your friend that, if she still needs healing, God will bring that about in His time and in her time. Put it in your GOD CAN as well.

In this phase, I found it necessary to be faithful with my Bible Reading and Prayer and Meditation. I sought His direction every step of the way, and He was faithful to see me through the process. I used the tool of Speed Writing prior to each amends. Writing in that way helped me to focus on the key points and not get hung up on inconsequential aspects. Once I had done that, I rehearsed what I would say in a calm, nonthreatening manner. Then I started approaching people. I prayed and put it in God's hands prior to each letter or encounter. In some cases, I wrote letters, and there was follow-up to that in return letters, visits, and phone calls. With some, I called and completed my amends on the phone, and with others I set a meeting time and then met with them in private. There were some amends for which I did not feel comfortable with a phone call or letter, but the distance was too great for a visit. Those I set aside until I would be with them naturally (like a family visit) and then found a time to sit and talk with them.

Fortunately, I did not have any financial restitution or criminal action to deal with, and mine turned out mostly amicable. I did have one friend tell me that I was not the person she thought I was, and there has been no contact since. I had to accept that and move on. I had done what I could, so I put that one in my GOD CAN for Him to deal with.

I tell you this just so you know it will not all be fun and roses. Some people may not be willing to accept your apology or repayment, and all you can do is accept that and move on. Do what you can. If you are left with unresolved issues or feelings, there are other ways to reach closure, which I discuss later. And then there are those situations where you apologize for what you thought was the problem only to find out it was strictly about the fact that, for instance, "you got Mom's ring after she died, and you knew I always wanted it!" You did not know, of course, and she never spoke up at the time. You finally give her the ring, and it's like there had never been a rift between the two of you. Family—you can't ever figure them out. It is amazing to me the number of family problems that surface with the loss of a loved one.

Spend some time in reflection with the following Bible verses. These are meant to help prepare you for making your amends. Do not think about how you are going to accomplish your list quite yet; just let the following Bible verses prepare your heart. Remember to use your journal and *write out* (don't just work in your head) your answers to the following questions. If you cannot resolve any questions, try going through the Tools and Exercises for suggestions to help you get past the impasse. And don't forget to include your AP if you get stuck in the process.

Matthew 5:9—"Blessed are the peacemakers, for they will be called Sons of God."

Being a peacemaker is sometimes a thankless job and not an easy one. Thank God it comes with a blessing! We can be sure that we are following God's will for us in making our amends.

Joshua 1:1–9—[paraphrased] After Moses's death, God told Joshua to gather the Israelites and cross into the promised land. God told him that he might have to fight for the land but promised that He would give Joshua every place where he set his foot. He promised that He would never leave him or forsake him but also admonished Joshua to obey all the law given to Moses and to not turn from it to the right or to the left. God advised Joshua to be strong and very courageous and then promised him that He would be with him wherever he went.

Our task, I think, is not nearly as difficult as moving thousands of complaining Israelites across the desert and fighting for the land on top of it all. But God promised that if Joshua would do as God commanded, He would give him every place he set his foot on. He admonished Joshua to meditate on His word and to not stray from it to the right or to the left. He advised him to not be afraid and promised to be with him wherever he went. And Joshua *did* prosper! Do you believe that God promises us the same thing? With your amends, focus on the scriptures, pray for His guidance; don't let fear get in your way, and God will be with you every step of the way.

Psalm 51:17—"The sacrifices of God are a broken spirit; a broken and contrite heart, O God, you will not despise."

The Revised Standard Version says, "The sacrifice acceptable to God is a broken spirit." Doing our amends can be a humbling and demoralizing experience. This scripture tells us to relish our humility as a sacrifice to God, as God loves a broken and contrite heart and will lift us up and support us.

Proverbs 16:20—"Whoever gives heed to instruction prospers, and blessed is he who trusts in the Lord."

Entrust each and every one of your amends to the Lord and pray for His direction. In that way, you will prosper. Don't get lazy and try to do it on your own; include God in each and every one of your amends, and you will prosper.

Proverbs 29:11—"A fool gives full vent to his anger, but a wise man keeps himself under control."

We need to pray for wisdom going into each and every one of our amends. In most cases, it was probably our anger that got us into this mess to begin with. It is entirely possible that when we go to make amends, the other person may not be willing to accept an apology and may bring up all the emotions and incidents that led up to the disagreement in the first place. It would be easy to fall right back into the old ways and lash back at them. In my story ("Making Amends" in Part 2) about the woman that we visited, she pushed all my old buttons, and I wanted to lash out at her the way I did the first time. But in my head, I told myself I was not the same person this day and prayed that God would give me self-control and wisdom. I guarantee I felt better leaving there with a clear conscience instead of giving in to my anger. A wise man keeps himself under control. Write about any incidents where you did not control your reactions. How did you feel?

Isaiah 43:18—"Forget the former things; do not dwell on the past."

Are we going to get better or bitter? By making our amends, we are getting better. We are putting the former things away so that we can be better. Hanging on to the past only makes us bitter.

Matthew 11:28—"Come to me, all you who are weary and burdened, and I will give you rest."

Write this verse down in your journal. If at any time in the midst of your amends you feel weary and burdened, just come back and read this verse. Then close your eyes and breathe deeply and let His rest soothe your soul.

Ephesians 5:21—"Submit to one another out of reverence for Christ."

One definition of *submit* is to yield yourself to another. We are told to submit out of reverence for Christ. When we do our amends, we are yielding ourselves to the person we have wronged for the purpose of setting things right—or as right as we can. We do it for them, for ourselves, and out of reverence for Christ, who suffered and died for us.

1 Thessalonians 5:15–18—"Make sure that nobody pays back wrong for wrong, but always try to be kind to each other and to everyone else. Be joyful always; pray continually; give thanks in all circumstances, for this is God's will for you in Christ Jesus."

Sound like a tall order? Maybe so, but I believe the key is in verse 17: "Pray continually." I like the American Standard Version of that verse: "Pray without ceasing." If we are in constant communication with God, it is He who makes it possible for us to always do that which is right. But how do we pray without ceasing? First, we have to recognize that prayer is simply communication between us and God—talking, asking, remarking, requesting, and thanking. It does not have to be head bowed with hands folded to be considered prayer. I have made a habit of talking to God throughout the day every day. In line at the grocery store I pray for the checker and people in line. I pray on the road—stranded cars, sirens, and I pray instead of cussing at the drivers who cut me off. At work—for my boss, my coworkers, our customers. At home—over the stove, doing the laundry, helping with homework, and especially dealing with teenagers. I believe that is the type of praying without ceasing that Paul was talking about. Inviting God into every waking moment of our lives, aware of His presence at all times. By inviting God into our daily life, we can manage the tall order of this passage—joyful always, kind to each other, no paybacks. In making our amends, we are embracing the spirit of this passage.

Philippians 4:6–7—"Do not be anxious about anything, but in everything, by prayer and petition, with thanksgiving, present your requests to God. And the peace of God, which transcends all understanding, will guard your hearts and your minds in Christ Jesus."

This would be a great scripture to use for meditation on the day you contact your people or on the day when you make amends. Make a note of this verse in your journal.

Proverbs 15:1—"A gentle answer turns away wrath, but a harsh word stirs up anger."

Let this be a guide as we decide how to approach our amends.

Step Nine Resolution

Made direct amends to such people whenever and wherever possible, except when to do so would injure them or others.

Now it is time to start actually making your amends. In summary, this is how making your amends should progress:

- Complete your amends list through the column for planned approach
- Meet with your AP to discuss your planned approach
- Use the tools of Bible Reading and Prayer and Meditation
- Rehearse what you will say
- Contact the person and set a time to get together or write letter
- Day of meeting: read your Bible, pray, meet
- Complete amends list with date of amends and results
- Meet with your AP to report results
- Follow up as needed

That is the process in brief. Now let's look at it in a bit more detail. Retrieve the amends lists started in Step Eight. These lists should already have the name of the person(s) with whom you need to make amends and the first column completed—the reason.

Now, complete the next column for each item—Planned Approach. This is not to be set in concrete and can be changed as the circumstances dictate. But for now, indicate how you think you should approach the amends with each person and how to make any financial or other restitution. Be creative, but mostly be sincere and sympathetic to their feelings. Following are some suggestions, but in no way are these the only options:

- Talk to them in person
- Talk to them on the phone
- Write them a letter and mail it
- Write them a letter and take it
- Write a Dear John letter and resolve the issue without meeting with the other person (See Tools and Exercises)

In addition to the actual contact with the person, there may be other amends such as financial or other restitution. Note your plan for that as well.

The person may not be available for a variety of reasons:

- You might have lost touch with them and do not know where they are. You should exhaust all avenues of trying to locate them, but if you cannot find them, you can still affect your amends. Use one or more of the methods described below for death, refusal.*

You may contact them, and they may refuse to talk to you.

- In that case, with sincerity and sensitivity, write them a letter and mail it or put it in the GOD CAN. Then follow up, for your benefit, with one or more of the methods described below for death, refusal.*

*Death, refusal, or unknown whereabouts—If you cannot meet with the person due to one of these reasons, you can do one of the following:

- Depending on the nature of the offense, there may be a family member with whom you can make amends or restitution.
- Go to the Tools and Exercises and employ one or more of the exercises to complete your amends. Or you may have an idea of your own as to how to obtain closure. If you do, I'd love to hear about it. From the exercises in this book, I found the following to be helpful:

Ghost Chair	GOD CAN	Make a project
Up in Smoke	Writing—Dear John	

- Once you have completed the amends, write your results on your amends sheet and put it in your GOD CAN.

In the event that the person should not be contacted because to do so would injure them or others:

- The example about whether to apologize to the friend with whose husband you had an affair serves to indicate that perhaps not all amends should be done directly. We need to prayerfully consider similar situations before we make matters worse. We need to examine our hearts to determine our motives. Matters such as this should be discussed with your AP to obtain an objective opinion. Discussing it with a minister for moral leadership would be another avenue. In the end, if the decision is made to not approach that person, then treat the amends as in the case of death/refusal.*

By now, you should have your planned approach column filled out. If not, complete that before continuing. You may change your approach as time goes on, but at least we have a starting point.

Make an appointment with your AP and go over each amends and planned action.

Date you completed your planned approach column on your amends list: _____

Date you met with your AP to discuss your plans: _____

Before you start contacting people, there is some preparation that should be done:

- Bible Reading—you can review some of the passages from above or refer to Suggested Bible Readings. Follow that with Prayer and Meditation.
- Rehearse what you will say—It would be a good idea to practice what you will say with your AP or in the mirror until it feels natural. Even if you do not want to actually rehearse, at least write out what you will say and go over it several times until it feels natural. Even though you will be apologizing and asking forgiveness, *how* it is said can make or break the situation. Make sure you *are* sincere and *sound* sincere.

Before you make your initial contact *and* on the day of your get-together or phone call or writing your letter, I would advise the following steps to be done before proceeding with contact. You might wonder why I would advise all of this for even just the phone call to set up an appointment. It is because you need to be prepared for anything. For instance, you may make a phone call with the purpose of just making an appointment to talk with them. They may refuse to meet and say something like, "If you have something to say, just say it now." If you had not fully prepared for the engagement, you may stumble and not present your case very well. Before your first contact, and again before any subsequent meeting, take care to do the following preparation:

- Spend some time with the tools of Deep Breathing or Breaststroke or any other method as a way to clear your mind.
- Read your Bible, pray, and meditate.
- Say a prayer right before you contact this person and before any subsequent meetings. Put it in your own words, but your prayer should include something like the following: "Father, I pray that you would give me the words to say and the actions to take that they will be acceptable in your sight. Send your Holy Spirit to join us so that a sense of calm will exist and plant peace and geniality in both of our hearts. If they do not respond kindly, Father, give me again the words to say and the actions to take to conclude our time together to the best of my ability. Thy will be done. Amen."

Now you need to make your initial contact:

Local people:
My suggestion is to get together in person for the amends. Although face-to-face time may seem a bit more threatening, I believe it also has a greater potential for better communication. The first step would probably be a phone call to set up an appointment and then get together. As mentioned in the previous section, be prepared to actually make your amends on the phone if needed.

People out of the area:
It may not be possible to meet with them, in which case you will need to decide whether to call or write. Either way, follow the previous section in preparation for either.

Deceased, refusal, or persons with unknown whereabouts:
Make the same preparations whether meeting a family member or even if there is no one to contact. Even though you may not be meeting an actual person, you need to do the same preparation. Just because you won't be meeting with a live person does not mean you don't want God's blessing in the process.

As each of the amends is completed, write the completed date on your amends list as well as a short phrase or key words to describe the outcome.

Make an appointment to share the results of the amends with your AP. You can get together with each and every item or get together and discuss three or four at a time or the whole list. Write the date that you shared the amends with your AP on your amends list.

Follow up:
Note on your list any follow-up needed. For instance, you may have settled issues, but there may still be some financial arrangements to be completed. Or your friend may have accepted your apology on the condition that you also apologize to his sister. Whatever follow-up actions you agreed to should be noted so that you do not forget to complete them.

Some warnings and thoughts:

You are dealing with a lot of variables here, a lot of "what if" situations. There is no way I can prepare you for every situation, and that is why it is so important to follow the preparation suggestions above. Do your Bible Reading and Prayer and Meditation. Put the situation in God's hands, and prayerfully ask Him to guide you through the process.

You should be prepared to accept the fact that just because you make amends doesn't necessarily mean the other person will accept your apology or extend forgiveness. You can only do what you can do. But if you are left with unresolved feelings, consider one or more of the suggestions above for how to deal with a deceased person as a means of closure.

Although you should not put off making your amends, there may be some that you cannot complete for months. Do not be dismayed if that is the case. Make an honest effort to do all that you can, and if there are some remaining, put them aside until the time and/or place is right. For now, you could treat the amends as if the person is deceased and use one or more of the suggestions above for how to deal with a deceased person. That would allow you some closure until you can fully make the amends. But do not use this approach as a method to just put off doing what can be done. And keep the incomplete amends nearby so they do not become forgotten.

Making your amends could jeopardize your current lifestyle today—especially if you have been living lies because of your transgression. There could be financial restitution or criminal proceedings. You will have to be the judge of how far you want or need to go to clear your conscience, to obtain forgiveness, and to make things right. Spend time in your Bible Reading and Prayer and Meditation time to ask for God's guidance. Speak to a professional counselor or an attorney as needed.

What to do with your amends list when all done?

- My suggestion for each one is to put it in your GOD CAN.
  As you put it inside, thank God for seeing you through the process and say something like "GOD CAN do for me what I can't do on my own."
  In six months or so, when you go through your GOD CAN, you will read through it and wonder why is seemed so hard at the time and thank God

for the healing that came with it. You can reflect on the time since then and the changes in your life. At that time, you can leave it in your GOD CAN, or you can burn it, representing the complete erasing of your sins that God's forgiveness extends to us.

Do you have to complete all your amends before going on to Step Nine A and Ten? The answer is no. You should take some time between Steps Nine and Ten to complete a substantial number of them. Do your best to complete the majority, but if there are some that will take a long time to complete or you have to wait for the right opportunity, set those aside to be completed later and move on to the next step. Just make sure to put the remaining amends lists someplace where you will not forget about them.

Date you completed all or a substantial number of your amends: _____

Do you have some amends that need to wait to be completed?_____

How many? _____ Where have you placed them to be completed later?_____

Date you shared your progress with your AP: _____

Amends List—Example

For the sake of space, I've listed three persons on one page.
But for the sake of clarity and enough writing space, I recommend each to be on a separate page.
The person's name and the first column were completed with Step Eight.
Now with Step Nine, complete the planned approach column and discuss with your AP.
Then complete your amends and the rest of the columns.

Person with whom to make amends:
1. Grandma Kelly 2. Friend, Kathy 3. Sister Sally

Reason amends needed	Planned approach	Date amends made	Results Follow-up needed?	Date shared with AP	Date forgave self
1. I wrote her a hurtful letter	Write letter asking for forgiveness	3/11	Received letter of forgiveness from her on 3/19	3/11 & 3/20	Still working on it
	Follow up with phone call	3/25	Called 3/25 and had a good chat	3/26	
2. She moved away before I was able to resolve dispute over Kevin	Unable to locate I will use tools of Dear John letter and Ghost Chair	4/22 4/28 5/2 5/10	Wrote letter and then did Ghost Chair. Was able to release anger & ask forgiveness. Letter in GOD CAN & did Up in Smoke	5/10	5/10
3. Dispute over inheritance	Talk to her in person	6/3	She refused to talk on phone. So wrote letter. Mailed one to her and put one in GOD CAN. Have done what I can for now, will pray for future opportunity and leave it in the GOD CAN for now.	6/10	6/10

STEP NINE A

R esolved pent-up anger and resentment toward those who had harmed us.
The principle behind Step Nine A is **freedom**. Although we certainly have the right to stay angry at those who have victimized us, it is not in our best interests to hang on to the anger and resentment. To allow their actions to define us keeps us their victim. To forgive and release the anger gives us freedom over our lives.

Colossians 3:13—"Bear with each other and forgive whatever grievances you may have against one another. Forgive as the Lord forgave you."

In Step Eight A, we identified those people with whom we had leftover anger and resentment as a result of their actions. It is time now to take action and complete the healing list started with Step Eight A. As a reminder, we are not looking for retribution; rather, we are resolving the anger and resentment that came as a result of those actions of others.

Keep in mind that our goal here is to forgive those who have sinned against us, and in that way, we will be relieved of the wounds that have been festering inside. Once we have forgiven, we can approach getting rid of the anger and restoring our self-esteem. But we might say they don't deserve our forgiveness. It doesn't matter whether they deserve it or not; we are not doing it for them. We are doing it for ourselves and in obedience to God. Remember that in making our amends in Step Nine, we were taking care of our side of the street only. The same applies here; we are taking steps to heal ourselves, not to cross the street and seek revenge. Granted, they may deserve our vengeance, but that is not our job here. Our purpose here is to restore ourselves.

I have an incredibly good friend whose husband was murdered on a high school campus where he was employed. He was shot and killed by a student for no apparent reason. Partway through the trial, I spoke with her, and she told me that she had forgiven the student. My mouth dropped open; I could not believe what she was saying. When I questioned her about it, she said she had to forgive him because if she didn't, it would eat her alive. She was still attending the trial, and she was hopeful for a life sentence but not out of hate or vengeance but for justice. She was content to let the legal system do their job and God to do His. Regardless of how things played out, this boy would have to answer to God one day. And she, too, would have to answer to God, but she would do it with a clean heart. I admired her so much and still do to this day. She is everything that a Christian should exemplify, and she does it with grace and with love in her heart. When I am tempted to be bitter and unforgiving, I have only to think of her, and my heart rejoices in knowing her, and I do the right thing.

Until I made my list of people and situations that I needed to forgive, I didn't realize how much anger I had stored up. I never manifested my anger to others; it was only directed at myself. Although I had really good skills and always had good jobs, I never felt like I did anything well enough—my self-esteem was in the gutter. This program was a lifesaver for me, and my friend's example paved my way to recovery.

I worked on each one of my issues separately until I felt that I had accomplished the goal of forgiveness and peace in my heart. And then I went on to the next. This process took me about six months on and off to complete. Throughout that time, I was faithful with my Bible Reading and Prayer and Meditation. I used many of the tools available in Tools and Exercises to express and release anger, determine the source of hurt, facilitate forgiveness, and gather facts.

The tools I used most were:

Dear John	Fill in the Blanks	Ghost Chair
GOD CAN	Grief Process	Up in Smoke

Once I felt free of all that baggage, it was time for me to work on my self-esteem. I accomplished that with a combination of:

God Talk	Mirror Talk
Personalize your Bible	Self-Affirmations

I continued my Bible Reading and Prayer and Meditation as well. I can't tell you exactly when I was finally a self-assured woman who finally had "her head on straight," but it came along in due time—in God's time.

Except for Filling in the Blanks about my father, not once did I feel the need to confront any people involved in any of those incidents. I made my peace with what had happened and was able to forgive in my heart and find peace. Unless there are criminal charges to be filed, I think it is best not to make contact, but each person will have to decide for themselves for each incident.

In Step Nine, we were making amends for actions we had taken, so it was necessary to seek out those we had harmed. In Step Nine A, we are seeking to heal our hearts. Seeking out our perpetrators might be counterproductive to healing. But if you feel that you have to, I guess you have to. Just be aware that you might be shaking up that beehive and will have to deal with the aftermath.

In addition to forgiving those people, I was also able to find forgiveness for myself as well. They might have victimized me, but I developed character defects (like overeating) as a result, and that part was on me. I can excuse the years of childhood eating, perhaps but as an adult, I had to take responsibility for my actions regardless of how they got started. The tools of God Talk and GOD CAN and Writing helped to bring that about.

Before you approach your healing list, spend some time in reflection with the following Bible verses. They are designed to help prepare your heart for healing. Remember to use your Journal and *write out* (don't just work in your head) your answers to the following questions. If you cannot resolve any questions, try going through the Tools and Exercises for suggestions to help you get past the impasse. And don't forget to include your AP if you get stuck in the process.

Colossians 3:13—"Bear with each other and forgive whatever grievances you may have against one another. Forgive as the Lord forgave you."

Has God ever forgiven you for anything? If yes (and none of us are without sin), then we are told to extend that forgiveness to others as well. It doesn't say that if it is just a little sin, you need to forgive. It doesn't give any dispensation for big crimes like murder and rape. It says to forgive whatever grievances you may have against someone. It is a tall order, but if my friend could do it, so can I. What about you?

Matthew 7:12—"So in everything, do to others what you would have them do to you."
Have you ever treated someone badly? Spoken to them in anger? How would you feel if someone did that to you? If we want to be forgiven, then we need to extend forgiveness. Simple as that.

Philippians 4:13—"I can do everything through him who gives me strength."
Has this Twelve Step program been a breeze up until now? It was not for me; it was hard work, but I did recognize that God was by my side, giving me the strength to see it through. And He will be here for this step as well.

Titus 3:10–11—"Warn a divisive person once, and then warn him a second time. After that, have nothing to do with him. You may be sure that such a man is warped and sinful; he is self-condemned."
To repeat, just because we forgive does not mean that what that person did to us is OK. Although we are to forgive, that action does not require us to have anything to do with that person again unless we want to. For instance, if the person who hurt you did so by hurting your feelings and has expressed remorse and you want to continue the relationship, by all means; I know that God would be pleased that you not only forgave but have softened your heart to accept that person as well. If, however, the person who hurt you did so by raping you, then you still need to forgive for yourself, but you are not in any way obligated to have anything to do with that person ever again. Also, just because you finally get to the point of forgiveness does not mean that you cannot report an illegal act to the police. In fact, you have every right to report any illegal activity but then leave it up to the authorities. In reporting illegal activity, we are not taking revenge but reporting a crime, as is required by law. But for our purposes here, you are not required to report to the police. Let your conscience be your guide and perhaps seek counsel from your AP or a professional.

Luke 17:1–4—"So watch yourselves. If your brother sins, rebuke him, and if he repents, forgive him. If he sins against you seven times in a day, and seven times comes back to you and says, 'I repent,' forgive him."

How many times are we expected to forgive others? No more than the number of times we expect to be forgiven by God ourselves. It is not easy to continually forgive the same person for the same offense over and over again. But do we really want God to limit the number of times He will forgive us?

Even if someone were to beat you every day, you are to forgive them every day if they repent. What about the alcoholic husband who beats his wife while drunk and then begs for forgiveness when sober? We are told to forgive every time—remember that forgiveness frees your heart from holding that hate inside you, so it is to your benefit to forgive. However, I don't read anything saying you have to stand there and take it. The Titus passage right above this one tells us to "have nothing to do with him." Leave. Get out of there. File a police report—let the authorities deal with his behavior.

Keep in mind that just because we forgive someone does not mean we have to necessarily trust them again. If someone has stolen money from us, we are to forgive, which is an action of the heart. But we would be prudent to not allow them access to our accounts and wallet again.

Matthew 6:14–15—"For if you forgive men when they sin against you, your heavenly Father will also forgive you. But if you do not forgive men their sins, your Father will not forgive your sins."

Have you withheld forgiveness for others? Has forgiveness from others been withheld for you? How did that make you feel? Do to others as you would have them do to you. Do you want God to forgive you? Then you need to extend that forgiveness as well.

Matthew 9:36—"When he saw the crowds, he had compassion on them, because they were harassed and helpless, like sheep without a shepherd."

I found this scripture when I was approaching my healing exercises, and it spoke to my heart. I felt harassed and helpless, and Jesus had compassion on me. It made me think of the "Footsteps in the Sand" story (see Addendum Three), and I felt lifted and cradled in His arms. I knew I could make it through these healing exercises with Him by my side and willing to hold me when needed. We often choose to go through life on our own, and even then, God is by our side to help us if we will let Him. Have you ever felt the hand of God? Felt a presence you could not explain? Experienced a miracle you could not explain? Have you ever done everything wrong and yet it all turned out OK? Some will call it karma or good vibes. I call it God. Write about a time that you needed help, and someone showed you compassion. How did that make you feel?

Romans 8:34b—"Christ Jesus, who died—more than that, who was raised to life—is at the right hand of God and is also interceding for us."

When we are overwhelmed and cannot even formulate thought, we need only to say "Jesus, speak for me as you know my needs even better than I." What a blessing. And as we approach these healing exercises, if the hurt has been such that you cannot fathom how to approach forgiving the act and healing your heart, you can ask Jesus to intercede for you until you can see the plan ahead. We are never alone.

Mark 5:25–34—

> And a woman was there who had been subject to bleeding for twelve years. She had suffered a great deal under the care of many doctors and had spent all she had, yet instead of getting better she grew worse. When she heard about Jesus, she came up behind him in the crowd and touched his cloak, because she thought, "If I just touch his clothes, I will be healed." Immediately her bleeding stopped, and she felt in her body that she was freed from her suffering. At once Jesus realized that power had gone out from him. He turned around in the crowd and asked, "Who touched my clothes?" "You see the people crowding against you," his disciples answered, "and yet you can ask, 'Who touched me?'" But Jesus kept looking around to see who had done it. Then the woman, knowing what had happened to her, came and fell at his feet and, trembling with fear, told him the whole truth. He said to her, "Daughter, your faith has healed you. Go in peace and be freed from your suffering."

This woman knew that if she partnered with Jesus, she'd be healed. That takes a tremendous amount of faith. Life is so much easier and better handled with a partner. Let God be that partner. Trust in Him as we go through this process and in all areas of our lives, and we will emerge freed from our suffering and enjoying

His peace even as the chaos goes on around us. Write about a big project that you tackled by yourself. How much easier would it have been to have a partner?

Proverbs 16:3—"Commit to the Lord whatever you do, and your plans will succeed."

Even if it feels impossible to forgive and release all anger from our heart, we can accomplish anything if we commit our plans to the Lord. For each and every item on your healing list, be sure to discuss with God your plan of action, and He will be faithful and help your plan to succeed.

Psalm 25:1–3—"To you, O Lord, I lift up my soul; in you I trust, O my God. Do not let me be put to shame, nor let my enemies triumph over me. No one whose hope is in you will ever be put to shame, but they will be put to shame who are treacherous without excuse."

Victims of abuse or crimes generally feel shame. It does not make sense, since we, as victims, did nothing wrong. Nonetheless, it is a common feeling. Putting our trust in God, we will never feel shame again. It is time now to start working on our healing list. Put your work in God's hands, and don't look back. Good things are in store for you.

Step Nine A Resolution

Resolved pent-up anger and resentment toward those who had harmed us.

Now it is time to start working on our healing list. In summary, this is how approaching your healing should look:

- Bible Reading
- Prayer and Meditation
- Complete your healing list through Planned Approach column
- Choose a planned approach for each healing
- Share your plan with your AP

- Do your planned exercises for each healing, one healing at a time
- Complete the healing list with date of healing and results
- Meet with your AP
- Follow up as needed

Now let's look at that with a little more detail.

Retrieve the healing lists started in Step Eight A. These lists should already have the name of the person(s) involved and the situation column completed.

Now, complete the next column for each item—Planned Approach. Almost all the exercises can be helpful in pursuit of that resolution. With each incident or feeling that you need to resolve, spend some time with the Tool and Exercise list to determine which one or more can best help with your issue.

For instance, I used Fill in the Blanks to gather more information so that I had all the facts. I used Ghost Chair to vent my anger and get in touch with the root cause of the anger. Once I got to the point of forgiveness, I used my GOD CAN to give those issues away and/or Up in Smoke to literally let those feelings float away. Once resolved, I found that I still needed to work on my self-esteem, which had taken a big hit as a result of some of those incidents. Using the tools of God Talk, Mirror Talk, Personalizing My Bible, and Self-Affirmations helped me to repair that lasting damage. And there may be other methods that you will think of or variations to the Tools and Exercises.

After studying the exercises, indicate in the approach column what method you plan to use in your quest for healing.

Date you completed the approach column on your healing list: _____

Next, it would be a good idea to get together with your AP to review your list and planned approach to get her approval, opinion, suggestions.

Date you met with your AP to discuss your plans: _____

You should approach each healing exercise as follows:

- Make sure you will not be interrupted and that you have allowed sufficient time.

- Spend some time with Deep Breathing or Breaststroke exercises or any other method as a way to clear your mind.
- Next, move on to a Bible Reading—you can review some of the passages from this chapter or refer to Suggested Bible Readings.
- Follow that with Prayer and Meditation asking God to send His Holy Spirit to be present and to guide you through the exercise.

As you complete each exercise:

- On your healing list, fill in the date of healing action and a short phrase or key words to describe the outcome in the results column.
- If you need to move on to another exercise in order to fully complete this healing, indicate that and follow the same steps for each exercise.
- Work on only one healing at a time and do not be in a hurry to go quickly from one to the next.

Make an appointment to share the results of your healing exercises with your AP:

- You can get together with each and every healing or get together and discuss three or four at a time or the whole list.
- Write the date that you shared the healing with your AP on your healing list.

Some warnings and thoughts:

Just as in Step Nine, you are dealing with a lot of variables. There is no way I can prepare you for every situation, so make sure to do your Bible Reading and Prayer and Meditation. Put the healing in God's hands and prayerfully ask Him to guide you through the process.

In Step Nine, it was necessary to seek out those we had harmed to make amends. In Step Nine A, we are looking for healing for ourselves. In most cases, it will not be necessary or advisable to seek out those who harmed us. We are not looking for retribution but for a healing and forgiving heart within us. There may be extreme cases where an attorney or the law may need to be contacted. For instance, if you were raped and you know who the rapist is, you may want to consider going to the police—we do not want others to suffer as we have. But under no circumstances should we contact the rapist or perpetrator ourselves. Again, the primary purpose in Step Nine A is for inner peace, not for retribution or even justice. Nothing we could do would ever make us feel good about what was done to us, but we can reach an inner peace and put the issue to rest.

Although you should not put off doing the healing exercises, there may be some that you cannot complete for months for whatever reason. Maybe you need to do a Fill in the Blanks exercise and the person that can help you with that is not available for a couple of months. Do not be dismayed if that is the case. Make an honest effort to do all that you can, and if there are some remaining, put them aside until the time and/or place is right. Keep your healing list nearby so it does not become forgotten.

Some of the issues you have may be more than you can deal with on your own. Cases of rape or other violent crimes are complicated to deal with. Spend time in your Bible Reading and Prayer and Meditation time to ask for God's guidance on how to proceed. If needed, speak to a professional counselor or minister and pursue that avenue of help instead of or in addition to the Tools and Exercises.

What should you do with each healing list when it's finished?

- For the completion, my suggestion is to celebrate each one. This is a time to rejoice as you experience a life free from shame and guilt. Let your imagination run wild.
  - Have a party or go on a picnic.
  - Go to the beach and celebrate.
  - Have a girls' or boys' day out.
  - Simply make a special dinner for you and a loved one.
- For the physical healing list, I suggest putting each one into your GOD CAN.
  - As you put it inside, thank God for seeing you through the process and say something like "I can't heal myself, but God Can."

In six months or so, when you go through your GOD CAN, you will read through them and thank God for the healing that came with it. You can reflect on the time since then and the changes in your life. At that time, you can leave it in your GOD CAN, or you can burn it, representing the complete erasing of your shame and guilt. That is God's love and grace extended to you.

Do you have to complete all of your healings before going on to Step Ten? The answer is no. You should take some time between Steps Nine A and Ten to complete a substantial number of them. Do your best to complete the majority, but if there are some that will take a long time to complete or you have to wait for the right opportunity, set those aside to be completed later and move on to Steps Ten and Ten A. Just make sure to put the remaining healing lists someplace where you will not forget about them.

Date you completed all or a substantial number of your healings: _____

Do you have some healings that need to wait to be completed? _____

How many? _____ Where have you placed them to be completed later?
_____

Date you shared your progress with your AP: _____

Healing List—Example

For the sake of space, I've listed three persons on one page.

But for the sake of clarity and enough writing space, I recommend each to be on a separate page.

For Step Nine A, fill in the remaining columns.

Person(s) Involved 1. Neighbor man 2. Guy from party 3. Myself

Situation needing healing	Planned approach	Date of healing action	Results	Date shared with AP	Follow up? Forgive self?
1. Childhood molestation	Speed Writing, Dear John letter, Ghost Chair, GOD CAN, Up in Smoke	8/12 8/22 8/30	Emotional but was able to express feelings & anger. Talked with another survivor. GOD CAN and Up in Smoke	8/13 8/23 8/30	Yes—forgave self. Will find organization that helps child victims to help support.
2. Date Rape	Go talk to girlfriend who was at same party. Dear John letter, Ghost Chair, GOD CAN, Up in Smoke	9/3	First time I ever told anyone. Very sympathetic. Expressed feelings & anger. Had a good follow-up with GOD CAN and burn party.	9/6 9/13	Yes, forgave self. Will be advocate for women's rights.
3. Child I never had	Talk with husband. Writing, Bible, Fill in the Blanks, Grieve	10/4 10/10 Oct & Nov	Husband was sympathetic. Tools all helpful. Worked through stages of grief.	Oct & Nov	No real forgiveness, just acceptance. Will look for hospital program volunteering with babies.

STEP TEN

Continued to take personal inventory, and when we were wrong, promptly admitted it.

The principle behind Step Ten is **perseverance**. Having cleaned up our side of the street does not mean that we will never mess up again. We are human and will make mistakes. The difference is that we now have the tools to work with and will make amends as soon as possible instead of letting years go by compounding the problem. But it will take perseverance to continually deal with situations in a timely manner.

Ephesians 4:26b–27—"Do not let the sun go down while you are still angry, and do not give the devil a foothold."

This step is looking to the future, so on the surface, it would appear that there is not any real action for us to take here except to resolve to do it. I know for myself that New Year's resolutions are seldom kept, and so I did not feel comfortable just making a simple resolution and moving on.

I felt the best way to keep this resolution was to instill some safeguards in my life that would ensure this practice. Over time, living this step has just become a part of who I am. I can't imagine myself allowing situations to get out of hand as I once did. But in the beginning, I needed reminders.

After the Bible Study below, I have listed some of the safeguards that I instituted. Read through those, and you may have other ideas as well on how you would like to safeguard Step Ten for yourself.

Spend some time in reflection with the following Bible verses. Remember to use your journal and *write out* (don't just work in your head) your answers to the following questions. If you cannot resolve any questions, try going through the Tools and Exercises for suggestions to help you get past the impasse. And don't forget to include your AP if you get stuck in the process.

Ephesians 4:26b–27—"Do not let the sun go down while you are still angry, and do not give the devil a foothold."

The emotion of anger and staying angry separates us from God. With it, we put up a barrier in our heart, blocking God out. Boy, does the devil like that. We need to resolve anger for the sake of our relationships and to be obedient to God, but primarily we need to do this so that the devil cannot get a foothold in our life. By now, you should have broken down all those barriers between you and God. Resolving to keep this step assures that those barriers will never build again. Do you have any remaining barriers?

Psalm 85:8—"I will listen to what God the Lord will say; He promises peace to His people—but let them not return to folly."

We have worked our way through nine steps. It was not always easy and at times was heart wrenching. What do you feel that you have gained with those nine steps? Would you want to put that in jeopardy by returning to your old folly? What circumstances in your life could lead to a return of your old ways?

Psalm 32:1–5—"Blessed is he whose transgressions are forgiven, whose sins are covered. Blessed is the man whose sin the Lord does not count against him and in whose spirit is no deceit. I acknowledged my sin to you and did not cover up my iniquity. I said, 'I will confess my transgressions to the Lord'—and you forgave the guilt of my sin."

David describes the transition we have made. Now that we have confessed our sins and sought forgiveness, we are *blessed*. That one word speaks volumes, but my favorite definition of *blessed* is "connected with God." If we can commit to this Step

Ten, then our blessings are not in jeopardy, but we all know how easy it is to slip back into old ways. Will you follow up and put safeguards in place to assure that won't happen? In what ways do you feel connected with God?

Psalm 139:23–24—"Search me, O God, and know my heart; test me and know my anxious thoughts. See if there is any offensive way in me, and lead me in the way everlasting."

Because it is so easy to fall back into our old ways, this is a great scripture to use as a prayer every day. Ask Him to keep watch over you and when He sees you going astray to lead you back into His ways. Consider posting this as a prayer somewhere in your house.

Proverbs 3:5–6—"Trust in the Lord with all your heart and lean not on your own understanding; in all your ways acknowledge him, and he will make your paths straight."

There are very few decisions that I make without entrusting the situation to God. It's not that I'm so holy or spiritual; I've just done it wrong so many times on my own that I finally learned my lesson. I used to say flippant things like "but I like a winding path." Believe me—I will take a straight and boring path anytime over the unpredictable and bumpy, winding path. How have you sabotaged the path that God has for you?

Proverbs 16:3—"Commit to the Lord whatever you do, and your plans will succeed."

As you consider what safeguards you will put in place, pray for God's will in making the decision and then commit that plan to the Lord with the expectation of success. Write out a prayer in your journal.

Proverbs 23:19–21—"Listen, my son, and be wise, and keep your heart on the right path. Do not join those who drink too much wine or gorge themselves on meat, for drunkards and gluttons become poor, and drowsiness clothes them in rags."

This scripture gives us just one more reason to stay on the right path. The consequences of unsavory behavior just are not worth it. Yet we will stray again, and then we will be sorry again, and then ask for forgiveness again, and then God will be faithful and forgive us again. Solomon advises us here to be wise and get off the merry-go-round. In what ways have you chosen the merry-go-round in the past?

Mark 14:38—"Watch and pray so that you will not fall into temptation. The spirit is willing, but the body is weak."

Step Ten states, "when we were wrong *promptly* admitted it." That is why it is crucial to watch and pray. Temptation to stray from the Christian lifestyle is all around us, and better people than us have fallen into the pit. We want to be good, but our body is weak. So we stay in prayer so that our sins will be pointed out to us immediately, and we can take corrective action promptly.

Romans 12:2—"Do not conform any longer to the pattern of this world but be transformed by the renewing of your mind. Then you will be able to test and approve what God's will is—His good, pleasing, and perfect will."

For the most part, God does not come into our home and tell us directly or in so many words just exactly what His will is for us. We need to live a godly life so that we can discern His will for us through our Bible Reading or Prayer and Meditation. If we conform to the pattern of this world, we get too cluttered up to hear Him. I cannot emphasis enough the importance in Bible Reading and Prayer and Meditation to determine God's will for us and to help us to keep our resolve with Step Ten.

1 Corinthians 10:12—"So, if you think you are standing firm, be careful that you don't fall!"

When we get too smug and think we have it all figured out (whatever *it* is), then sure as shooting we're in for a fall. It is one thing to be assured and competent, but if we ever forget where we once were, what it took to get to this point, and the role that God played in our recovery, then we risk losing it all.

Philippians 3:13b–14—"Forgetting what is behind and straining toward what is ahead, I press on toward the goal to win the prize for which God has called me heavenward in Christ Jesus."

This was my mantra throughout my recovery. Whenever I was frustrated or tired or thought I just couldn't make one more stride toward recovery, I would read this scripture, and I'd just keep putting one foot in front of the other. I have a great deal of respect for Paul, so when I consider that he, too, had moments of weakness, it makes me feel better about myself, knowing that I can go on. We need to surround ourselves with whatever it takes to motivate us—for me, it is scripture (and sometimes the comics *Family Circus* and *Maxine*). What motivates you?

Romans 12:17–18, 20–21—"Do not repay anyone evil for evil. Be careful to do what is right in the eyes of everybody. If it is possible, as far as it depends on you, live at peace with everyone. If your enemy is hungry, feed him; if he is thirsty, give him something to drink. In doing this, you will heap burning coals on his head. Do not be overcome by evil, but overcome evil with good."

Christians are held to a higher standard—by other people, that is. We are all sinners in this world, but if we profess to be a Christian, non-Christians will hold a sinning Christian as proof that Christianity is not the way. To spend eternity in heaven, we have only to accept the free gift offered by God through His Son Jesus Christ. Good works don't get us into heaven. However, good works serve as a good witness to our fellow man. Now that we have put all our affairs in order through the first nine steps, let's continue to live in a godly fashion, not only for ourselves, but as a witness for our Lord and Savior, Jesus Christ. What actions do you have that are contrary to biblical principles? That appear to be non-Christian? Anger? Cursing? Lust?

Step Ten Resolution

Continued to take personal inventory, and when we were wrong, promptly admitted it.

To just say that you will continue to take personal inventory and promptly admit mistakes is one thing—doing it is another. We should consider some ways that we can safeguard our future by putting some controls in place. Following are some safeguards that I recommend making a regular part of life.

Bible Reading and Prayer and Meditation improve our Bible knowledge, keep us in regular communication with God, and are regular reminders to keep our relationships healthy. It would be hard to go to the Lord in prayer if we are hardening our hearts to family or friends, so these things will help safeguard our resolve to maintain healthy relationships.

Read and put into action the Conflict Resolution tool. This is a proven method of resolving conflict in a nonthreatening manner. Resolve to use this method regularly to settle differences before they get out of hand and blown out of proportion.

Ephesians 4:26b–27—"Do not let the sun go down while you are still angry, and do not give the devil a foothold."

Post this scripture somewhere in your house as a reminder to keep sin out of your life, to thwart the devil, and to maintain healthy relationships.

Psalm 139:23–24—"Search me, O God, and know my heart; test me and know my anxious thoughts. See if there is any offensive way in me, and lead me in the way everlasting."

Post this scripture somewhere in your house as a daily prayer.

Put on your thinking caps—I'm sure you can come up with other ideas on how to ensure regular monitoring of this Step Ten promise.

Date you became willing to commit to an ongoing practice of taking periodic personal inventory and then making amends as needed: _____

What kinds of safeguards will you initiate to ensure that? _____

Date you shared that decision with your AP: _____

STEP TEN A

C ontinued to take personal inventory, and when we found ourselves vulnerable, took appropriate action to avoid being a victim again.

The principle behind Step Ten A is **value**. In a lot of my group therapy sessions, I met others, like myself, who had been victims. We all asked each other, "How did they know they could victimize me?" I do not actually have a simple answer to that, but it often follows that "once a victim, always a victim." As a result of this program, we have realized that we are loved and valued, that we are worthy of securing our safety. We have resolved to never be a victim again.

1 John 3:1—"How great is the love the Father has lavished on us, that we should be called children of God! And that is what we are!"

Again, as in Step Ten, this step is looking to the future, and the best way to ensure our resolution to this step is to put some safeguards in place. One reason that victims often fall prey to being victims again is because with each experience, our self-worth is devalued, and we don't feel we deserve any better. The best safeguard I know is to become confident, self-assured, assertive, self-sufficient, and at the same time loving and caring and always seeking God's will in our lives. Of course, we should be careful to not take that to the extreme and become self-centered, arrogant, or aggressive, or to treat others as beneath us. We should already be on our way to achieving this through our work in Step Nine A. The emphasis there, however, was in healing from past victimizations. Here, we need to set some safeguards in place to help us to keep that resolve as we move forward. I have listed several safeguards in the section after the Bible Study. Be sure to read through those and consider other ideas of your own to incorporate into your daily life.

Spend some time in reflection with the following Bible verses. Remember to use your journal and *write out* (don't just work in your head) your answers to the following questions. If you cannot resolve any questions, try going through the Tools and Exercises for suggestions to help you get past the impasse. And don't forget to include your AP if you get stuck in the process.

1 John 3:1—"How great is the love the Father has lavished on us, that we should be called children of God! And that is what we are!"

And what does every parent want for their children? Happiness, love, success, and contentment. God wants all of that for us as well. He does not want us to ever be a victim again and will support us as we put safeguards in place so that nothing like what we have experienced before will ever happen again. Write a prayer asking God to help you determine the best safeguards for you.

Matthew 10:29–31—"Are not two sparrows sold for a penny? Yet not one of them will fall to the ground apart from the will of your Father. And even the very hairs of your head are all numbered. So, don't be afraid; you are worth more than many sparrows."

What do we do with those things we value? We take steps to keep them safe and protected. We put money in the bank to keep it safe. We give regular maintenance to our car to keep it in good running order. We place boundaries on our children to keep them safe. This passage tells us how much we are valued—He even knows the number of hairs on our head. But we live in a fallen world where people have free will, so bad things do happen. For that reason, we should not sit back and do nothing, saying, "God will save me." God works in many ways. There is the story of a man whose town was in the midst of a flood. A rescue truck was sent to get him for evacuation. "God will save me," he responded and closed the door. When the floods reached the second story of his house, a rescue boat came and told him to get in. "God will save me," he responded and closed the window

Sherry L. Miller

of the second story bedroom. When the flood reached the roof line, a helicopter hovered over the roof where he was huddling and sent down a hook. He refused the line, stating, "God will save me." When next we see him, he is at the gates of heaven asking why God didn't save him. He was told, "We sent a truck, then a boat, and then a helicopter—why didn't you get in?" God will be there for us, but we have to do our part as well.

Matthew 6:26—"Look at the birds of the air; they do not sow or reap or store away in barns, and yet your heavenly Father feeds them. Are you not much more valuable than they?"

Here is yet another testimony of our value. In my bleak years, I would read this and say, "Birds—that's all I am worth?" I knew I was worthless. But the verse does say that I am *much more valuable* than a bird. So if God will care for just a little bird that is not even made in His image and has no free will, how much more will He care for me? In a better frame of mind, I could understand the message—I hope you can as well. If not, do some Speed Writing about this verse.

Titus 2:11–12—"For the grace of God that brings salvation has appeared to all men. It teaches us to say 'No' to ungodliness and worldly passions, and to live self-controlled, upright, and godly lives in this present age."

Living a self-controlled, upright, and godly life is the best way to safeguard our safety. By choosing a Christian lifestyle, we are setting boundaries of what is right and wrong, what is acceptable and unacceptable, and we communicate that to others in the way that we live our lives. Boundaries protect us from those who do not have self-control and who may want to harm us. Have you set personal boundaries? Are you consistent with the boundaries you set? See Boundary Settings in Tools and Exercises.

Matthew 6:8—"Your Father knows what you need before you ask him."

Couples who have been married twenty years or more often know what the other is going to say before it is said and can anticipate each other's needs. That is how our heavenly Father knows us. Only someone highly interested in us and who loves us would know what we need before we ask. If God loves us that much, then we need to love ourselves as well and put those safeguards in place.

Romans 8:16—"The Spirit himself testifies with our spirit that we are God's children. Now if we are children, then we are heirs—heirs of God and coheirs with Christ, if indeed we share in His sufferings in order that we may also share in His glory."

We are in the will. We have an inheritance. Only loved ones do that for each other. So if I haven't convinced you yet—*you are loved by God*. He cares deeply what happens to you and wants you to care as well.

Mark 12:28–29a, 30–31—"One of the teachers of the law asked Jesus, 'Of all the commandments, which is the most important?' Jesus answered, 'The most important one is this: Love the Lord your God with all your heart and with all your soul and with all your mind and with all your strength. The second is this: Love your neighbor as yourself. There is no commandment greater than these.'"

Generally, we love those who love us (unless it is a stalker, of course, and that is not real love anyway). We have established that God loves us, so why wouldn't we love Him back? It is a natural thing to do. And then we are told to "love your neighbor as yourself." I got stuck on that part because I didn't love myself. God loved me, and I loved Him back. And I actually did extend love to others, but if I had done it at the level of self-love, it would have been a pitiful love. Through this program, I did learn to love myself as God loves me. In Step Nine A, you should have worked on self-esteem exercises (as needed). With all that love abounding, I know you will safeguard your safety.

Ephesians 6:10–18—

> Be strong in the Lord and in his mighty power. Put on the full armor of God so that you can take your stand against the devil's schemes. For our struggle is not against flesh and blood, but against the rulers, against the authorities, against the powers of this dark world and against the spiritual forces of evil in the heavenly realms. Therefore, put on the full armor of God, so that when the day of evil comes, you may be able to stand your ground, and after you have done everything, to stand. Stand firm then, with the belt of truth buckled around your waist, with the breastplate of righteousness in place, and with your feet fitted with the readiness that

comes from the gospel of peace. In addition to all this, take up the shield of faith, with which you can extinguish all the flaming arrows of the evil one. Take the helmet of salvation and the sword of the Spirit, which is the word of God. And pray in the Spirit on all occasions with all kinds of prayers and requests.

Read through this passage several times. Close your eyes and see yourself suited up, ready for battle. See the arrows of the evil one bounce off the breastplate. This is how we keep ourselves from being vulnerable to the evil in this world and beyond. Truth, righteousness, peace, faith, salvation, Holy Spirit, word of God. These are our weapons—incorporate them in your daily life for the ultimate protection.

Mark 11:25—"And when you stand praying, if you hold anything against anyone, forgive him, so that your Father in heaven may forgive you your sins."

We did this in Steps Eight A and Nine A, and now in Step Ten A, we are making a commitment to continue making this a way of life. Are you committed to this?

Step Ten A Resolution

Continued to take personal inventory, and when we found ourselves vulnerable, took appropriate action to avoid being a victim again.

Consider including some or all of these in your regular routine as a way to safeguard your resolution of keeping Step Ten A as a part of your daily life:

- Bible Reading and Prayer and Meditation improve our Bible knowledge, keep us in regular communication with God, and strengthen our relationship with Him as His child. It ensures that as we become the self-assured person God wants us to be, we don't forget about how He got us to this point and try to go it alone again.

- In becoming the self-assured person that God would have us to be, we aspire to being assertive but not aggressive. Read through the definitions of those two attributes under Conflict Resolution in Tools and Exercises.
- Staying physically well and fit can help us to feel confident in ourselves as well. You might consider joining a gym or exercise class.
- Personal Boundaries—Read through Personal Boundaries in Tools and Exercises and consider including some or all those suggestions in your daily life.
- If you have a proven disability, such as PTSD, you might want to consider getting a service dog or even just an emotional support dog for at home.
- There are several exercises in Tools and Exercises that address the topic of self-esteem. Go through them and perhaps do just one at a time in a revolving cycle for as long as you feel is necessary.
- Put on your thinking caps—I'm sure you can come up with other ideas on how to maintain good self-esteem and a commitment to Step Ten A.

Date you became willing to commit to an ongoing practice of taking personal inventory and taking appropriate action to avoid being a victim again: _____

What kind of safeguards will you initiate to ensure that? _____

Date you shared that decision with your AP: _____

STEP ELEVEN

S ought through scripture, prayer, and meditation to improve our conscious contact with God, praying only for the knowledge of His will for us and the power to carry that out.

The principle behind Step Eleven is **attunement**. Attunement means "to bring into harmony." Through our actions of Prayer and Meditation, we are connected to God intuitively so that His will for us is more easily understood.

Psalm 25:4–5—"Show me your ways, O Lord, teach me your paths; guide me in your truth and teach me, for you are God my Savior, and my hope is in you all day long."

Seeking God's will can seem to be rather elusive—just how is God going to make His will known to us? When we get the idea to do something or decide how to handle a situation, how do we know if it is our idea or God's? In the devotional book *Jesus Calling*,[13] each day's reading is written from the perspective of Jesus talking to us personally. On March 8, it describes the process of seeking His will as follows:

> To find Me and hear My voice, you must seek Me above all else. When you are determined to get your own way, you blot Me out of your consciousness. Instead of single-mindedly pursuing some goal, talk with Me about it. Let the Light of My Presence shine on this pursuit, so that you can see

---

[13] Sarah Young, *Jesus Calling*, Copyright© 2004 by Sarah Young. Used by permission of Thomas Nelson, www.thomasnelson.com.

it from My perspective. If the goal fits into My plans for you, I will help you reach it. If it is contrary to My will for you, I will gradually change the desire of your heart. Seek Me first and foremost; then the rest of your life will fall into place, piece by piece.

God speaks to us in many forms. When we read the Bible, He is speaking to us through the written word. When we pray, we are opening a channel for discussion—we present our requests, give thanks, and praise His name. In meditation, we allow for quiet time in which God can speak to us. There are several ways to approach the Bible. We can attend Bible Study at church or work. We can simply pick up the Bible and start reading. Or we can use a devotional book that helps to guide our daily scripture time. There is no wrong way to approach the Bible—just get in there and explore.

The best sermon I ever heard on the subject of prayer advised that the primary purpose of prayer is to change us so that we are more usable for God's purpose. We can pray for things, events, and people if the motivation is right, and all requests should be presented in the format of "if it be your will..." He defined prayer as that dynamic of the Christian life whereby we take our stubborn self-centered will and bring it into submission of His will.

After that sermon, my prayer life became less about me and more about furthering God's kingdom and determining His will for me and how I can be used to accomplish His will. And the scripture that has most defined my prayer life is from 1 Thessalonians 5:17, where it simply says, "Pray without ceasing." It is the concept of God being by our side all the time. He accompanies me at home with housework, at work, on the road driving, at kids' activities, hiking in the mountains, at church, at parties and, yes, in the bathroom. I keep Bible Study reading material in the bathroom, and we have some surprisingly good discussions there. Praying without ceasing is simply having an ongoing conversation with God as if He were your best friend doing all of life's activities with you each and every day. He is a wonderful companion.

I talk to God throughout my day, and I sing praises to Him and with Him—in the car, in the shower, and doing the dishes. I will tell you that having Him as a constant companion keeps life on an even keel, helps with my decision-making, and bats away depression. Are you old enough to remember the Mikey commercial? "Try it; you'll like it."

Meditation is time that we set apart to just sit still, be quiet, and listen. We can precede our meditation with a request for guidance in a certain area of our life or simply tell God that we are here for His purpose and for Him to make His will known to us. And then, just sit quietly. It is a good idea to keep a notepad and pen with you, and if you sense a message, write it down and obey. One day while I was meditating, I sensed the message *Go to a Christian bookstore for a devotion book.* I was a little puzzled by that, but I have learned to trust what comes to me in meditation. I was away from home staying in a hotel, so I went to the internet and found two Christian bookstores in the area. One of them in particular jumped out at me, so that was where I went. To make a long story short, the young woman who helped me turned out to be the reason I was sent there. She had specific needs that I was in tune with, and I was able to help her that day with counseling and prayer. God's ways are magical, but we have to be still long enough to hear.

Spend some time in reflection with the following Bible verses. Remember to use your journal and *write out* (don't just work in your head) your answers to the following questions. If you cannot resolve any questions, try going through the Tools and Exercises for suggestions to help you get past the impasse. And don't forget to include your AP if you get stuck in the process.

Psalm 25:4–5—"Show me your ways, O Lord, teach me your paths; guide me in your truth and teach me, for you are God my Savior, and my hope is in you all day long."

How does God show us and teach us? Through His word, the scriptures, the Bible. How can we see and learn if we do not read? Yes, He does speak to us in other ways—sermons at church, evangelists on TV, friends, books by Christian authors—but the only place we read *His* word is in the Bible. He will guide us and teach us, but we need to read. When I open my Bible, I generally start with a prayer asking God to help me understand what I am reading and to show me how to incorporate it in my life. What stands in the way of regular Bible Reading for you?

Luke 22:42—"Father, if you are willing, take this cup from me; yet not my will, but yours be done."

These were the words of Christ in the Garden of Gethsemane as He awaited the soldiers He knew were coming to take Him. He was in human form and knew the suffering that awaited Him. But even in that moment, He taught us how to pray. Yes, His flesh was weak, and He wanted to be spared what was to come. But He still left the decision in His Father's hands: "Not my will, but yours be done." That is how we are to pray. Are you willing to subject yourself to God's will?

Psalm 119:105–106—"Your word is a lamp to my feet and a light for my path. I have taken an oath and confirmed it, that I will follow your righteous laws."

I like things that I can visualize. In the dark, we stumble around, but in the light, the path is apparent. God's word, the Bible, is our light. The whole of Psalm 119 is 176 verses, so I am not going to write it down for you here. But it is a good read, so dust that Bible off and read the whole of Psalm 119. What it does so beautifully is highlight the benefits of doing God's will, which is our goal here in Step Eleven—to find God's will and the power to carry it out.

Isaiah 30:21—"Whether you turn to the right or to the left, your ears will hear a voice behind you, saying, 'This is the way; walk in it.'"

We will not hear that voice, though, if we are not faithful in Bible Reading and Prayer and Meditation. We need to stay in touch with God to hear His voice. The Bible and prayer are how we stay in touch.

Luke 6:46–49—

Why do you call me, "Lord, Lord," and do not do what I say? I will show you what he is like who comes to me and hears my words and puts them into practice. He is like a man building a house, who dug down deep and laid the foundation on rock. When a flood came, the torrent struck that house but could not shake it, because it was well built. But the one who hears my words and does not put them into practice is like a man who built a house on the ground without a foundation. The moment the torrent struck that house, it collapsed and its destruction was complete.

Our foundation is our knowledge of God and His word. Studying the Bible is the same as laying the foundation. If we try to live a Christian life without the knowledge of what God wants us to do, how we should live, and the teachings of Jesus, we will soon collapse into our old ways because we did not build the foundation to support our lifestyle. Find a church that teaches strong biblical truth. Join a Bible Study where you can learn from other Christians. Develop a personal relationship with our Lord. There is your foundation.

Romans 8:26–27—"The Spirit helps us in our weakness. We do not know what we ought to pray for, but the Spirit himself intercedes for us with groans that words cannot express. And He who searches our hearts knows the mind of the Spirit, because the Spirit intercedes for the saints in accordance with God's will."

And here is one of the best benefits of that gift of the Holy Spirit. When we don't even know what we want or how to pray, just ask the Holy Spirit, and he will pray for us. He knows us better than we know ourselves and is faithful to intercede on our behalf.

Philippians 4:6–7—"Do not be anxious about anything, but in everything, by prayer and petition, with thanksgiving, present your requests to God. And the peace of God, which transcends all understanding, will guard your hearts and your minds in Christ Jesus."

God Can calm the chaos. This is the passage that my whole book is based on. Our lives will always contain some element of chaos as we navigate our way through life here on earth. But if we will present our requests and thanksgiving to God through prayer, He will see us through it. But this is the important part: He will not just see us through it, but through it with *peace* in our heart. Our lives can be crumbling down around us, and yes, we might be worried and have lots of decisions to make and not like the situation, but we will work our way through it with peace in our hearts. Turmoil vs. tranquility. It is a priceless gift offered by God at the expense of just a prayer.

James 1:22—"Do not merely listen to the word, and so deceive yourselves. Do what it says."

The Sunday Christian is that person who puts on the Sunday face, picks up his Bible, attends church, and then goes about the rest of the week acting as a non-Christian. This passage says that we deceive ourselves calling ourselves Christians just because we go to church once a week. If we are not willing to take action on what we hear at church, we are only fooling ourselves as to our real intent. If we really want to be a Christian, it is a daily job, not just for Sundays. Being a Christian is full-time, but it is a joyful, easy load. Can you commit to daily prayer in pursuit of a full Christian lifestyle?

James 4:13–15—"Now listen, you who say, 'Today or tomorrow we will go to this or that city, spend a year there, carry on business and make money.' Why, you do not even know what will happen tomorrow. What is your life? You are a mist that appears for a little while and then vanishes. Instead, you ought to say, 'If it is the Lord's will, we will live and do this or that.'"

Boy, have I learned this lesson. My husband and I summarize this passage this way: "Man plans, and God laughs." We only think we are in control of our universe. I also say it this way: "Plan for the future, but live for today." We do have to make plans, after all. We all live by day planners and schedules and calendars. The parent-teacher meeting goes on the calendar as well as Little League practice, doctor appointments, family reunions, piano lessons, and on and on. But once the plan is made and the calendar noted, we should say "God willing" and place it in God's hands, knowing that He knows what is best for us and will give us whatever we need to make the adjustments to our schedule. We need to live each day fully present to the goings on around us.

1 John 5:14–15—"This is the confidence we have in approaching God: that if we ask anything according to His will, He hears us. And if we know that He hears us—whatever we ask—we know that we have what we asked of Him."

Now, I found this logic confusing at first. We need to ask it in His will. But if we believe and know that He hears us, He will give us what we have asked. So that dream house in the mountains? The kicker is that if we are truly willing to accept His will for us, then we will not expect anything that is not in God's will for us. I said at the beginning of this step study that "Prayer is that dynamic of the Christian life whereby we take our stubborn self-centered will and bring it into submission of His will." So then my feeble mind said, "Well, then why do I need to pray at all if my input means nothing?" God does want to know the desires of our heart and will fulfill those as they fit into His plan for us. But the most compelling reason to pray is that God wants to have a relationship with us. Think of your best friend. How often do you talk, do things together, laugh together, cry together? God wants to spend those moments with us, but if we never pray (which is conversation with God), then what kind of a relationship is it? If we ignored our best friend, how long would they remain our best friend? We are to make our requests known to God, trust that He knows what is best for us, and then communicate with Him the same way we would with any friend—just for the joy of being together.

Step Eleven Resolution

Sought through scripture, prayer, and meditation to improve our conscious contact with God, praying only for the knowledge of His will for us and the power to carry that out.

Once again, it is one thing to say we will do it and another thing to follow through and actually do it. One way to safeguard this decision is to make a plan for how that will be carried out.

- Choose your space. Set an area aside where you will do your Bible study and prayer. If you have a favorite easy chair or if you enjoy sitting at the kitchen dinette watching the birds in the backyard or if you eat your lunch in your car at work, any of those or others can be your regular reading/ prayer space. Put your Bible there along with devotional guides. Plan to sit with a cup of coffee or tea or your favorite soda and spend some time with God.

- Choose your time. Determine a time of day that you will usually be able to set time aside to be with God. You notice I said "usually." God knows that things come up, and there will be occasional times when the time will not work out. Don't beat yourself up for that, but get back into the routine as quickly as possible.

- Plan your time with God. Have a plan on how you spend your time with God. It should be broken into three parts: Prayer, Bible Reading, and Meditation in any order. Prayer is a time to give thanks to God and to present our requests. Meditation is a time to clear our minds and allow God's presence to be with us. We read the Bible to learn and to determine God's will for us. Decide how you will approach that reading. It could be with a devotional guide—they can be found at churches, Christian bookstores, and on the internet. Some people simply read the Bible straight through. Some read one book at a time. My suggestion would be to start with the gospels—Matthew, Mark, Luke, and John followed by Acts, Ephesians, 1 and 2 Corinthians, and Philippians. The gospels recount the life of Christ and His teachings. Acts follows the disciples after Christ's death and resurrection and recounts many of the ways that the prophecies of the Old Testament were fulfilled in Christ. Ephesians, Corinthians, and Philippians are written by Paul with instructions on how to incorporate the teachings of Christ into our daily life. Don't worry if you don't do it perfectly every day. Just make an honest effort, and it will become easier and more natural over time.

Date you committed to a regular time of Bible Reading, Prayer, and Meditation:

_____

Where will you do your Bible study, prayer, and meditation? _____

What time of day will you do it? _____

What is your plan for how you will approach it? _____

Date you decided to commit to seeking God's will and the power to carry it out:

_____

Date you shared your decisions with your AP: _____

STEP TWELVE

H aving had a spiritual awakening as the result of these steps, we tried to carry this message to others and to practice these principles in all our affairs.

The principle behind Step Twelve is **gratitude**. In thanksgiving for our recovery, we now make ourselves available to anyone still in need. We readily share our experience, strength, and hope.

2 Corinthians 1:3–4—"Praise be to the God of comfort, the Father of compassion who comforts us in all our troubles *so that we* can comfort those in any trouble with the comfort we ourselves have received from God."

It was this twelfth step and this passage from 2 Corinthians that led me to write this book. I have sanity because of these Twelve Steps, and I worked them from a Christian perspective just as I have laid out here in this book. So it was a combination of God in me and the Twelve Steps that saw me through to full recovery. How can I not want to share that with the world, with anyone who will listen?

At one point, I was suicidal. At another point, I was unable to function. I had times when all I could do was rock in the rocking chair. I had other times when I cried for no reason. I could put on a brave face to others, but inside myself and at home, I was a mess. I had times when I was fully functional in and outside of home, which at one point led the doctors to think I was bipolar, as my father was. But that turned out not to be the case. PTSD better fit what I was going through. I probably could have made it through the last thirty years without this program, but not happily. Not fully functioning. Not with good health. Not with loving, intact relationships. I thank God every day for my fully functioning life, loving relationships, good health, and modest financial stability (who couldn't use more?).

When we find a fantastic recipe, we oftentimes share it with others. When we find a real bargain at the store, we can't wait to tell others. When someone compliments us on our clothing, we anxiously tell them where we got it and, if it was on sale, how much it cost. When we read a good book, we pass it on to others. After we've had a spiritual awakening, when someone compliments us on our lifestyle, why not tell them how we got that way? When someone comments on our beaming smile, why not share with them why we can radiate love and contentment? When a friend is struggling, why not share our story? We used the format of the Twelve Steps to reconnect with God, and through His Son, Jesus Christ, we found peace, love, contentment, and joy in our lives. His Holy Spirit is with us every moment of the day and night, encouraging and guiding us.

Spend some time in reflection with the following Bible verses. Remember to use your journal and *write out* (don't just work in your head) your answers to the following questions. If you cannot resolve any questions, try going through the Tools and Exercises for suggestions to help you get past the impasse. And don't forget to include your AP if you get stuck in the process.

2 Corinthians 1:3–4—"Praise be to the God of comfort, the Father of compassion who comforts us in all our troubles *so that we* can comfort those in any trouble with the comfort we ourselves have received from God."

None of us are particularly happy with some of what we have had to endure, but by the grace of God, we made it through and have a story to tell. Others are out there who have not yet found help. Because of those folks, I have been open about my experiences. I have shared at women's retreats about my experience, and it never fails that at least one or two women will approach me after the meeting to tell me that they, too, were molested as a child and, until now, had never told anyone. They thank me for sharing because it opens the door for them to begin healing as well. We don't have to air our dirty laundry to the world, but we should be attuned to the needs of others in such a way that we are open to sharing as God directs us.

Psalm 13:6—"I will sing to the Lord, for he has been good to me."

I love to sing praise songs in the car. It lifts my spirits, and if others are with me, it can lift theirs as well. When my daughter and I were active with JOY Company (see "Joy—A Story of Faith" in Part Two), I used to sing with the company members in the car. I'd teach them new little ditties when I could remember all the words. I'd sing along, and when there was a lapse in my memory, I'd continue the tune in a "la la" fashion until the words connected in my head again. They called it the "Miller Method," and they used to laugh at me. It served as more than just fun, though, as I taught them that if they ever lost the words onstage, it was truly a way to see their way through the song until the words caught up with them. Sharing our knowledge, whatever our expertise, opens the door for other kinds of sharing as we are led by God.

Psalm 28:6–8—"Praise be to the Lord, for He has heard my cry for mercy. The Lord is my strength and my shield; my heart trusts in Him, and I am helped. My heart leaps for joy and I will give thanks to Him in song. The Lord is the strength of His people, a fortress of salvation for His anointed one."

A lot of people don't have the source for strength that we have through our Lord. When we live a joyful life and other people see that, they will want what we have. And when they ask, be willing to share your source of strength with them. Write in your journal what you would tell someone when asked, "How do you manage to live a joyful life in the midst of this crazy world?"

Psalm 86:12–13—"I will praise you, O Lord my God, with all my heart; I will glorify your name forever. For great is your love toward me; you have delivered me from the depths of the grave."

When we are newly in love, head over heels in love, we can't help but beam from within and tell the whole world. I love my Lord that same way, so it is only natural to want to share it with others. Are you comfortable sharing your faith and your recovery with others? For many of us, it is hard to express our faith to others. Pray about it and ask God to help you to be open to opportunities as He presents them. Write out that prayer in your journal.

Psalm 150—"Praise the Lord. Praise God in His sanctuary; praise Him in his mighty heavens. Praise Him for His acts of power; praise Him for His surpassing greatness. Praise Him with the sounding of the trumpet, praise Him with the harp and lyre, praise Him with tambourine and dancing, praise Him with the strings and flute, praise Him with the clash of cymbals, praise Him with resounding cymbals. Let everything that has breath praise the Lord. Praise the Lord."

Psalm 150 is the last of the psalms, and it goes out with a bang—trumpets, harp, lyre, tambourine, dancing, strings, flute, cymbals. Just imagine the symphony, all in praise to God. So I never understand it when churches get hung up on the style of music that should be allowed in the church. Psalm 100 tells us to "Make a joyful noise unto the Lord." We are truly advised to praise God with abandon. Let us praise Him in all aspects of our lives and in all manner of praise.

Matthew 5:14–16—"You are the light of the world. A city on a hill cannot be hidden. Neither do people light a lamp and put it under a bowl. Instead they put it on its stand, and it gives light to everyone in the house. In the same way, let your light shine before men, that they may see your good deeds and praise your Father in heaven."

The words to the children's song based on that scripture are as follows:

This little light of mine, I'm gonna let it shine.
This little light of mine, I'm gonna let it shine.
This little light of mine, I'm gonna let it shine.
Let it shine, let it shine, let it shine.

This song can go on as long as you'd like. Replace the words "This little light of mine" with the following or make up other locations:

Hide it under a bushel? No!
Don't let Satan blow it out
Shine all over [name of your street]
Shine all over [name of your city]
Shine all over [name of your state]
Shine all over [name of your school]

Let us all let our light so shine.

Psalm 78:4—"We will not hide them [the teaching of our fathers] from their children; we will tell the next generation the praiseworthy deeds of the Lord, His power, and the wonders He has done."

The Native Americans passed on the stories from one generation to the next in the oral tradition. Some of the tribes call them storytellers. Native art stores and trading posts sell many versions of the storyteller—an elder with many children sitting on the lap listening to the stories of the old one. That is what we should all be doing, no matter what our culture. One of my favorite songs is called "I Love to Tell the Story":

> I love to tell the story
> Of unseen things above,
> Of Jesus and His glory,
> Of Jesus and His love.
> I love to tell the story,
> Because I know it's true;
> It satisfies my longings
> As nothing else would do.
> I love to tell the story,
> 'Twill be my theme in glory
> To tell the old, old story
> Of Jesus and His love.

Let us all be anxious to tell the story.

1 Timothy 1:15–16—"Here is a trustworthy saying that deserves full acceptance: Christ Jesus came into the world to save sinners—of whom I am the worst. But for that very reason I was shown mercy so that in me, the worst of sinners, Christ Jesus might display His unlimited patience as an example for those who would believe on Him and receive eternal life."

This was written by Paul to Timothy. Before his conversion, Paul (then Saul) persecuted Christians. In his mind, that made him the worst of sinners, yet he was shown mercy. Paul spent the rest of his life spreading the Good News of Jesus Christ. There have been times in my life when I felt I should be doing more in the pursuit of spreading the word, but I eventually learned that God can and does use us wherever we are. When I was working as an assistant manager for a china and crystal outlet store, I often questioned God, asking if there wasn't something else I should be doing with my life and still pay my bills. I mean, china and crystal, how frivolous. But I became friends with many of my employees and helped several of them through life crises. As a manager at a campground, I had employees reach out to me for help in their lives. I looked back over my work history and realized that God truly had used me in each of those places. We just have to be open to letting Him use us where we are.

1 Peter 3:15–16—"In your hearts set apart Christ as Lord. Always be prepared to give an answer to everyone who asks you to give the reason for the hope that you have. But do this with gentleness and respect, keeping a clear conscience, so that those who speak maliciously against your good behavior in Christ may be ashamed of their slander."

This scripture is referring to evangelizing to those who have requested you to talk with them. In sharing our experience, strength, and hope, we don't want to ram it down their throats. We should not act superior or talk down to them, and we should be respectful. If, after a time, the person simply does not want to hear any more, we will need to recognize that God must have a different plan. We all have our part in the overall scheme of things, and I decided a long time ago that I am not generally a closer, but I am a seed planter. I talk to a lot of people and share my story, but I seldom see the conclusion. I have to trust that God will send someone else to water and fertilize those seeds until the time is right in God's time. Are you a planter or a fertilizer or a closer? How do you see God using you?

1 Peter 2:11–12—"Dear friends, I urge you, as aliens and strangers in the world, to abstain from sinful desires, which war against your soul. Live such good lives among the pagans that, though they accuse you of doing wrong, they may see your good deeds and glorify God on the day He visits us."

Good deeds are not what assure us of life in eternity—that is a free gift offered by God through His Son Jesus Christ. But good deeds are how we are measured by other people here on earth. If we profess to be a Christian and then live ungodly lives, what kind of a message does that send? Atheists just love to see a sinful person claiming to be a Christian. We are all sinners, of course, but by ungodly men's standards we, as Christians, are held to a higher standard. There are many ways of witnessing for our Lord, but I believe the best is in how we live our lives. If we profess to be a Christian and others can see the goodness and love in us, then we are witnessing what God can do in our lives. The biggest compliment any Christian could get, I believe, is for someone to say to them, "I want what you have."

Step Twelve Resolution

Having had a spiritual awakening as the result of these steps, we tried to carry this message to others and to practice these principles in all our affairs.

You can simply make the commitment, but I have found that it is helpful to have some symbol of that commitment as a regular reminder. For me, the doll I made as a symbol of the turning point in my recovery sits in my bedroom as a reminder of where I have been and where I am now (See "Bridging the Gap" in Part Two). I am so thankful for that recovery, and she serves as a reminder that I want to share that recovery with others. In Step Three, I purchased a plaque that states, "Christ is head of this household." It hangs in my entryway where I pass it each day, and it serves as a reminder of the choice to live for Him and by His will. Although these two items were made/purchased for other steps, I use them with this step to symbolize my full recovery and commitment to a changed lifestyle. My suggestion is that you choose something that you will display as a symbol of your recovery and commitment to a changed lifestyle.

Date you committed to incorporating these principles in all your future affairs:

_____

Date you committed to share your experiences and hope with others: _____

What symbol will you make or purchase as a reminder of that commitment?
_____

Where will that symbol of commitment be displayed?_____

Date you shared these decisions with your AP: _____

The Great Commission

After Jesus's resurrection, He was seen by the disciples on several occasions. For details, see the final chapters of Matthew, Mark, Luke, and John. His final act before going to His heavenly home is what we have come to call the Great Commission. As in our Step Twelve, Jesus asks us to carry His message to others.

Matthew 28:16–20

"Then the eleven disciples went to Galilee, to the mountain where Jesus had told them to go. When they saw Him, they worshiped Him; but some doubted. Then Jesus came to them and said, 'All authority in heaven and on earth has been given to me. Therefore, go and make disciples of all nations, baptizing them in the name of the Father and of the Son and of the Holy Spirit, and teaching them to obey everything I have commanded you. And surely I am with you always, to the very end of the age.'"

Mark 16:19

"After the Lord Jesus had spoken to them, He was taken up into heaven and He sat at the right hand of God."

Addendum One

KEY BIBLE VERSES

Our Salvation

"For God so loved the world that He gave His one and only Son, that whoever believes in Him shall not perish but have eternal life" (John 3:16).

Hope to Endure Suffering

"Not only so, but we also rejoice in our sufferings, because we know that suffering produces perseverance; perseverance, character; and character, hope. And hope does not disappoint us, because God has poured out His love into our hearts by the Holy Spirit, whom He has given us" (Romans 5:3–5).

Paul Struggled Too

"I do not understand what I do. For what I want to do I do not do, but what I hate I do" (Romans 7:15).

Our Responsibility to Others

"Do not destroy the work of God for the sake of food. All food is clean, but it is wrong for a man to eat anything that causes someone else to stumble. It is better not to eat meat or drink wine or to do anything else that will cause your brother to fall" (Romans 14:20–21).

Permissible vs. Beneficial

"'Everything is permissible,'—but not everything is beneficial. 'Everything is permissible,'—but not everything is constructive...Do not cause anyone to stumble" (1 Corinthians 10:23, 32).

The Reason I Wrote This Book

"Praise be to the God and Father of our Lord Jesus Christ, the Father of compassion and the God of all comfort, who comforts us in all our troubles, *so that we* can comfort those in any trouble with the comfort we ourselves have received from God" (2 Corinthians 1:3–4).

Saved by Grace

"For it is by grace that you have been saved, through faith—and this not from yourselves, it is the gift of God" (Ephesians 2:8).

Our Protection

Finally, be strong in the Lord and in His mighty power. Put on the full armor of God, so that you can take your stand against the devil's schemes. For our struggle is not against flesh and blood, but against the rulers, against the authorities, against the powers of this dark world and against the spiritual forces of evil in the heavenly realms. Therefore, put on the full armor of God, so that when the day of evil comes, you may be able to stand your ground, and after you have done everything, to stand. Stand firm then, with the belt of truth buckled around your waist, with the breastplate of righteousness in place, and with your feet fitted with the readiness that comes from the gospel of peace. In addition to all this, take up the shield of faith, with which you can extinguish all the flaming arrows of the evil one. Take the helmet of salvation and the sword of the Spirit, which is the word of God. And pray in the Spirit on all occasions with all kinds of prayers and requests. With this in mind, be alert and always keep on praying for all the saints. (Ephesians 6:10–18)

What Kept Me Going

"Not that I have already obtained all this, or have already been made perfect, but I press on to take hold of that for which Christ Jesus took hold of me. Brothers, I do not consider myself yet to have taken hold of it. But one thing I do: Forgetting what is behind and straining toward what is ahead, I press on toward the goal to win the prize for which God has called me heavenward in Christ Jesus" (Philippians 3:12–14).

The Promise of Peace in the Midst of Chaos

"Do not be anxious about anything, but in everything, by prayer and petition, with thanksgiving, present your requests to God. And the peace of God, which transcends all understanding, will guard your hearts and your minds in Christ Jesus" (Philippians 4:6–7).

Contentment in the Midst of Chaos

"I have learned to be content whatever the circumstances. I know what it is to be in need, and I know what it is to have plenty. I have learned the secret of being content in any and every situation, whether well fed or hungry, whether living in plenty or in want. I can do everything through Him who gives me strength" (Philippians 4:11b–13).

Addendum Two

HOUSE CLEANSING CEREMONY / DEMON RELEASE

If you have doubts of the reality of demonic powers, read my story "In God's Time" in Part Two. After I had been confronted by demons, someone in my Bible Study gave me this prayer to release all demons from my life and home. The origin of this prayer is unknown.

Use this prayer to release yourself and your household from demons. Each time it states "me and mine," name each person in your household. Following are a few scripture references to read before the prayer.

Exodus 20:4–6, Exodus 34:7, Matthew 8:16, Matthew 9:32–33, Mark 9:14–29, Romans 6:4, Galatians 2:20, Galatians 3:13–14, Ephesians 1:7, Ephesians 2:5–6

Prayer of Renunciation and Affirmation

As a child of God purchased by the blood of the Lord Jesus Christ, I here and now renounce and repudiate the sins of *me and mine* and all the sins of my ancestors. As one who has been delivered from the power of darkness and translated into the kingdom of God's dear Son, I cancel out all demonic working that has been passed on to *me and mine*. As one who has been crucified with Jesus Christ and raised to walk in newness of life, I cancel every curse that may have been put upon *me and mine*. I announce to Satan and all his forces that Christ overcame all evil and sin for *me and mine* when He hung on the cross. As one who has been crucified and raised

315

with Christ and now sits with Him in heavenly places, I renounce any and every way in which Satan may claim ownership over *me and mine*. I declare *me and mine* to be eternally and completely signed over and committed to the Lord Jesus Christ. All this I do in the name and authority of the Lord Jesus Christ.

Prayer of Victory

In the name of Jesus and in His blood, there is victory! Jesus Christ has trod upon the head of the serpent and also conquered its power over *me and mine*. Hallelujah!

Jesus Christ has abolished death—in the hearts of *me and mine* as well. He has overcome death.

The Lamb, the Lion of Judah, has overcome Satan's power and the power of sin in the lives of *me and mine*.

Jesus has put all His enemies under His feet and in the lives of *me and mine* as well. The enemy has been overcome.

Jesus has come to destroy the works of the devil. They are destroyed and in the lives of *me and mine* as well.

Jesus has redeemed me from every power of sin, for He says, "If the Son makes you free, you will be free indeed." This truth avails for *me and mine*. We have been redeemed from the bondage of sin.

Me and mine know that our Redeemer lives. He redeems *me and mine* and re-molds each of us into a new creature. Jesus sets *me and mine* free. Hallelujah!

Jesus has disarmed His enemies and made a public show of them. Jesus is victor over every power of the enemy, also whenever Satan tries to oppress *me and mine*.

In the name of Jesus and in His blood, there is victory! Jesus has the keys of death and Hades. No longer can the enemy harm *me and mine*, rage as he will. *Me and mine* are redeemed. Jesus is victor! Hallelujah!

Satan, in the name of Jesus Christ, *be gone*. You have no place in the lives of *me and mine*. You have no place in the homes or hearts of *me and mine*. Jesus has overcome the works of evil, and we claim His protection.

(Source Unknown)

After this, say a prayer of thanksgiving in your own words, thanking God for all that he has done for you and for the gift of His Son, Jesus Christ. Thank Him for the power of His name.

Hallelujah! Christ Rules!

Addendum Three

MEMORIZED PRAYER AND SCRIPTURE

There is an importance to memorized prayer as well as the memorization of scripture and songs. Howard Rutledge found that to be true in the seven years that he was in a POW camp in Vietnam. He endured brutal treatment and was sometimes left for days shackled in excruciating positions. Rats the size of cats crawled around his cell.

In an effort to find solace, Rutledge thought back to his Sunday School days and tried desperately to recall Bible stories and songs from his childhood. He and fellow POWs in nearby cells struggled to rediscover their faith. As best they could, they would communicate through cell walls to help each other recall scripture verses and Bible stories. Everyone knew the Lord's Prayer, the Twenty-Third Psalm, and John 3:16, and over time, their jogged memories remembered more.

Looking back, he realized the importance of memorizing verses from the Bible. He said that simply thinking about one memorized verse could make the whole day bearable. In his book *In the Presence of Mine Enemies*,[14] he said, "I would pray, hum hymns silently, quote scripture, and think about what that verse meant to me. The enemy knew that the best way to break a man's resistance was to crush his spirit in a lonely cell. Scripture and hymns might be boring to some, but it was the way we conquered our enemy and overcame the power of death around us."

---

[14] Howard and Phyllis Rutledge, *In the Presence of Mine Enemies,* Baker Publishing, 1973.

I hope that no one reading this book ever experiences life in a POW camp or is a victim of rape or kidnapping or any other of the atrocities that man has imposed on his neighbor. But having a memorized arsenal can provide a great peace of mind in those circumstances or in everyday circumstances when you just need to connect with God but cannot form the words—such as at the bedside of a dying family member or at the scene of a car accident or when someone is hurt on the Little League field.

The Lord's Prayer can be found at the end of this list of prayers, but not because it is the least important. To the contrary, I saved it for last because I consider it the most important and because I have included a study of the prayer.

Some Common Mealtime Prayers

My family was partial to these first two mealtime prayers. I can hear the tone and the cadence of my Uncle Wally's voice every time I repeat this first one.

We thank the Lord for this our food,
For life and love and every good. Amen.

My family is of German descent. My maternal grandmother grew up in the Dakotas, where she spoke English in her everyday life, but the Lutheran church and her confirmation were conducted in German. This next prayer is of German origin, so I have listed it here in German, as well as including the English version that we always prayed.

Komm Herr Jesus,
Sei unser Gast,
Und segne was Du uns bescherret hast.

(English translation)
Come, Lord Jesus,
Be our guest.
And let this food to us be blest.

I have also heard the following ending:
And let these gifts to us be blest.

This prayer is one that I first heard at Vacation Bible School as a child and introduced it to my family. For a change, we would occasionally use this one as well.

> *Thank you for the world so sweet,*
> *Thank you for the food we eat,*
> *Thank you for the birds that sing,*
> *Thank you, God, for everything. Amen.*

My daughter and I participated in the Indian Maidens mother/daughter program through the YMCA for several years. At mealtimes, we most often sang the "Johnny Appleseed Song." We still use this prayer today when we have extended family gatherings. We stand in a circle holding hands and sing together:

> *Oh, the Lord is good to me,*
> *And so I thank the Lord,*
> *For giving me the things I need,*
> *The sun and the rain and the apple seeds,*
> *The Lord is good to me.*
> *Amen—Amen*
> *Amen, Amen, Amen (in quick succession)*
> *A—men (held out)*

Some Common Bedtime Prayers

This is probably one of the best-known prayers that children say at night. In spite of that, some people find it to be a bit too "heavy" for children. I, on the other hand, like this prayer. Death is a certainty in life, and this puts it in proper perspective—that each day is precious, and that death is not something to be feared, for our next home is in heaven. It is the version that I grew up with and still say every night.

> *Now I lay me down to sleep,*
> *I pray the Lord my soul to keep.*
> *If I should die before I wake,*
> *I pray the Lord my soul to take.*
> *If I should live for other days,*
> *I pray the Lord to guide my ways.*

That is the only bedtime prayer I used growing up, but in researching, I found these next two and like them very much as well:[15]

Father, we thank thee for the night,
And for the pleasant morning light;
For rest and food and loving care,
And all that makes the day so fair.
Help us to do the things we should,
To be to others kind and good;
In all we do, in work or play,
To grow more loving every day.
—Rebecca Weston 1890

The day is done;
O God, the Son,
Look down upon
Thy little one!
O Light of Light,
Keep me this night,
And shed round me
Thy presence bright.
I need not fear
If Thou art near;
Thou art my Savior
Kind and dear.
—Author Unknown

[15] David Peach, "What Christians Want to Know," www.whatchristianswanttoknow.com/10–popular–bedtime–prayers, accessed 2019.

Anytime Prayers
The Serenity Prayer

The Serenity Prayer is repeated every single day at twelve step meetings across the nation. It is said that Bill W., the founder of AA, said of the Serenity Prayer, "Never had we seen so much AA in so few words." They instituted the use of it in their meetings in 1942. In their group setting, they use "us and we," but for individual use, I like the "I and me" version better. This is the most common version of this prayer as adapted from the prayer by American theologian Reinhold Niebuhr (1892–1971).[16]

> *God, grant me the Serenity to accept*
> *The things I cannot change.*
> *Courage to change the things I can.*
> *And the Wisdom to know the difference.*

A Prayer by which to Exercise

I have a difficult time motivating myself to exercise. So I wrote the following prayer to repeat as I walk, to remind myself of the benefits of exercise.

> *I'm keeping off the weight, With every step I take,*
> *So I can be in shape, For any hike I take.*
> *I chase away the blues, With every step I choose,*
> *My focus on the Lord. My ultimate reward.*

Scripture to Memorize
John 3:16 (NIV)

This verse is at the core of all Christianity and therefore the most memorized scripture.

> *For God so loved the world*
> *That He gave His one and only Son*
> *That whoever believes in Him*
> *Shall not perish*
> *But have eternal life.*

---

[16] Serenity Prayer, www.wikipedia.org, accessed 2019.

I memorized this verse as a child from the King James Version:

For God so loved the world
That he gave his only begotten Son
That whosoever believeth in Him
Shall not perish
But have everlasting life.

The Twenty-Third Psalm

This is one of the most memorized pieces of scripture and is often repeated in times of crisis or when comfort is needed.

The Lord is my shepherd,
I shall not be in want.
He makes me lie down in green pastures,
He leads me beside quiet waters,
He restores my soul.
He guides me in paths of righteousness
For His name's sake.
Even though I walk through the valley of the shadow of death,
I will fear no evil,
For You are with me;
Your rod and your staff,
they comfort me.
You prepare a table before me
In the presence of my enemies.
You anoint my head with oil,
My cup overflows.
Surely goodness and love
Will follow me all the days of my life,
And I will dwell in the house of the Lord forever.

Another comforting story, though not from scripture, is
"Footsteps in the Sand"[17]
An elderly man, who had lived his life
Left this world to go and meet his Maker.
He asked the Lord a question.
"As I'm looking down on the paths I've trod,
I see two sets of footprints on the easy paths.
But down the rocky roads I see only one set of footprints.
Tell me, Lord, why did you let me go down all those hard paths alone?"
The Lord smiled and simply replied,
"Oh, my son, you've got that all wrong!
I carried you over those hard paths."

The Lord's Prayer

Jesus gave this prayer to His disciples as a model of how to organize our prayer life. It is recorded in Matthew 6:9–13. The words read slightly different from one version of the Bible to another, but the most commonly used version as a prayer is as follows:

Our Father, who art in Heaven,
Hallowed Be thy name.
Thy Kingdom come,
Thy will be done,
On earth as it is in heaven.
Give us this day our daily bread,
And forgive us our trespasses,
As we forgive those who trespass against us.
And lead us not into temptation,
But deliver us from evil.
For thine is the kingdom and the power and the glory,
Forever and ever.
Amen.

---

[17] If you check the internet, you will find many versions of this poem and many claims as to the authorship. Most just list "Anonymous." This anonymous version, from a small-town newspaper in Iowa, July 1978, is from Wikipedia.org, Footprints (poem).

A Bible Study that I attended one time broke the Lord's Prayer down as follows:

Our Father, who art in Heaven
This opening shows an intimacy coupled with respect and a healthy distance.

Hallowed be thy name
This is the motivation of the prayer—to set Him apart as holy.
We are saying that in our world and in our life, we want Him to be seen as holy.

Thy Kingdom Come
This is the evangelization of the prayer. We are praying that all will be brought into His presence and that God will use the petitions of our prayer as an instrument to His glory.

Thy will be done on earth as it is in Heaven
This is the submission of the prayer. We are submitting our will to God's will.

Give us this day our daily bread
This is the provision of the prayer. We are praying for things, people, circumstances, and His will in all of that.

Forgive us our trespasses as we forgive those who trespass against us
This is the confession of the prayer. We are acknowledging our wrongs with the understanding that we must also extend forgiveness to those who have wronged us.

And lead us not into temptation but deliver us from evil
This is the protection of the prayer. We are acknowledging His power and putting our lives in His hands.

INDEX

Abuse 29–31, 102

Addendum One—Key Bible
    Verses 312

Addendum Two—Demon
    Release 315

Addendum Three—Memorized
    Prayer 317

Against All Odds 92

Angels Among Us 90

Bible Reading 122

Bible Verses, Key 312

Block Wall 123

Boundary Setting—Personal 125

Boundary Setting—Time 128

Breaststroke 129

Bridging the Gap 50

Conflict Resolution 130

Dear John 163

Deep Breathing 132

Demons / Evil Spirits 75, 315

Doll / Craft for Healing 14, 50, 145

Establishing Relationships 82

Father's Day 44

Fill in the Blanks 133

Footsteps in the Sand 323

Force Field 73

Foster Parenting Guide Dog
    Puppies 105

From the Heart 46

Ghost Chair 134

GOD CAN 136

God Talk 138

Good Boy, Cochise 108

Great Commission, the 311

Grief/Grieving 141

Guide Dogs—see Service Dogs

Have a Plan 139

Holding On 69

Hurt List 140

In God's Time 75

Innocence Lost 102

Journal, Behavior 166

Journal, General Daily 165

Journal, Relationship 165

Journals 165

JOY—A Story of Faith 61

Kiva 18–19, 114

Lingering Love—Sherry 40

Live for Today 144

Lord's Prayer 323

Love Your Neighbor as Yourself 97

Making Amends 53

Medical Profession 146

Mirror Talk 147

Mythical Character 148

Native American—see Storyteller

Normalcy in the Midst of Chaos 42

Part One—Qualification 1

Part Two—Perspectives 33

Part Three—Tools and Exercises 115

Part Four—Biblical Path to Calm the
Chaos 117

Personal Relationship with Christ xi,
11–13

Personalize Your Bible 150

POW 317

Prayer and Meditation 151, 317

Pregnancy, Teen 8

Priority Jar / Walnuts and Rice 153

Project or Craft 145

Relationship Affirmations 154

Relationship Chart 155

Rutledge, Howard 317

Self-Affirmations 158

Self-Help Groups or Counseling 159

Serenity Prayer 321

Service Dogs 18, 105–114

Speed Writing 162

Step
One 193

Two 200

Three 207

Four 214

Five 221

Six 227

Seven 234

Eight 242

Eight A 250

Nine 259

Nine A 272

Ten 284

Ten A 290

Eleven 296

Twelve 304

Stepmother—Not So Evil After
All 57

Storyteller 308

Suicide Kills 37

Talk to Someone 159

Therapy Dogs—see Service Dogs

Tithing 67

Twelve Steps from a Christian
Perspective 183

Understanding 111

Up in Smoke 160

Visualization 161

Walnuts and Rice 153

What is Family? 84

Writing 162

WWJD 161

ABOUT THE AUTHOR

Sherry is a Christian woman of 70 years, a wife of 43 years, a mother to a 53-year-old daughter and a Stepmother to a 52-year-old daughter and a 49-year-old son. She says that 70 does not make her feel old—the ages of her children do. Jim and Sherry have 5 grandchildren aging in range from 14–25 years old who live in 4 distinctively different areas of the United States—California, North Dakota, Texas, and Virginia. They are actively engaged as Aunt and Uncle to 9 nieces and nephews, 10 grand nieces and nephews and 4 "adopted" niece and nephews who reside in yet 5 more states. Jim and Sherry spent 10 years as Full Time RVer's which afforded them the opportunity to visit them all regularly. What is a Full Time RVer? Amy would tell you her parents were Gypsies; Kay would tell you her parents were Trailer Trash; and Brian would tell you his parents were Homeless. All of that is true as they divested in almost all material possessions after retiring from law enforcement and retail management and traveled the country with a Truck and 5th Wheel Trailer and no "fixed to the ground" permanent residence. They worked about 4-5 months of the year at seasonal jobs throughout the United States and spent the remaining months being tourists or visiting with family and friends. Some of their seasonal Workamper jobs have included running a Christmas Tree/Pumpkin Patch Lot; Working the Sugar Beet Harvest; Being busy little "elves" at an Amazon.com fulfillment center; Flying to the bottom of the Grand Canyon with a 2010 Census group to perform the Census with the Havasupai Indian Nation; Running a Fly Fishing Shop; Working the Angel's Baseball Spring Training Camp;

and a great deal of writing has taken place in the wilds of South Texas where they worked as Oil Rig Gate Guards. When not working or visiting, Jim enjoys reading and bowling and Sherry enjoys writing, photography, hiking and the canine love of her life was her PTSD service dog, Kiva, who passed at age 13. Since leaving the highway, they have settled in San Antonio, Texas near their younger grandchildren and are active at church, bowling and raising Guide Dogs for the Blind.

Sherry has shared parts of her personal story at Christian Women's Retreats and states that every single time at least one woman approaches her to say, *thank you for your willingness to share* and then to tell her about when they were molested or raped as a child. It is Sherry's desire, God willing, that with this book she can reach more victimized women through the written word and as a speaker.

Made in the USA
Columbia, SC
13 January 2022

53505489R00205